John Addington Symonds

An introduction to the study of Dante

John Addington Symonds

An introduction to the study of Dante

ISBN/EAN: 9783741158506

Manufactured in Europe, USA, Canada, Australia, Japa

Cover: Foto ©Andreas Hilbeck / pixelio.de

Manufactured and distributed by brebook publishing software (www.brebook.com)

John Addington Symonds

An introduction to the study of Dante

AN INTRODUCTION

TO THE

STUDY OF DANTE.

BY

JOHN ADDINGTON SYMONDS, M.A.,

LATE FELLOW OF MAGDALEN COLLEGE, OXFORD.

> Hail Poet, who for mortal men dost pour
> Strong wine of words that burn and sense that sears,
> Drawn from thy bleeding bosom's fiery core,
> And tempered with the bitter founts of tears!

LONDON:
SMITH, ELDER & CO., 15, WATERLOO PLACE.
1872.

PREFACE.

THESE Chapters on Dante were originally composed as Lectures. My sole purpose in writing them was to make the study of Dante's works more easy to English readers. To Fraticelli's invaluable edition of the *Divine Comedy* and minor works of Dante, and to his *Life of Dante*, I am indebted for nearly all the material of which I have availed myself. The Dean of St. Paul's *Essay* was unknown to me, nor had Miss M. F. Rossetti's *Shadow of Dante* appeared, before the composition of the following pages. My debt to Mr. D. G. Rossetti's unique work on the *Early Italian Poets*, and to Dr. Carlyle's Translation of the *Inferno*, will be acknowledged in the notes. It remains to be mentioned that the photograph which forms a frontispiece to this volume is taken from a mask of Dante's face given to me by the late Mr. Kirkup of Florence.

Clifton, July, 1872.

CONTENTS.

CHAPTER I.

EARLY ITALIAN HISTORY.

(i.) Diversity a Characteristic of Italian History.—(ii.) The Lombard Conquest of Italy.—(iii.) The Papacy.—(iv.) The Southern States and the Normans.—(v.) The Maritime States: Venice, Genoa, and Pisa.—(vi.) The Lombard Towns.—(vii.) The Causes of the Decay of Liberty in the Italian Cities 1

CHAPTER II.

DANTE'S LIFE BEFORE EXILE.

(i.) Birth and Ancestry of Dante.—(ii.) His Education under Brunetto Latini.—(iii.) His first Meeting with Beatrice.—(iv.) The *Vita Nuova*.—(v.) Dante's Studies after the Death of Beatrice; his gradual Idealization of her.—(vi.) The Beginning of Discord in Florence; Dante's Priorate, Marriage, Military Service; the Confusion of political and private Quarrels; Dante's political Idealism 10

CHAPTER III.

DANTE'S LIFE IN EXILE.

(i.) His Embassy to Rome, Exile, Residence at Arezzo, and Friendship with Uguccione.—(ii.) In Lunigiana with the Marquis of Villafranca.—Visit to the Convent del Corvo, and Frate Ilario's Letter.—(iii.) Dante at Paris, at Milan. Letter to the Princes and Peoples of Italy. The Treatise *de Monarchiâ*.—(iv.) Letter to Florentines. Letter to Henry. Henry's Death. Dante Retires to Gubbio. Letter to the Italian Cardinals.—(v.) Visits Uguccione at Lucca. Battle of Monte Catini. Dante's Letter to a Friend, refusing to return in Disgrace to Florence.—(vi.) At Can Grande's Court. Change to Ravenna. Embassy to Venice. Death.—(vii.) The Question of the Veltro.—(viii.) Dante's Personal Appearance and Qualities 61

CHAPTER IV.

THE SUBJECT AND SCHEME OF THE "DIVINE COMEDY."

(i.) Definition of the Epic.—Dante's Comedy one of the Triad of Supreme Poems—(ii.) Various Theories about its Subject.—(iii.) Dante's Account of his Poem in the Letter to Can Grande. —(iv.) Why he called it a Comedy.—(v.) Its Originality.—(vi.) An Apocalypse and not an Allegory.—(vii.) The Allegories of the Purgatory.—(viii.) The Allegories of Virgil and Beatrice.— (ix.) Dante's names for Virgil and Beatrice.—(x.) The Frigidity of the Element of Symbolism in Virgil and Beatrice 92

CHAPTER V.

THE HUMAN INTEREST OF THE "DIVINE COMEDY."

(i.) Dante's Personality, untainted by symbolism, the main Interest of the *Divine Comedy*.—(ii.) Dante's Satire: the Cities of Italy.— (iii.) Dante's Animosity against Boniface.—(iv.) Filippo Argenti,

Alberigo: the Severity of Dante.—(v.) Dante's Hatred of Treachery and Lukewarm Indifference.—(vi.) His Liberality: the Story of Manfred: Dante's Treatment of Lovers: his Boldness: Cacciaguida's Warning.—(vii.) Dante's Pride: Respect for Noble Ambition: Estimate of Fame.—(viii.) The gentler and more amiable aspects of Dante's Character.—(ix.) Nature of the Human Interest of the Episodes of the *Divine Comedy*.—(x.) Hell: Farinata, Jason, Semiramis, Ulysses: Maestro Adamo: the Harpies' Forest: the Transformation of Men and Serpents.— (xi.) Purgatory: Difference of the Atmosphere of Hell and Purgatory.—(xii.) The Human Interest of the Purgatory: Casella, Buonconte, Sordello, Adrian, Statius, Forese Donati.— (xiii.) The Transition from Purgatory to Paradise: the State of the Saints: Light, Joy, and Love, the Triune Element of Paradise: their Charity and Contentment.—(xiv.) The Relation of the Spheres to the Celestial Rose explained.—(xv.) The Peculiarity of Dante's *Paradise*, and the Faculties required for its Appreciation.—(xvi.) The Human Interest of the *Paradise*: Piccarda, Donati, St. Francis and St. Dominic: Mars, Cacciaguida: Jupiter, the Eagle: Saturn: the Vision of Paradise itself: the Mystic Rose: St. Bernard's Prayer: the Beatific Vision............ 130

CHAPTER VI.

THE QUALITIES OF DANTE'S GENIUS.

(i.) Definiteness, Intensity, Sincerity, Brevity.—(ii.) Mechanism of the *Divine Comedy*: Its Cosmography: the Line traced by Dante in his Journey: the number of Days spent by him *en route*.—(iii.) The Geography of the *Inferno*.—(iv.) Smallness of Scale in Dante's World: Phlegethon, Nimrod, Lucifer, the Cornices of Purgatory.—(v.) Dante's Faculty of Vision: his Pictures: his Illustrations from Actual Scenes.—(vi.) Descriptions of Morning and Evening in Purgatory: View of the City of Dis.—(vii.) Dante's Similes.—(viii.) The Compression and Brevity of Dante's Thought.—(ix.) The Chief Faults of the *Divine Comedy* are Grotesqueness and Obscurity 184

CHAPTER VII.

THE QUALITIES OF DANTE'S GENIUS.

(i.) The Sublimity of Dante: compared with Milton's: Fuseli and Blake: Orcagna and Michael Angelo: Dante's Sublimity not Pictorial but Moral: Dante and Shakspere: Milton and Æschylus.—(ii.) The relation of the *Divine Comedy* to the Plastic Art of Italy: *Purgatorio* Canto 12, and the Pavement of Siena Cathedral: *Purgatorio* Canto 10, and the Bas-reliefs of the Tuscan Sculptors: Inter-dependence of the Fine Arts in Italy.—(iii.) The Metre of the *Divine Comedy*: compared with Homer's Hexameter and Milton's Blank Verse: Laws of the Terza Rima.—(iv.) Dante's Gift of a Voice and Language to Italy and Europe: the Study of Dante in Italy: the Conditions under which he will necessarily meet with Neglect and Attention 217

CHAPTER VIII.

THE POETRY OF CHIVALROUS LOVE.

(i.) Difference between Classical and Mediæval Conceptions of Love.—(ii.) Chivalry and Feudalism.—(iii.) Platonic Love.—(iv.) Prose Romances and Provençal Poetry.—(v.) Italian Lyrists.—(vi.) Depth of Thought and Feeling introduced into the Poetry of Love in Italy.—(vii.) Dante and Guido Cavalcanti: Cino da Pistoja and Petrarch: Guido Guinicelli.—(viii.) Dante and Petrarch 237

INTRODUCTION

TO

THE STUDY OF DANTE.

CHAPTER I.

EARLY ITALIAN HISTORY.

(i.) Diversity a Characteristic of Italian History—(ii.) The Lombard Conquest of Italy—(iii.) The Papacy—(iv.) The Southern States and the Normans—(v.) The Maritime States: Venice, Genoa, and Pisa—(vi.) The Lombard Towns—(vii.) The Causes of the Decay of Liberty in the Italian Cities.

I.

THE essential characteristic of Italian History is Diversity—diversity of race and language, diversity of political interests, of internal development, of traditional customs. It is to this diversity that we can trace the strength as well as the weakness of the Italians. There is no modern nation which, on the whole, has produced so much as the Italians in Science, Literature, and Art. This pre-eminence they owe to the variety of conditions offered by their several and disjoined states, which has proved not only favourable to the growth of individual character, but has also served to stimulate by generous emulation, to educate by mutual comparison, and to intensify by long-continued rivalry. No nation, on the other hand, has hitherto so completely failed to attain constitutional stability or historical unity, owing to deep-seated differences and divisions in its very elements. These diversities, which have stimulated spiritual liberty, have been a fatal source of national instability. If from one point of view it is impossible to understand the greatness of the achievements of the Italian intellect without regarding Italy as a whole, from another point of view it is impossible to comprehend the history of the Italians, to appreciate the conditions under which their greatest men have had to work, without taking note of the complete disintegration of the race. The unity of Italy is an ideal, based partly on the unity of her literary language—a language which, when written, is one, when spoken is a hundred; partly upon the shadow of a mighty name—the name of Rome. Before the eyes of patriots like Dante, and enthusiasts like Petrarch, the unity of Italy has ever floated like a glorious dream. But the division of Italy into separate, hostile, mutually restrictive elements, is not an idea, not a dream, but a fact and a reality, which

Dismemberment of Italy.

we can easily trace from the dissolution of the Roman Empire to the formation of the present kingdom of Italy.

During the whole of this long period—a period of at least thirteen centuries—there has never been a central point in Italy; no nucleus like that round which, as in the case of France and England, the scattered atoms of the national system could gather to form one organized whole. Rome, which should have been this centre, to which the patriots turned in their enthusiasm, and which the tyrants dreaded in their selfishness, remained a source of weakness, rather than of strength, owing to the conflicting claims of feudal emperor and spiritual Pope, which had their root and basis there. While reading Italian history, our attention is constantly divided in the north between the cities of Milan, Verona, Pavia, Mantua, Ferrara, Bologna, Parma, and the maritime states of Venice and Genoa; in the centre, between Florence, Pisa, Lucca, Siena, Arezzo, each of which pursues a separate policy; in the south, between Rome and the loosely compacted States of the Church, and the unquiet kingdom of the Two Sicilies. Each state, each city, each prince, each lord, each bishop, has a separate and usually a selfish plan of action. The leagues which bind them into transient unity shift according as the will of individuals, the caprice of popular assemblies, or the dread of foreign force dictates. Internal jealousies are complicated by the interference of foreign powers. France, Germany, and Spain oppress the Italian States, and meddle with the course of Italian politics. To complete this tissue of complexity, all minor discords are fomented and encouraged by the interminable antagonism of spiritual and imperial potentates. Pope and emperor, representatives of adverse social and political principles, are like, if such a thing were possible, two magnets between which the restless needle of Italian diplomacy is incessantly wavering. To follow history under these conditions is like attempting to steer a straight course up a stream, the bed of which is for ever shifting, forming fresh shoals and opening unexpected channels in obedience to laws which can be but imperfectly determined.

II.

In order to understand the position of Italy in the age of Dante some retrospect over her preceding history is requisite. Modern history began with the foundation of Theodoric's Gothic kingdom at Ravenna in 489. But it was the conquest of the Lombards which really decided the future of Italian politics. To what they did and what they failed to do we may attribute the permanent dismemberment of Italy into separate masses. To begin with, the Lombards never thoroughly subdued the whole peninsula, and consequently never fused it into one. Alboin, their leader, died before he had completed his work of conquest, and where he left it, there it stayed. He founded the seat of his kingdom at Pavia, making the plain of the Po, between the Alps and Apennines, one province. This country still bears the name of Lombardy. It formed the solid portion of the Lombard conquest. But Alboin failed to take Venice; and Venice grew, unnoticed, to be an independent state of the first magnitude, with institutions peculiar to herself, and with unconquerable jealousies. Alboin, again, failed to wrest Ravenna and the five cities of Romagna, called Pentapolis, from the Greek Emperors. Here we get a second block detached from the supreme power in Italy. Rome, too, remained untouched by the Lombards, although their power extended over Tuscany and Umbria. Again, in Southern Italy, they never got possession of the maritime cities of Bari, Amalfi, and Naples, which, continuing faithful to the empire of Byzantium, developed for themselves a free constitution. In the south, however, the Lombards did found a duchy, called Benevento. This duchy, though independent of the Lombard kingdom of Pavia, kept its Lombard princes for many generations, and formed a separate mass embedded in the loosely compacted elements which eventually formed the Norman and then the French kingdom of the Two Sicilies. One result of this imperfect conquest of the Italian peninsula by the Lombards was, that all the malcontents among the Roman population who had means or vigour to escape, took refuge in the still

unsubjugated provinces. Thus the exiles who gathered
together at Venice, in Rome, at Ravenna, and on the
southern coast-line, formed at once separate, mutually
suspicious, and self-reliant communities, with distinct
interests and with peculiar national qualities, maintained by intermarriage through a long period of time.
The great political outcome of the so-called Lombard
conquest was therefore the dismemberment of Italy at a
very early period into those great blocks, which, broadly
distinguished from each other, have never since attained
to perfect fusion. The Valley of the Po, or Lombardy
proper, Venice, Romagna, Tuscany, Rome, and those
southern districts which, after the Norman Conquest,
became the kingdom of Naples—these are the parcels
which make up what we call Italy. Add to these com-
ponent parts the maritime towns of Genoa and Pisa,
which developed themselves at an early period by trade,
and we have already the chief elements of Italy distinguished. It is interesting to observe how these elements
maintained their individuality in spite of all external
changes. The Lombards were conquered by the
Franks. Charlemagne was crowned at Rome and
Pavia in 800. The Empire was transferred from the
Franks to the Germans. The dynasties of the Saxons,
the Franconians, and the Hohenstauffens succeeded each
other between 900 and 1250. Emperor after emperor
came to assume the iron crown in Lombardy, the golden
crown at Rome; states changed their leaders and their

forms of government; cities rose and fell in importance; but yet the broad divisions of Italy remained unaltered. When the spirit of intellectual freedom appeared in Italy and animated poetry and art, these distinctions became more accentuated instead of being softened. The special character of each district and each city expressed itself in painting, sculpture, architecture, poetry, with subtle but undeviating individuality; so that the study of Italian politics, Italian literature, Italian art, is really the study not of one national genius, but, if I may so express myself, of a whole family of cognate geniuses, grouped together and obeying the same laws, but producing markedly different results.

III.

Having insisted on the dismemberment of Italy, which, in my opinion, dates from the failure of the Lombard Conquest, I wish now, as briefly as possible, to review the affairs of each of these separate parcels of the Italian nationality before the age of Dante. I need scarcely dwell at length upon the successive steps by which the See of Rome became detached from Byzantine and barbarian rule, and lost its purely spiritual character. Yet the influence of the Papacy upon Italian politics was so important, and Dante's indignation against the temporal usurpation of the Pontiff formed so strong a portion of his creed, that some notice of the phases through which Rome passed will be necessary. While the Byzantine emperors were still clinging with a feeble grasp to their Italian domains, Rome was governed by a duke in the name of the Emperor of the East, and owed no allegiance to the Lombards; at this time the Pope had no secular power. But the spiritual ascendancy of the Holy See was growing every year and spreading over Western Europe; so that in 752, when the Iconoclastic Heresy of Byzantium caused the division of the East and West, the Pope found himself the most important functionary of Europe, though holding an anomalous position in Rome. The Frankish Emperors appealed to his religious sanction for their title, and in return granted to the chair of St. Peter political privileges and feudal suzerainties in the Exarchate. These temporalities bred corruption. The Popes became princes, generals, judges, men of worldly power. Then followed the period of degradation, during which Theodora and Marozia made and unmade Pontiffs at their pleasure; when Otho the Great was justified in stigmatizing the Vicar of Christ as guilty of crimes which would have disgraced the lowest actor; when John XII., wearing the tiara at seventeen, died of the wounds he received in a disgraceful brawl at night. It was only the vitality of the Christian creed, and the superstition which attached to Rome, that maintained the Papacy through this period of anarchy. Then came the resurrection of the Holy See under Hildebrand. He first conceived the idea of uniting pontifical supremacy and temporal power in the single person of the Pope. Finding the whole Western world ready to embrace his spiritual yoke, and perceiving the feebleness with which his predecessors had allowed themselves to rank as merely feudal barons, he defied Henry IV., and caused him to do bare-kneed penance through four winter days in the courtyard of Canossa, in order that all men might see that Christ's Vicar had no equal on the earth. He also gained for the Church the vast inheritance of the Countess Matilda (chosen by Dante at the end of the *Purgatorio* as a symbol of zeal for the Church). Hildebrand again, by destroying the feudal character of the bishoprics, and centralizing the whole system of Latin Christianity at Rome, added to the force and efficiency of the Papacy. He failed, indeed, in his attempt to found a theocracy in Europe : he did *not* absorb the Empire in the Church ; but he established the Church as a counterpoise to the Empire, and bequeathed to Italy the interminable strife between the two powers that claimed the sacred seat of Rome. Hildebrand's strife with Henry IV. was continued by Alexander III., who opposed Frederick Barbarossa, and by Innocent III., who used the minority of Frederick II· to consolidate the Papal temporalities. The hatred of the Popes for the Suabian Emperors during the reign of Frederick II. became so virulent that at last they took the fatal step of calling in French aid to extirpate the house of

Hohenstauffen. It was to this crime against the unity of Italy that Dante alludes at the end of the 32nd canto of the *Purgatorio*, when he speaks of the Church and her gigantic paramours, "puttaneggiar co' regi." To this selfish and short-sighted policy of the Popes must be attributed the greater portion of the weakness of Italy. Machiavelli says of them: "In this way the Pontiffs at one time by love of their religion, at other times for the furtherance of their ambitious schemes, have never ceased to sow the seeds of disturbances, and to call foreigners into Italy, spreading wars, making and unmaking princes, and preventing stronger potentates from holding fiefs they could not learn to rule."

IV.

Passing to the Southern States, it is not necessary to trace the history of the Duchy of Benevento, and the development of the coast towns of Amalfi and Naples, though some tribute should be paid in passing to the brave little town of Amalfi, which founded the Hospital of St. John at Jerusalem, coined gold money, gave laws to Naples, and encouraged science at a time when all Europe was buried in ignorance. Historically of more importance is the subjugation of the Duchy and the coast republics by the Normans in the first half of the eleventh century. This page of history reads like a romance. Forty horsemen going on a pilgrimage to

Monte Gargano on the Adriatic—a mountain hallowed by the apparition of an angel, like St. Michael's Mounts in Cornwall and in Normandy, and other "guarded mounts" and high places of religious mystery —defended the Christians of Southern Italy against the Saracens, and placed their feet upon that fruitful soil. Shortly after followed one Drengot, a Norman rover, attended by one hundred knights, who fought with the Goths for the sea-town of Bari, and settled at Aversa. Next came the great family of Hauteville—Tancred, the father, with his five sons, William Iron Arm, Drogon, Unfroi, Roger, and Robert Guiscard. This brood of heroes, supported by a handful of adventurers, rested not till they had subdued the whole of Southern Italy, reducing Goth and Saracen and Lombard to their rule. Nor were they satisfied with this. In 1061, Roger, with three hundred knights, set forth for the conquest of Sicily. In a few years he had entirely mastered the island, and fused it into one kingdom with the previously conquered provinces of Naples, Apulia, Calabria, Benevento. Of the heroic simplicity of these self-made monarchs an old story gives some idea. It is said that, in Sicily, Roger and his wife could not appear together in public, as they possessed but one mantle.

Nor was the Norman conquest of the Two Sicilies one of mere marauders. On the contrary, the heirs of Tancred administered the country well, and made good laws. Unhappily for Italy they appealed to the Pope for their title, and thus gave him a pretence to the suzerainty of Southern Italy. Another misfortune was the termination of their dynasty in an heiress Constance, who married Frederick Barbarossa's son. The Two Sicilies thus became involved in the rancorous animosity of the Popes against the Suabian Emperors. In order to extirpate the heirs of Frederick,[*] Clement IV. called in the aid of the French arms, and invested Charles of Anjou with the sovereignty of the Two Sicilies. From this time forward Italy was never free from French as well as German interference. In the course of a few years the French yoke became intolerable to the people of Sicily, who threw it off by the massacre known as the Sicilian Vespers. This led to the division of the kingdom of Naples from that of Sicily, and to the introduction of a Spanish ruler into the latter. Naples and Sicily henceforward proved a perpetual source of misery to Italy. Divided from the rest of the country by the Papal States, coveted by Frenchmen and by Spaniards, used as a lure by Popes for selfish purposes, of sufficient independent importance to turn the scale in any diplomatic intrigues, the Neapolitan kingdom was fatal to national coherence.

[*] This was the policy of Innocent IV. in 1253 after the death of Frederick II.; but it was not carried out till the reign of Clement and the battle of Grandella, near Benevento, in 1266, when Manfred was killed. The Popes thus ended their war with the House of Suabia triumphantly, but paved the way for their own exile to Avignon.

V.

In the Papacy, and in the Two Sicilies, we have seen fruitful causes for the disruption of Italy of which Dante so bitterly complains.

If we next turn to consider the three great maritime powers—Venice, Genoa, Pisa—we shall be struck with two chief points: first, the vigour of their development, and the splendour to which they rapidly rose; secondly, their bitter jealousy and unpatriotic refusal to act in concert for the good of Italy. Wordsworth, in one of his finest sonnets, says, that Liberty has two voices, one of the mountains, the other of the sea. The truth of this is manifest. Ever since the days of Solon, when Athens was acquiring her supremacy by maritime adventure, seamen, by their familiarity with two elements, by their habitual contempt of danger, by their independence of houses and encumbrances of every sort, have been foremost in the battles of national freedom. Both Venice and Genoa, owing to their geographical position, and the nature of their population, had the best opportunities of training a noble race of sailors. Venice, unconquered by the Lombards, and pent within the solitudes of her lagoons, became the resort of all exiles and daring persons. Genoa, shut in by the Ligurian mountains from the rest of Italy, and perched upon a barren coast, was both difficult to attack, and not worth pillaging. Each city had to gain the very necessaries of life by piracy and trade. Pisa, less isolated, but still secluded in some measure from the rest of Tuscany by sheltering hills, was driven to defend herself upon the sea from the attacks of Saracens. So it happened that Venice, Genoa, and Pisa began their national existence with a contest for bare life. But they soon turned defence into offensive warfare. Venice directed her attention to the East, annexed the shores of the Adriatic, and shared the empire of Byzantium with the leaders of the Fourth Crusade. Genoa appropriated the Riviera as far as Monaco westward, and Spezzia to the south. Pisa wrested Corsica and Sardinia from the Saracens. All three states profited by the Crusades, combining works of piety with mercantile sharp practice. Their fleets were of service for transport, convoy, and defence to the Crusaders. Venice, for instance, made a commercial contract by which she undertook to provide for the transport and commissariat of the western armies in the Fourth Crusade, agreeing to convey 4,500 horses with 9,000 grooms, 4,500 cavaliers, and 20,000 infantry, to supply food for nine months, and to maintain an armed escort of fifty galleys, receiving in payment 80,000 silver marks, and half the booty. In addition to such gains, the Venetians, Genoese, and Pisan merchants acquired vast private wealth by banking and trading on the shores of the Levant. But as they grew in prosperity and power, their mutual jealousy increased. The weaker were successively swallowed up by the stronger. Pisa, after helping to destroy her early rival, Amalfi, was herself overwhelmed after a series of bloody naval battles by the Genoese; and the Genoese in the fourteenth century * were in their turn crippled by the Venetians, who remained sole masters of the Mediterranean. In each case we have a struggle for the championship of the sea between two Italian cities, beginning with petty squabbles, which raised the *esprit de ville* so strong in Italy, and caused the Republics to put their whole force into the duel, and ending with some decisive blow like the battle of Meloria, by which the weaker was permanently disabled.

VI.

While the invasions of Saracens, and the necessity of gaining a livelihood at sea were forming the maritime states, the Lombard and Tuscan towns were rising into independence by quite a different discipline. During the invasions of the Goths, the Lombards, and the Franks, the old Roman municipalities, deprived of their walls, and exposed to recurring visitations of pillagers, had presented no resistance, but had been mere pens of sheep preyed on by ravening wolves. Misery, and the

---

* The first disagreements between Venice and Genoa arose in 1293 from a skirmish between four Venetian and seven Genoese galleys near Cyprus. SISM. iii. 163.

brutalizing influences of barbarous despotism, annihilated the old classical culture and luxury; but they inured the people to privation, and restored their physical strength. Instead of being elegant but enervated Romans, the citizens became rude but vigorous Italians. Left to themselves by the impotent emperors of the East, they enclosed their towns with walls, trained a militia, and established a municipal government, which to some extent resembled the old Roman organization. Each city elected two yearly consuls to act as supreme judges in peace, and as generals in war. They were supported by a privy council called Credenza, and a deliberative senate, as well as by a popular assembly. The city was divided into quarters for civil and military purposes, each quarter providing a body of mounted cavaliers and heavy infantry; and every male citizen was obliged, between the years of eighteen and seventy, to appear armed at the sound of the tocsin with at least a sword.*

* When the people went forth to battle they were generally preceded by a car, which, like the Ark of the Israelites, served for a rallying point, and was regarded with superstition as peculiarly sacred. Villani (vi. 75) gives a curious description of the Car of Florence: "The Carroccio of the people of Florence was a waggon upon four wheels, all painted red; and had two great red masts, between which stood and fluttered the great standard of the State, half gules, half argent; and a pair of oxen housellcd with red cloth drew the car. This Carroccio our ancestors used for triumphal pomps; and when they went to war, the Counts and Knights drew it from San Giovanni to the piazza of the new market, and gave it to the people; and the best and bravest of the burghers were appointed to lead it forth to battle; and round it gathered the whole force of the State. And when the host was ready, and for a month before, a bell was placed

The history of the rise of these free burghs has been so vigorously sketched by Sismondi, that I need not repeat it. It is enough to call attention to two points —first, the gradual emancipation of the Lombard and Tuscan cities from the yoke of the Emperor; secondly, their policy with regard to the noble families. The towns of Lombardy acquired their independence separately: this deserves especial notice. Though bound together by a league, they never attempted any scheme of federal government like that which gave consistency to Switzerland. Each burgh acted for itself, and was ready on the smallest provocation to quarrel with its neighbours in the effort to consolidate its own power. Throughout their contest with Frederick Barbarossa, we find the Pope opposed to the Emperor as the champion of freedom against the oppressor, as the patron of the burghs against the feudal suzerain. The Popes, being essentially spiritual potentates, swaying a kingdom in the consciences of men, found it favourable to their interests to annihilate the political despotism of the Empire, and by undermining the feudal fabric to gain a more unlimited supremacy over the minds of

upon the gate Sante Marie, which sounded day and night, as warning of war to the foemen. This was called by some La Martinella, by others the Bell of Asses. And when the Florentines would go afield, the bell was taken from the gate and placed in a wooden shrine upon the car, and the host was guided by its sound. By these two customs of the Carroccio and the Bell was ruled the lordly pride of our people of old, and of our fathers in their wars."

the people they pretended to liberate. It was thus that in the great struggle between Guelf and Ghibelline, the former was always the popular and democratic party, the latter the aristocratic and restrictive. At the same time, while the Popes were favouring political liberty, they trampled on freedom of thought; the Emperors, on the contrary, encouraged scepticism in order that men might be more ready to revolt against the Church. The Ghibelline ranks comprised freethinkers, but despotic politicians; the Guelfs were loyal in religion, but rebellious against discipline. It is easy to conclude from this complexity of interests and crossing of principles, how impossible it was for the Italian cities to gain coherence or fixity of constitution.

Besides fighting with the Empire the burghs were always at feud with the nobles. These nobles were mostly of foreign origin, talking not Latin nor the vulgar Italian, but a barbarous Tedesco. In course of time the weaker of them, and those who lived near the city walls, were induced or compelled to become burghers. But against the stronger nobles—those in particular who owned castles far away from towns—the burghs protected themselves with force. At the end of the thirteenth century the city of Turin could show a live Count of Savoy imprisoned in an iron cage, and Alessandria a Marquis of Montferrat in a similar condition. This proves the animosity subsisting between the cities and the feudal lords. It was war to the death between them; war without quarter, war without humanity.

In the midst of these contests, on the one side with the Empire, on the other with the nobles, the cities of Lombardy won their way through two centuries of continued and indomitable energy to freedom. The Emperor, Frederick Barbarossa, acknowledged their independence in 1183, by the Treaty of Constance, and the nobles were, if not destroyed, at least suppressed or brought into superficial harmony with the burghers.

What follows this splendid upward progress to liberty is a steady and dismal descent to slavery. One after the other these cities, mutually suspicious, divided by factions, separated from each other by conflicting interests, animated no longer by a common object, bound together by no permanent federation, threw the inestimable boon of liberty away.

VII.

The causes of the loss of freedom in the Italian cities were chiefly these:—A total want of cohesion between the several states; the insecurity of life and property in each city, owing to hereditary feuds, faction, and a bad system of government; the imperfect fusion of the noble families with the burghers, which not only gave rise to innumerable petty quarrels, but also facilitated the growth of tyrants. Each of these points deserves separate consideration: to a proper understanding of the conditions under which Dante lived and developed his genius, they are all-important. In the first place the cities of Lombardy and Tuscany, and the maritime powers of Venice, Genoa, and Pisa, never made common cause or pursued a systematic course of united policy. Had they done so after the peace of Constance, when Lombardy and Tuscany were at the height of prosperity, when Venice swayed the whole Levant, and Genoa and Pisa divided the Western Mediterranean, there is little doubt but that their federation would have been too powerful for Pope or King of Naples to resist. But it seemed impossible for Italians to regard their peninsula as one land geographically, or as one nation. Each city preferred a policy of self-aggrandizement, and the ruin of its rival, to the common good of Italy. Nor was there any monarch among them strong enough to subdue them to a unity of subjection. This, from one point of view, was no doubt a blessing; but it was also a source of interminable wars and wasting jealousies. When the Emperors sought to rule Italy as a single nation, the Popes opposed them; when Charles of Anjou aspired to form a monarchy from the Alps to Brindisi, the Ghibelline party proved too strong for him. When the Visconti indulged the same dream, they were immediately thwarted by diplomacy. Thus the Italian cities grew every year to be more disconnected, more suspicious of each other, more accustomed to shifting alliances, more keen in the prosecution of separate and selfish plans. They were as distinct from one another as the Greek States, but with an enormous inferiority of circumstance. For whereas the Greeks were unassailed by any great foreign power (except only at one moment by Persia), the Italians were surrounded by political forces of the greatest magnitude—by France, and Germany, and Spain, and Islam, all ready to prey upon them. The Greeks, again, were in a high degree capable of self-government, and had a high respect for established law; but the Italians gained their independence while still uneducated, and without any adequate conception of what a national constitution should be. Another disadvantage peculiar to the Italians was the presence in the midst of them of so anomalous a power as the Papacy. I have already pointed out how the Popes, in order to maintain their state as petty princes, neutralized the Empire, and how they scrupled not to sow dissensions by inviting foreigners into the kingdom of Naples. Nor again was the long but undefined title of the Emperor for the time being to exercise sway over Italy without its peculiarly baneful consequences. The entrance of the Emperor into Italy was always the signal for reviving old feuds and agitating old party cries; while the perpetual antagonism between Guelf and Ghibelline,* mixing itself up with local dissensions and family disagreements in each city, utterly destroyed the possibility of permanent peace. It is curious to notice how municipal factions and domestic grievances were embittered by the Guelf and Ghibelline dispute with which they crossed and intertwined. It is only necessary on this topic to allude to the history of the Bianchi and Neri of Pistoja, which took root in Florence, or rather was engrafted on the vulgar jealousy of two rival houses, the Cerchi and Donati, and ended by splitting the Guelf city into Black and White or ultra-Guelf and lukewarm Ghibelline. Bologna furnishes another notable instance. There a private quarrel between the families of Gieremei and Lambertazzi led to the one espousing Guelf and the other Ghibelline principles. Alliances with neighbouring towns were formed. A civil war began. In the end 12,000 Bolognese citizens were exiled, and one half of the city was destroyed by the inhabitants who remained as victors on the scene of contention.

* The insane fury of the Guelf and Ghibelline parties, which began in the Wars of Investiture between Hildebrand and Henry IV., which was intensified in the struggle for freedom, carried on by the Lombards, under the authority of Pope Alexander III., against Frederick Barbarossa, which was stimulated by Innocent III. in the interest of Papal aggrandizement during the minority of Frederick II., became so rooted in Italy during the prolonged warfare carried on by Frederick II. with the Popes Innocent III., Honorius III., Gregory IX., and Innocent IV., that the Italians lost sight of their original just motives of rebellion against imperial servitude, and cared only for the immediate success of one or the other party.

The Nobles.

The second cause of Italian enfeeblement was the imperfect fusion of the nobles with the burghers. By the middle of the twelfth century there were few noble families that had not in some way or other established connections with the towns. Muratori has preserved charters of citizenship, under which the aristocratic houses undertook to spend at least a portion of each year as burghers within the walls of the cities they had severally adopted. But these nobles did not lose their territories or seignorial rights by becoming citizens. They preserved their castles, their vassals, their habits of the chase, their love of arms. Unlike the burghers, with whom they made alliances,* they lived independently of commerce and manufacture, and consequently were able to devote time and attention to the prosecution of hereditary feuds and party-quarrels, or to the acquisition of more than their fair share of

---

* It was the habit of the nobles in Italian towns to cluster together by families in great blocks of houses, surmounted by huge towers, and provided with iron chains at their basement, called Serragli, which could be thrown across the street to form barricades. When one party happened to be in exile their antagonists destroyed their towers: thus, at Florence, thirty-six Guelf towers were thrown down in 1248, including the Toringhi of the height of 250 feet (MALASPINA, 94, 95). One Tuscan town, San Gemignano, still remains to show what must have been the street architecture of Florence, and of all the principal cities of that period. Towers, massive, bare of ornament, high as steeples, emerge in a thick cluster from a mass of sullen fortresses with tiny windows. The whole town, enclosed in a narrow circle of walls, bristles like a sheaf with these gloomy watch-towers. During successive party-victories the old street architecture of Florence was gradually altered; and in 1250 the forts of the nobles were pulled down by a decree of the people (GIOVANNI VILLANI, vi. 42; SISMONDI, ii. 319).

political influence. The nobles thus became in two ways dangerous to the liberties of the burghs, either by throwing the citizens into a state of faction, or by assuming a tyranny. It is difficult to say which cause of disturbance was the more dangerous. The latter, however, was the more permanent. In order to explain the growth of the tyrannical power acquired by noble families in the free cities of Italy, it is necessary to consider the third evil of which I spoke—the insecurity of life and property, and the inadequacy of the political system in the towns.

The sense of law which never failed to control the citizens of Sparta and Athens, and which formed the religion of the ancient world, was absent in Italy. Mediæval Europe seemed devoid of this great principle of internal order. It was not Law, but the individual Will, which determined feudal history. But in Italy there was no one regnant and supreme will of an acknowledged ruler controlling a hierarchy of subordinate governors. The Emperor, the Pope, the King of Naples, were neither of them strong enough to stand alone, though strong enough to check each other's policy. As a consequence of this weakness, the annals of the Italian republics offer a miserable spectacle of suffering and crime and revolution—of internecine civil wars begun by trifles ended in national disasters.

In course of time the populations grew so weary of discord that they were willing to sacrifice liberty to quiet. Having no palladium in law, they sought it in despotism. It was thus that the institution of the Podestàs and the Captains-general began. In a society where open crimes, vendettas, violences, were of daily occurrence, the administration of criminal justice became of paramount importance. The officer whose business it was to suppress riot and punish lawlessness was made an autocrat, called Podestà, invested with military power, and invariably elected from a neighbouring city. Now the nobles were the only idle, well educated, vigorous men, trained to martial discipline of all kinds, who had abundant leisure. To make a noble Podestà was natural. When he became Podestà, to proceed to be a despot was easy for him. In this way Milan, in 1242, gave supreme power to Pagano della Torre; Bologna, in 1276, wearied out with the quarrels of the Lambertazzi, invited Charles of Anjou; Florence, in 1300, sought a pacificator in Charles of Valois; Pisa, in 1285, made Ugolino Captain-general.[*] Other nobles, who had no opportunity of rising to the dignity of Podestà or Captain-general,

[*] Innumerable instances might be adduced of the alternations of tyranny from which the great Italian cities suffered. Otho Visconti, Archbishop of Milan, got Matteo, his kinsman, afterwards called Il Grande, made Captain-general in 1287, and in 1294 caused the people to confirm for him the title of Imperial Vicar. In 1290 Alberto Scotto managed to be elected by the vote of the people Captain and Signor of Piacenza; in 1302 he was strong enough to displace Matteo Visconti. In 1303 Ghiberto di Correggio caused himself to be proclaimed Signor-general of Parma. Among minor nobles may be reckoned Antonio Fisiraga of Lodi, Count Rusca of Como, Venturino Benzone of Crema, the Cavalcabi of Crema, the Brusati of Novara, the Avvocati of Vercelli, &c.

formed companies of mercenary soldiers* who were ready to foment the jealousies of cities and subserve the schemes of tyrants. The names of Guido Guerra, Guido Novello, Buoso de Doara, the Marquis Pelavicino, and Guido da Montefeltro are familiar to all readers of Dante. Sooner or later all the Lombard and Tuscan cities fell beneath the yoke of some great house. In the time of Dante there were Visconti and Della Torri at Milan, Della Scalas at Verona, Carraras at Padua, Correggios at Parma, Estes at Ferrara, Gonzagas at Mantua, Sismondi and Lanfranchi at Pisa, Colonnas and Orsini at Rome; not to mention Malaspinas, Malatestas, Montefeltros, and the host of minor nobles in Romagna.

It is needless to dwell upon the crimes and vices of these aristocratic usurpers—to point to the prisons of the Torri and Visconti, or to describe the butcheries, starvations, tortures, mutilations practised by Eccelino da Romano.† It is more instructive to consider the results

* The first regular Company of Adventure was the disbanded troop which had fought from 1282 till 1302 for Sicily, against the House of Anjou in Naples (*see* SISMONDI, iii. 160; VILLANI, viii. 50). The changes in the arms used in warfare, and the preponderance of cavalry (described by SISMONDI, ii. 374), threw military power into the hands of nobles, and encouraged them to adopt war as a profession.

† Of the prisons of Eccelin, Rolandini (vii. 8) writes: "There, of a truth, were weepings and gnashings of teeth; there was anguish and wailing; there, too, were worms and perpetual darkness and stench and pains that dried the blood and marrow,—thirst, hunger, terror, trembling, groaning, sighs that no man heard. Here did men find that there was something worse than death." A crusade was preached against Eccelin because he was a Ghibelline. This is probably the reason why we hear so much about his vices. Charles of Anjou, a scarcely less horrid tyrant, was praised and petted by the Church, being a good Guelf.

of their selfish policy. Like the despots who gained sway in the Greek towns after the old Homeric monarchies had been dissolved, and before the new period of constitutional order had commenced, these tyrants were the worse for having had to court the populace in the first instance, or to wrest power from the mob on whom they trampled. They had all the selfishness of an aristocracy, none of its nobleness. They combined the suspicious intriguing spirit of party-leaders with the ferocity of brigands and the inhumanity of autocrats. Each despot was jealous of his neighbour, cruel to his kin. Domestic tragedies—poisonings, imprisonments, treacheries, frauds of guardians, oppressions of the weaker by the stronger members of a ruling house—were encouraged by the facility of revolution, which the peculiar constitution of semi-republican, semi-despotic governments afforded in the midst of hungry competitors and rival States. The pages of Dante are filled with this eminently tragic matter.

At the risk of some repetition I must revert to the causes which prevented Italy from shaking off the yoke of these despots. Had the Italians been able to work out their history without foreign interference, they might have lived through the age of the tyrants, just as Athens, Thebes, Corinth, Sicyon, Megara, Syracuse, lived through theirs, and passed on to a period of constitutional freedom. Then the growing enlightenment of the Italian commonwealths, by educating a truer sense of national existence, might have introduced some principle of abstract equity like that which the great lawgivers of Greece made paramount. But alas for Italy! she never had this chance. Germany, France, and Spain were on her borders. The Papacy was in the midst of her. Three hungry neighbours regarded her fertile plains and prosperous cities as their pillage-field and cockpit. An anomalous spiritual power, combining pretensions to the authority of heaven with vices sprung from hell, a corporation more persistent in its selfish policy than any dynasty of princes could have been, prevented coalition by pitting town against town, despot against despot, fomenting discord for the sake of self-advancement. When the Tuscans and Lombards had once adopted the insane policy of making France and Germany the arbiters in their disputes, and of countenancing in the Papal See a system of intrigue, which was not Italian so much as European, their prospects of independence were utterly ruined. It was then as if the States of Greece before the age of Pericles had been subject to the continual interference of a flourishing Persia, a greedy Macedonia, a heartless Carthage, and, moreover, had established in the midst of them, say at Delphi, a selfish theocracy regardless of their interest, but rendered potent by superstition and by unbounded wealth.

Italy was at this point of total internal dismemberment and of subjection to foreign interference when

Dante began to write. The worst, indeed, had not yet come. But all the elements of discord and disruption were in full activity. This is why spirits like Dante and like Petrarch, nursed in the traditions of a glorious past, regarding their country as the rightful seat of a Supreme Empire, looking back to the great days of Rome and forward to the possibilities of political reconstruction, cried so passionately for a Deliverer, a political Messiah, who should curb unruly mobs, suppress tyrannical usurpers, and make of prostrate party-mangled Italy once more a single splendid State. The Selva Selvaggia—that wild, and rough, and stubborn wood, whose bitterness was scarce less terrible than death—in the midst of which Dante found himself at the beginning of his journey, is a true metaphor, not only for the trouble of the poet's soul, but also for the civil and political confusion of his nation.

CHAPTER II.

DANTE'S LIFE BEFORE EXILE.

(i.) Birth and Ancestry of Dante—(ii.) His Education under Brunetto Latini—(iii.) His first Meeting with Beatrice—(iv.) The *Vita Nuova*—(v.) Dante's Studies after the Death of Beatrice: his gradual Idealization of her—(vi.) The Beginning of Discord in Florence: Dante's Priorate, Marriage, Military Service: the Confusion of political and private Quarrels: Dante's political Idealism.

I.

DANTE—or, as he was christened, Durante *—the son of Aldighiero and Bella Alighieri, was born at Florence, in May, 1265. Of his ancestors thus much is evident through the mists of a very nebulous antiquity—that they were noble among the citizens of Florence, and that their primitive name was not Alighieri, but Elisei. Tradition differs about the origin of the Elisei. Some of Dante's

---

* It is singular that Durante, the enduring one, and Alighieri, the wing-bearer, should have been the two names of this poet who, having borne in his lifetime the strokes and buffets of fortune, after death has lasted through all time, and who, of all the singers of the world, has soared the highest.

biographers trace them to the Roman colonists of
Florence in the time of Julius Cæsar. Others, and these
are the majority, derive them from one Eliseo, of the
noble Roman house of Frangipani,* or bread-breakers—
so called by reason of some eminent act of public
charity—who is said to have settled at Florence in the
days of Charlemagne, or soon after. In any case the
Elisei were noble in Florence, possessing castles in the
country round, and towered houses in the city. They
dwelt within the old pomœrium in the Via degli
Speziali, near the Mercato Vecchio : this in itself was
a sign of ancient and noble blood.

Our most interesting and important information
respecting Dante's ancestry is to be gathered from his
own poems. It is clear from Ser Brunetto's speech,
Inferno xv., from Cacciaguida's, *Paradiso* xvi., and from
allusions to the state of Florence in *Purgatorio* vi. 125,
and *Inferno* xvi. 73, that Dante prided himself upon
his nobility, and upon his descent from the purest
blood of Florentine citizens. He drew a marked
distinction between the Roman and the Fiesolan
element in Florence, regarding the latter' as alien
and intrusive. From Brunetto's speech there can be

---

* The arms of the Alighieri "party per pale or and sable a bar arg.,"
resemble those of the Frangipani "party per pale gules and az a bar arg.,"
more than those of the Elisei, "party per fesse chequy az and or and
arg." It was not till the end of the sixteenth or beginning of the seven-
teenth century that the Alighieri of Verona took the canting arms "Az a
wing or" in allusion to their name—Aligeri.

no doubt that he claimed connection with the former. Again, the reticence of Cacciaguida concerning his forefathers—

> Chi el si furo, ed onde venner, quivi,
> Più è tacer, che ragionare onesto : *

resulted from humility and not from shame.

The change in the name of Dante's family from Elisei to Alighieri took place thus:—Cacciaguida degli Elisei, who was born in 1106, married Aldighiera degli Aldighieri of Ferrara, and had a son by her, whom he called Aldighiero. This son gave his Christian name to his descendants, while a brother of Cacciaguida's continued the line and name of the Elisei. Cacciaguida followed Conrad III. to the Crusades in 1147, was knighted by him, and died at the age of 42 in Holy Land. His great-great-grandson, the poet,† met his soul among the martyrs and confessors of the faith upon the blood-red cross of Mars. Of the other ancestors of Dante little is known, and of that little there is nothing worth recording. The Alighieri, who had dropped the harsh sounding *d* in their name, lived at the centre of Florence, in the Sesto di Por' San Piero. They were Guelfs; their kindred of the Elisei being Ghibelline.

---

* "Who they were, and whence they came, it is more honourable to pass in silence than to speak of in this place."

† *Paradiso* xvi.

II.

Dante, I have already said, was born at Florence, and was christened Durante. We have his own authority (*Purgatorio*, xxx. 55) for shortening his Christian name, and we know from his own mouth that he was born and christened at Florence. In *Inferno* xxiii. 94, he says:—

> I' fui nato e cresciuto
> Sovra 'l bel fiume d' Arno alla gran villa *—

and again in *Paradiso* xxv. 6:—

> Con altra voce omai, con altro vello
> Ritornerò poeta, ed in sul fonte
> Del mio battesmo prenderò 'l cappello.†

That he saw the light for the first time in the middle of May is also to be gathered from a passage in the *Paradiso* (xxii. 110). These otherwise trivial details gain some value when we can record them in the very words of a poet whose style turned everything he touched to gold.

Born under the Gemini, Dante, according to the superstitions of his day, was destined to a career distinguished by its brilliancy; nor was his birth unaccompanied by omens. His mother, Bella, says Boccaccio, dreamed that she gave birth to him beneath a laurel tree, beside a fountain, and that the infant fed on laurel

---

* "On Arno's beauteous river, in the great city, I was born and grew."
—CARLYLE's Translation.

† "With altered voice, with altered hair, shall I return as poet, and above the fount of my baptism assume the crown."

leaves, and on the water of the spring, till he became a shepherd, and crowned himself with branches of the tree. Thereafter he fell to earth and rose up a peacock.

Dante lost his father at the age of nine or ten; but his education was carefully conducted by Brunetto Latini, one of the best scholars of his day. That Dante loved his master, though his rigid sense of justice, and perhaps, also, the exigences of his poem, forced him to put Brunetto in a very ugly part of Hell, is clear from their dialogue in the 15th canto of the *Inferno*. He seems to have taught Dante rhetoric, poetry, and the elements of mathematics, helping him to study the works of Virgil, Lucan, Ovid, and Statius. Such was the meagre education of a lad in Florence of the thirteenth century. Dante's philosophical and theological studies belong to a later period of his life. His biographer, Bruni,* however, relates that Dante while a youth applied himself with success to painting and to music. It has been conjectured that Casella may have taught the poet music: at any rate, Dante delighted in his melodies; for in the *Purgatorio* (ii. 106) we find him addressing Casella thus:—

<pre>
        Se nuova legge non ti toglie
        Memoria, od uso all' amoroso canto,
        Che mi solea quetar tutte mie voglie.†
</pre>

---

* Leonardo Bruni, called Aretino, some time Chancellor of the Florentine Republic: born 1369, died 1444.

† "If the new law of thy life robs thee not of the memory or practice of that love-laden song which used to give rest to all my longings."

Of Dante's practical acquaintance with the art of painting we learn somewhat from the pretty story in the 35th section of the *Vita Nuova*. "On that day which fulfilled the year since my lady had been made of the citizens of eternal life, remembering me of her as I sat alone, I betook myself to draw the resemblance of an angel upon certain tablets." In the days of his youth Giotto had not arisen yet, and the cry was still for Cimabue; so we may conclude that Dante's angel was both stiff and grim, at least as solemn as the sceptred and winged archangels of that master at Assisi. That the critical faculty of Dante was delicate and highly developed is evident not only from what he says about Da Gubbio and Franco in *Purgatorio* xi., but far more from his extraordinary descriptions of imaginary bas-reliefs and sculptured pavements in the *Purgatorio*. There can be no doubt that Dante's genius was modified, and his divine faculty of vision intensified by his early application to painting.

III.

In his ninth year the greatest event of Dante's life happened to him. His father took him to a May-day feast at the house of Folco Portinari, a rich citizen of Florence. There Dante saw for the first time Beatrice, the daughter of his host, a little girl of eight, more fit to be an angel, says

Boccaccio, than a girl. "Her dress, on that day,"* says Dante, "was of a most noble colour, a subdued and goodly crimson, girdled and adorned in such sort as best suited with her very tender age. At that moment,† I say most truly that the spirit of life which hath its dwelling in the secretest chamber of the heart began to tremble so violently that the least pulses of my body shook therewith; and in trembling it said these words:—Ecce deus fortior me, qui veniens dominabitur." These are strange and definite words to describe the impression produced upon a boy of nine by a girl of eight. Yet they bear the indubitable seal and certain signs of truth. We may compare them with the chapter in which Alfieri relates the intense emotions of his childhood, or, in order to display the truth of their analysis of passion, may set them beside this splendid passage from the Phædrus of Plato:—"When the real lover beholds a godlike face, the form and very image as it were of beauty, he shudders first,

---

* ROSSETTI's Translation.
† Compare the description of the effect on Dante of her greeting, section xl., and of the sudden sight of her—what Plato would have called her ὄψις ἀσπράττουσα—section xiv. Compare also the words of the canzone "E' m' increse di me," as follows:—

        La mia per una parola sostenne
        Una passion nova
        Talch' io rimasi di paura pieno :
        Ch' a tutte mie virtù fu posto un freno
        Subitamente sì ch' io caddi in terra
        Per una voce che nel cor percosse.

and is surprised by some of his old awe; then gazing fixedly, pays it reverence as though it were a god; and did he not fear to be thought mad, he would sacrifice to his beloved as to the statue of a god." What Dante in early manhood recorded in the *Vita Nuova* he repeated after the sternest trials of his life in the *Divine Comedy* :—

> E lo spirito mio, che già cotanto
>   Tempo era stato, ch' alla sua presenza,
>   Non era di stupor tremando affranto,
> Sanza dagli occhi aver più conoscenza,
>   Per occulta virtù, che da lei mosse,
>   D' antico amor senti' la gran potenza.
> Tosto che nella vista mi percosse
>   L' alta virtù, che già m' avea trafitto
>   Prima ch' io fuor di puerizia fosse,
> Volsimi alla sinistra col respitto,
>   Col quale il fantolin corre alla mamma,
>   Quando ha paura, o quando egli è afflitto,
> Per dicere a Virgilio : Men che dramma
>   Di sangue m' è rimasa, che non tremi :
>   Conosco i segni dell' antica fiamma.*
>   —*Purgatorio*, xxx. 34—48.

The language, both in the *Vita Nuova* and in the *Purgatorio*, is plain enough. Yet, in spite of distinct evidence and of common sense, there have been found

---

* "And my spirit, which had now so long time been unstonied by the trembling caused by her presence, without receiving more knowledge from the eyes, by a hidden virtue that moved from her, felt of ancient love the mighty puissance. As soon as on my vision smote the sublime virtue which already had pierced me before I had passed from boyhood, I turned to the left with the anxiety with which a child runs to its mother when it is afraid or sad, to say to Virgil : Less than a drachm of blood is left within me that trembles not ; I recognise the traces of the ancient flame."

critics and biographers who deny that Beatrice was a real person at all. Gianmaria Filelfo, who pretended to write a life of Dante in the fifteenth century, was the first to promulgate this absurd* view: critics as acute as Biscioni† and the elder Rossetti, perverted by the desire to find political allegories in everything connected with Dante, and distracted by the idealizing spirit of persecuted Italian patriotism, have warmly supported a similar theory. That, however ingeniously defended, it militates against the truth of Dante's life, and renders it impossible to understand him, cannot be doubted by any unprejudiced and cool-headed reader. That it destroys the beauty and poetry of his history and reduces his warm-hearted humanity to an enthusiasm for an abstraction, is evident. So pernicious, indeed, is the mere suggestion of the heresy, that I shall take this occasion of saying, as it were, *in limine*, what I have to say about Beatrice and her influence over the life of Dante.

* *Vita Dantis* (ed. Florence, 1828) p. 20. "Ego æque Beatricem, quam amâsse fingitur Dante, muliebrem unquam fuisse opinor, ac fuit Pandora, quam omnium Deorum munus consecutam esse fabulantur poetæ. Scripsit, dicet ille (*i.e.* Boccachius) ad amicam cantiones. Scripserunt et Poetæ somnia, quæ figurata ratione majus aliquid complectantur."

† See FRATICELLI's Introduction to the *Vita Nuova*, p. 26. Rossetti does not deny that Dante's earliest affection was fixed upon "the little girl Beatrice Portinari, whom he began to love before he had passed from the years of boyhood;" but he interprets the title *Vita Nuova* and the name *Madonna* by reference to the allegorizing practice of the Ghibelline poets in such a way as to make it uncertain whether Dante was writing the history of his early love or of his political conversion.

IV.

To begin with, let us take a closer look at the *Vita Nuova*.* We have already seen how Dante first met Beatrice on May-day at her father's house. From this time forward, Love, he says, became his constant lord. "He oftentimes commanded me to seek if I might see this youngest of the angels: wherefore I, in my boyhood, often went in search of her, and found her so noble and praiseworthy that certainly of her might have been said those words of the poet Homer, She seemed not to be the daughter of a mortal man, but of God."† For nine years he waited on her thus, until when he had reached his eighteenth year, he chanced to meet her in the street walking between two ladies, and received her salutation. This was a memorable day; for it made Dante a poet. He returned to his chamber and fell asleep while thinking of her courtesy. Then, says Dante, "there appeared to be in my room a mist of the colour of fire, within the which I discerned the figure of a lord of terrible aspect to such as should gaze upon him, but who seemed therewithal to rejoice inwardly that it was

---

* The title simply means "Youthful Life," as would appear, if from nought else, from the following line (*Purgatorio* xxxi. 115):—
  Questi fu tal nella sua vita nuova.
Dante, in *Convito*, *Tratt*. iv. 24, divides the life of man into four parts, the first of which ends in the twenty-fifth year. This was Dante's age at the time of Beatrice's death.

† Rossetti's Translation.

a marvel to see. Speaking, he said many things, among the which I could understand but few; and of these, this: *Ego dominus tuus.*"* In his arms he bore a lady clothed with only a blood-coloured cloth, and in one hand he held a flaming heart. This was the first of many visions in which Love appeared to Dante, to warn and comfort him, and after seeing it Dante wrote the first Sonnet which he published.

The apparitions of Love are among the most touching and graceful incidents in the *Vita Nuova*. At one time he appears upon what Dante called "the way of sighs," "like a pilgrim, lightly dressed and with coarse raiment." At another time he came and sat by Dante's bed in the fashion of a youth "dressed in whitest raiment and thinking deeply." Again he stood by Dante's side when Beatrice, among her maidens, passed by, pointing out his lady and strengthening him to look on her. Each of these visions is related with artless simplicity, and with the fidelity of a painter carefully tracing on his canvas the form he has imagined. We feel that Dante saw Love thus, that he habitually externalized, made personal, the passion of his heart. It is thus that poets are the true myth-makers, for after no other fashion but this of fervent poetry did myths begin and take their splendid shapes in Greece. The Love, so realized by Dante, is a definite personage, such perhaps, as Burne Jones in his most inspired moments might

* ROSSETTI's Translation.

present to us with form and colour. No Love is he of Sappho or Anacreon, to descend from heaven with flaming chlamys on his shoulder, breaking hearts as winds rend oaks and forging souls upon his anvil—nor yet the Erôs of Alexandrian poets, to wanton bee-like among flowers—nor yet, again, such a winged nursling of the gods as, in the silver age of Athens, was seen by Praxiteles on poplar bough or pediment in the gymnasium. The difference between the love which "withdrew Dante's thoughts from all mean things,"* and that elder brother of his who shook the soul of Sappho with "bitter-sweet impracticable" violence, distinguishes their several appearances. A skilful artist might paint companion-pictures of the fiery-faced inexorable God of Greece and of that sympathizing youth whose eyes are filled with tears, who sighs, and bears the comfort of low, tender mystic words to his servant in his sleep. Dante's love was half religious; his lord was the cloistral spirit of those heavenly aisles in which Madonna's hymns are sung. The spirit of Æolian Hellas and of Tuscan Italy had not much in common: therefore Erôs, who is everywhere one Lord, and makes his faithful "wear upon their face his ensign," † came from heaven to Sappho in whirlwind and in splendour, to Dante in twilight and humility and calm.

We cannot follow all the incidents related by Dante

* *Vita Nuova*, xiii. † *Ibid.*, iv.

in his book of Love. Each is a picture; and each was the occasion of a poem. He is in church, and chooses from the crowd a lady whom he makes the screen of his real love for Beatrice. He passes the bier of a gracious maiden, and remembers to have seen her in the company of Beatrice. He receives the salute of Beatrice and tells us how for joy thereat he found no other word but Love in all his heart, and how his eyes became the shrine where every man might look on very Love. The father of Beatrice lies dead, and ladies passing from the house of mourning see in his wan face sorrow no less than hers. He is sick, and in his dream he beholds the angels carrying to heaven the soul of Beatrice like a little cloud of perfect whiteness. He tells us how, "crowned and raimented with humility, she walked among men," and how they said as she passed by, "this is no woman; rather it is one of heaven's most radiant angels." After she is really dead he sits down to paint the picture of an angel, and certain "men to whom it was needful to pay honour" interrupt him. Still carrying the burden of his loss about, a "gentle lady, young and very fair," looked kindly on him from a window with such sorrow in her eyes, "that all pity seemed in her to be gathered into one."

All these incidents, and many more of the same kind, are related with touching reverence. They are so many jewels in the memory of Dante, the thoughts which, if we may use the exquisite imagery of Shelley, he piles for "Love himself to slumber on." Interspersed with sonnet and canzone, and with quaint glosses and interpretations, these anecdotes form a book perfectly unique in its kind—steeped in all the melancholy of Dante's soul, glowing with his fervour and intensity, almost terrible in its tenderness. There is no book of the sort which reveals to us a spirit so profound, so tenacious of its thought, so loyal in its feeling, so pure and radiant and strong in spite of feminine tremulousness of emotion. Those who complain that Dante is stern and hard and pitiless would do well to study the *Vita Nuova* attentively. It tells a different tale of him from that which is recorded in the 8th and 33rd cantos of the *Inferno*. And yet he is in all respects the same Dante. Notably the same is he in his love of classification, arrangement, and precise order. He dissects his love-songs with the keenest criticism, laying bare the secret of his art and the sources of his inspiration. Even in the *Vita Nuova* there is nothing unplanned, unpremeditated. It is in every way a young book, pliant, and luxuriant when compared with the mature fruit of those later years which turned the poet's soul to adamant by tribulation. Yet even as the calculating artist of the *Divine Comedy* is already noticeable in the *Vita Nuova*, so may we affirm that the stream of youthful tenderness is not dry in the heart which wept for Francesca, and melted like wax beneath the words of Beatrice upon the Holy Mount.

At last the day of mourning came. Dante was engaged in writing a canzone in his lady's praise when "the Lord of Justice called my most gracious lady to be glorious beneath the banner of that blessed Queen Mary, whose name was always of greatest reverence in the words of saintly Beatrice." Here he notices a fact which strangely illustrates the temper of his mind. Beatrice died on the ninth day of the month, which, according to the Syrian calendar, was the ninth month of the year, and the year itself was that in which the perfect number ten reached its ninth completion in the century—that is, it was the year 1290. It will be remembered that he saw her first in her ninth year; that he wrote his first sonnet in her honour after the lapse of another nine years; and that her first salutation was made him in the ninth hour of the day. His dream of her in sickness happened on the ninth day after he had been taken ill. In this recurrence of the number nine he sees a deep and mystical significance. The number of the spheres that move is nine, and thus all the celestial influences were united in favourable conjunction at her birth. The root of nine is three, and the Trinity is three; therefore, argues Dante, Beatrice was continually accompanied by the number nine to show that she was herself "a nine, that is a miracle whereof the root is nought but the marvellous Trinity." This

Death of Beatrice. 45

process of reasoning, this profound attention to minute details, and straining of irrelevant coincidences, is very characteristic of Dante. We shall find it running through all the creations of his genius, and giving a peculiar tone to his imagination.

After Beatrice's death, Dante was indeed desolate; and the town of Florence seemed to him to mourn. The pilgrims passing through the "dolorous city" touched him with sadness, because they knew not of her name, and could not tell what made the streets so sad. He wrote a letter* to the chief men of the State, beginning *Quomodo sedet sola civitas ;* so seriously did he believe that all men sorrowed with him in his affliction. At last after a year "it was given to me," says Dante, "to behold a very wonderful vision; wherein I saw things which determined me that I would say nothing further of this most blessed one, until such time as I could discourse more worthily concerning her. And to this end I labour all I can; as she well knoweth. Wherefore if it be His pleasure through whom is the life of all things, that my life continue with me a few years, it is my hope that I shall yet write concerning her what hath not before been written of any woman. After

---

* We may reflect, not without humour, upon the grave citizens of Florence receiving in conclave (if so it reached them) this eloquent epistle of the forlorn poet. Was their sunshine clouded, were there no ballot boxes and votes of banishment, no cakes and ale and civic banquets left, because, forsooth, this youngest of the angels had been taken from her desolate husband and her love-lost worshipper.

the which, may it seem good unto Him who is the Master of Grace, that my spirit should go hence to behold the glory of its lady: to wit, of that blessed Beatrice who now joyeth continually on His countenance qui est per omnia sæcula benedictus. Laus Deo." *

V.

With this promise of the *Divine Comedy*, and with this prayer, which was heard and answered, Dante closed the *Vita Nuova*. We must resume the history of his life from other sources. What the studies were with which Dante strove both to console himself for the loss of Beatrice, and also to prepare himself for the great work in which he wished to praise her, we gather from the *Convito*. The grief in which he was at first buried resembled that described by St. Augustine in the fourth book of the *Confessions*. He found no consolation in study or in business, and everything which was not she for whom his heart was bleeding seemed to him more sad than death. "However," says the poet, in the third chapter of the second part of the *Convito*, "after some time my mind, which strove to regain strength, bethought itself (since neither my own consolations nor those of friends availed me aught) of having recourse to the method which had helped to comfort other spirits in distress.

* Rossetti's Translation.

I took to reading the book, not known to many students, of Boethius, wherewith, unhappy and in exile, he had comforted himself. And hearing also that Tully had written another book in which, while treating of friendship, he had used words of consolation to Lelius in the death of his friend Scipio, I read that also. And as it happens that a man goes seeking silver, and far from his design finds gold, which hidden causes yield him, not perchance without God's guidance, so I who sought for consolation found not only comfort for my tears, but also words of authors and of sciences and of books, weighing the which, I judged well that philosophy, the lady of these authors, of these sciences, and of these books, was a thing supreme. And I imagined her in fashion like a gentle lady, nor could I fancy her otherwise than piteous; wherefore so truly did I gaze upon her with adoring eyes that scarcely could I turn myself away. And having thus imagined her I began to go where she displayed her very self, that is in the schools of the religious, and the disputations of philosophers; so that in short time, about thirty months, I began so much to feel her sweetness that her love chased away and destroyed all other thought in me."

This remarkable passage helps us to understand how the image of Beatrice became identified in Dante's mind with that ideal of divine philosophy which ruled the minds of his masters Boethius and Cicero. After the study of these words we comprehend Dante's transition from the worship of Beatrice as a living woman to his worship of her as the symbol of Theology. We see the idea of Philosophy taking form in his essentially definite and picturesque imagination, and growing into life beside the image of Beatrice. At last there is a point at which the radiant visions melt into each other and are one. The last sentence and the last sonnet of the *Vita Nuova* mystically and covertly hint at this transition, and prepare us to conceive of the process by which Dante occupied with the thought of Beatrice, and intent at the same time upon the splendour of science revealed to him in study, was about to fuse the past and future of his soul in the apotheosis of his lost but living love. The death of Beatrice seemed at first to snap the thread of his life. But in those thirty months of study he was engaged in gathering up the broken strands and knotting them into imperishable strength. Dante had always loved Beatrice more as an idea than a reality: the end and object of his service was a salutation. Therefore it was not difficult for him, when death required it, to dispense with the reality and embrace the idea. Beatrice had become a need of his soul since the age of nine: he could not live without her. But it was not Beatrice in the flesh to whom he clung. He lost her for a moment, and then found her again — found her where no change of time or death could take her from him any more. Perhaps it would be impossible just so to idealize the wife or mistress who has shared our daily joys and sorrows. But to idealize the dream of passionate youth into the apocalypse of thinking manhood is far easier; and the death of the mortal object of the soul's desire renders such alchemy more possible. Beatrice was the thought which gave to Dante's soul its unity, the ceaseless rhythm of its song.

> Dal primo giorno, ch' io vidi 'l suo viso
> In questa vita infino a questa vista,
> Non è 'l seguir al mio canto preciso.*

His adoration for her never flagged :—

> Al suo piacere e tosto, e tardo
> Vegna rimedio agli occhi, che fûr porte,
> Quand' ella entrò col fuoco, ond' io sempre ardo.†

But this adoration changed its tone and temper. In the boy it was passionate worship of his lady's smile; in the man it was thoughtful and ecstatic communion with the spirit which revealed to him all truth. Dante knew this, and therefore he makes Beatrice ‡ herself enjoin on him the necessity of such idealization: like

---

* *Paradiso* xxx. 28. "From the first day that I saw her face in this life until this vision, the sequence of my song was never cut." In this passage he is describing the supreme radiance of Beatrice, for which he found no adequate words; therefore, for the first time, he says, at this point my song failed me.

† *Paradiso*, xxvi. 13. "At her pleasure, soon or late, let come the remedy to these eyes that were gates, when she passed in with the fire that ever burns me."

‡ *Purgatorio*, xxxi. 46—60. This passage, when rightly considered, destroys the possibility of Beatrice's having been a mere εἴδωλον.

Diotima, in Plato's *Symposium*, she bids him ascend from the first signs and types of beauty to the abstract and the real, passing from the love of some one beautiful being to the great wide sea of beauty itself. When we come to discuss the *Divine Comedy*, we shall see how far Dante was artistically successful in his idealization of Beatrice. It is enough now to have explained the transition from the *Vita Nuova* to the *Convito*, from the worship of Beatrice alive, to the adoration of Beatrice in heaven. Having done this, I must turn to a very different side of Dante's life, and set forth the political condition of Florence at his time.

VI.

In order to make Dante's position as a patriot and politician clear, it will be necessary to take a survey of that entangled thicket of parties, factions, fierce hostilities and frigid treacheries—that "selva selvaggia" of Guelf and Ghibelline, Neri and Bianchi, Cerchi and Donati, Secchi and Verdi, in the midst of which the poet found himself in middle life without a path. Our best way of piercing this wild wood will be first to consider those domestic quarrels in Florence and Pistoja which added peculiar bitterness to party politics, and then to explain the position of the great factions of the Guelfs and Ghibellines when complicated by minor and more private sources of disturbance.

From 1115, the date of the death of the Countess Matilda, until 1215, Florence enjoyed peace, and advanced in civil liberty. In the latter year the tranquillity of the horizon was disturbed by a storm which, gathering from a cloud at first no bigger than a man's hand, grew to overspread her sky and blot out all her sunshine. Buondelmonte de' Buondelmonti, a noble youth of Florence, was betrothed to a lady of the Amidei family, when the fancy took him to jilt her and to marry one of the Donati.* This was reckoned a great insult to the Amidei, and their anger against the Donati waxed the fiercer, inasmuch as it was thought that the mother of the bride had enticed away the bridegroom from his first allegiance. The Amidei reckoned among their kindred and allies some of the most powerful Florentine families, notably the Uberti and the Lamberti. These conspired to wipe the insult out with blood; and in the fatal year of 1215 they killed Buondelmonte on the Ponte Vecchio beneath an old statue of Mars which stood there.

> Conveniasi a quella pietra scema,
> Che guarda 'l ponte, che Florenza fesse
> Vittima nella sua pace estrema.†

Buondelmonte's murder left a heritage of woes for

---

* *See* VILLANI, v. 38. References to the affair are to be found in the *Divine Comedy: Inferno*, xxviii. 106; *Paradiso*, xvi. 136—147. The beginning of troubles at Pistoja was also a family squabble; so, but more romantic, was the beginning of parties at Bologna with the unhappy loves of Bonifazio Gieremei and Imelda Lambertazzi, 1273.

† *Paradiso*, xvi. 145. "It was ordained that at the broken stone which guards the bridge Florence should slay a victim in her last hours of peace."

Florence. His family and their supporters, numbering thirty-nine of the chief houses of the state, became Guelfs: the Uberti, heading the remaining thirty-three great families, ranged themselves as Ghibellines. It was thus that in mediæval Italy a private vendetta could plunge a tranquil city into a worse than civil war—worse, because the strife of Guelf and Ghibelline was interminable.

Frederick the Second made use of these domestic feuds to set his foot in Florence, hitherto unanimously Guelf. We need not relate how Ghibellines exiled Guelfs in 1249; how they in turn were driven out in 1258; how Farinata degli Uberti headed the great faction of the Empire; how, finally, after many ebbs and flows of fortune, the Guelf party got the upper hand a little while before the birth of Dante. The Alighieri, we may remark, were Guelfs throughout this struggle.

Hitherto no mention has been made of Blacks and Whites, the names which play so large a part in all memorials of Dante's time. But we are going to hear of them. Yet before we pass on to this topic it will be well to trace the few events in Dante's life which preceded the epoch of the feuds of the Bianchi and the Neri. Being a noble by birth, of good fortune and of able person, he naturally took his place among the chivalry of Florence during the wars which the Guelf party waged against Arezzo and Pisa. We know from his own poem that he was present at the battle of

His Marriage.

Campaldino*, and the evacuation of Caprona.† In the year 1292, two years after the death of Beatrice, he was in Florence: it was then that, worn out with grief, and pressed by the solicitations of his friends, he married Gemma Donati—perhaps ‡ the lady of the piteous eyes who drew his heart toward her in his grief, as he relates at the end of the *Vita Nuova*. After saying that Gemma bore him seven children during ten years of married life, that she did not accompany him in exile, and that Dante never mentions either her or his seven children, we may dismiss her from our notice. There is no reason to suppose that she was a bad wife ; § Boccaccio's and Manetti's stories being probably mere gossip. In a town so small as Florence every citizen of ability and fortune was a statesman : ‖ but in order for

---

* *Inferno*, xxii. 4. † *Ibid.* xxi. 94.

‡ This is an inference of Fraticelli's (*Vita di Dante*, p. 109), who calls attention to the fact that the houses of the Alighieri were placed back to back with those of the Donati at Florence. If this explanation of the passage in the *Vita Nuova* (section xxxvi.) be thought too matter of fact, we may suppose that the lady in whom "all pity seemed to be collected" was an allegory of the transient solace he found at this time in mere study. But as Beatrice was a real woman, it seems more consistent with Dante's plan in the *Vita Nuova*, to believe that the lady at the window was also a reality.

§ See FRATICELLI, *Vita di Dante*, p. 109. Leonardo Bruni, who, as a chronicler and grammarian, had no sympathy for love-stories, is very severe on Boccaccio for having represented Dante's wife as "tutta d'amore, di sospiri e di cocenti lagrime piena." Indeed Boccaccio's notice of the life of Dante is full of the faults usual with a novelist's narrative of fact.

‖ Florence at the time of Dante was governed by three Councils and the Signoria. The Signoria consisted of six Priors of the Arts, to whom was added the Gonfalonier of Justice in the year 1306. The executive power was vested in this chamber, and supported by a body of 2,000

a Florentine to take office in the government, it was requisite for him to be thirty years of age, and to be enrolled in one of the seven arts or guilds, the chiefs or priors of which constituted the supreme administrative Council. Accordingly, about the year 1295, Dante entered the Art of the Physicians, the sixth among the seven privileged Arti of Florence. This guild traded not merely in drugs, but also in spices and all Oriental produce, including precious stones. So thoroughly republican was Florence, that her nobles were obliged to be merchants before they could be ministers. It will be remembered that her proudest family, than which no other has been more illustrious in Europe, was called de' Medici—of the physicians. Well, Dante entered the Arte degli Speziali, and in 1300 he was elected Prior. The year 1300 brought new miseries to Florence, and blasted Dante's civil life more thoroughly than 1295 had been able to affect his personal happiness.

soldiers. The Councils were severally of the People, of the Capitudini, and of the Podestà. The Council of the People, numbering 300, was elected by lot. That of the Capitudini consisted of the chief men in the arts of the two first ranks, and of other officials of distinction. That of the Podestà (who himself was always a foreigner) was composed of 90 or 100 members, nobles, commoners of eminence—an assembly of representative notables. Laws having received the sanction of the Priors were successively presented to the three Councils, and then submitted to the Consiglio Generale, in which the several chambers were united. They then, if ratified, became valid. It may be further remarked that the Priorate lasted only two months, and that the Signoria consulted another subordinate body of advisers call Collegi in their deliberations. Any citizen aged thirty, belonging to an Art, and of Guelf principles, might hold office in any of the above capacities except that of Podestà.

Faction and sedition, like plagues and malignant fevers, are contagious. The new curse came from Pistoja—Pistoja * which Dante calls the lair of noxious beasts. This little town, which the modern traveller from the north to Florence, sees outspread beneath him like a puzzle, as the express train from Bologna sweeps down the curves of the Apennine railway, harboured in the thirteenth century two families of Cancellieri. They were descended from the same ancestor, but were the families of separate mothers, one of whom was named Bianca. Hence half the Cancellieri were called Bianchi, and another half, for the sake of distinction, Neri. These cousins do not seem to have lived in less than ordinary mediæval amity, until a lad of the Neri wounded one of the Bianchi in a quarrel, and was sent by his father to apologize at the house of the injured man. The head of the Bianchi branch did not see fit to treat the matter lightly. He took the youth and chopped his right hand off upon a dresser, and bade him tell his father that, "Injuries are effaced with blood and not with words." Here, indeed, was enough to set Pistoja by the ears. One half of the citizens sided with the Neri and another half with the Bianchi, and the city was possessed by internecine warfare.

Now came the turn of Florence. At first the Florentine citizens contented themselves with securing the leaders of both Pistojan factions and imprisoning

* *Inferno*, xxiv. 125.

them in Florence. They might as well have sprinkled fire and brimstone through every street. Among their own families were two, the one old and poor, called Donati, the other rich but recent, called Cerchi. The former were headed by Corso de' Donati, the latter by Viero de' Cerchi; and, I need not add, they were at feud. The Donati took the part of the Cancellieri Neri; the Cerchi that of the Cancellieri Bianchi. In this way, through the private enmities of two Pistojan and two Florentine houses, the state of Florence was divided between Black and White. All this while Florence was ostensibly Guelf. The Neri and Bianchi were subdivisions, which, in time, became respectively pure Guelfs and disaffected Guelfs, but which, in their commencement, were wholly unpolitical. After the same fashion Arezzo, properly a Ghibelline city, had its Secchi and its Verdi, pure and disaffected Ghibellines. The private rancours of the Bianchi and the Verdi drew them gradually away from their old political allegiance, and forced them to seek allies among their former foes. It was in this way that the standing quarrel of Guelf and Ghibelline proved so disastrous to Italian towns.

About these august and time-honoured parties a few words must be said before returning to Dante. Upon the ruins of the Roman civilization, there sprang up two powers—the Papacy and the Empire—both temporal, both claiming the supremacy. Both, too, were traditionally cosmopolitan: the Vicar of Christ pretended to be the *servus servorum* of entire humanity, while Rome, from which the Emperors derived their sceptre, still represented the metropolis of the inhabited world. The Papacy, however, became by degrees more exclusively Italian. The Empire, in like manner, grew more genuinely German through the influence of the Electors, who were German powers. Italy lay between the two, forming the battle-field of the Pope's friends, who called themselves Guelf, and of the Emperor's, who called themselves Ghibelline. A third power, in course of time, intervened and complicated matters: France gave material assistance to the Papacy, and plagued the States of Italy with foreign interference. At last, in Dante's days, the King of France transferred the Papal See to Avignon, caused a schism, and sorely muddled the old humdrum course of Guelf policy.

The Church of Rome, true to the spirit of Christianity, and to its own principles of organization, sided with the popular governments in Italy, fostered the growth of municipalities, and, while allowing the free cities of Italy to exist, endeavoured to become the arbiter and referee in all their quarrels. The Imperial policy, on the other hand, in general was to maintain the cause of the nobles against the commons, and to support feudalism. Such strongly marked antagonism of Pope and Emperor, representing as they did conflicting principles, was disastrous for Italy. All Italian schemes of policy were vitiated by the double influences between which states, cities, and individuals wavered. The minds of thinkers as powerful as Dante could not escape from the thraldom of Papal and Imperial supremacy: to believe in two co-equal rulers, divinely appointed to hold sway in Rome, was an article of faith. But, what was worst, the nation, torn between two extremes, was prevented from pursuing a free development from within, and failed to attain stability or unity. The Popes, being not dynastic but elective, and less Italians than Churchmen, never conceived the idea of organizing Italy into one confederation on any basis possible in the Middle Ages. It was their policy to pit the various towns and states against each other, and to appeal for aid to France. But, while they did not unite Italy themselves, they prevented the Emperors from doing so. Many eager Italian patriots, Dante among the number, still dreamed that the Emperor might fix his seat of power at Rome, and make one nation from the Alps to Brindisi. But the time for this had really passed away. Every year made the Empire more German, and France more powerful in the affairs of Italy. The genuine warfare of Guelf *versus* Ghibelline began to languish. In Dante's days Guelfism was a disorderly spirit of democracy fostered by the Popes, and directed for selfish purposes by France. The Ghibelline faction, grown weak, was composed of nobles and anti-Guelfs, rather than of true Imperial partizans. The very names of Bianchi and Neri, Secchi and Verdi, Donati and

Cerchi, as we have before seen, proved that the old strife had been made more turbid by the mixture of domestic discords. Politics in Italy degenerated into a hopeless tangle of factions and confused interests, so nicely balanced that a private quarrel was sufficient to upset a state. It was no season for a great and patriotic man to espouse the simple cause of either Guelf or Ghibelline, Neri or Bianchi. We shall not, therefore, be surprised to find Dante first renouncing Guelfism, and then keeping clear of Ghibellines, and finally creating, as he said, a party for himself. Not that he—the most impassioned of politicians, who would have enforced Solon's law and slain the citizen who stood aloof in party strife—the most severe of moralists, who set self-seeking citizens in a limbo severed from the joys of heaven and from the tragic pains of hell—can be counted among the Vigliacchi or the Lukewarm. The very thought of such a thing moves laughter, it is so absurd. No : he was more than a Ghibelline in his bitter rancour against the temporal Papacy and France, in his enthusiastic zeal for the imperial supremacy. He escaped from the parties of his time through the intensity of his partizanship and the acumen of his views. He became a theoretical politician, an ardent and impassioned doctrinaire, an inspired prophet, standing outside existing factions and clinging tenaciously to the dream which he had formed of a future and better state of things, destined by the Providence of God to supersede factions and restore the divine order of the world. Upon his conception of that order hinged all his theories. The double idea of the Papacy as a spiritual power supreme over the souls and eternal interests of men, of the Empire as a temporal power supreme over the lives and mundane interests of men, lies at the root of his treatise *De Monarchiâ*, pervades the *Divine Comedy*, reappears in his Ethics and Psychology.

CHAPTER III.

DANTE'S LIFE IN EXILE.

(i.) His Embassy to Rome, Exile, Residence at Arezzo, and Friendship with Uguccione—(ii.) In Lunigiana with the Marquis of Villafranca: Visit to the Convent del Corvo, and Frate Ilario's Letter—(iii.) Dante at Paris, at Milan: Letter to the Princes and Peoples of Italy: the Treatise *De Monarchiâ*—(iv.) Letter to Florentines: Letter to Henry. Henry's Death: Dante Retires to Gubbio: Letter to the Italian Cardinals — (v.) Visits Uguccione at Lucca: Battle of Monte Catini: Dante's Letter to a Friend, refusing to return in Disgrace to Florence—(vi.) At Can Grande's Court: Change to Ravenna. Embassy to Venice: Death—(vii.) The Question of the Veltro—(viii.) Dante's Personal Appearance and Qualities.

I.

DANTE, we saw, was Prior in the year 1300, when the feuds of the Cerchi and Donati broke out in Florence. It was, therefore, his business with his colleagues to prevent the spread of faction, and especially to guard against the resuscitation of Guelf and Ghibelline disputes. The measures for public safety which they took were these. They banished the leaders of the Donati to Castello della Pieve, and those of the Cerchi to Serrezzano. Among the latter was Dante's earliest and best friend, Guido

Cavalcanti, the poet. This circumstance proved calamitous to Dante: for Guido falling ill at Serrezzano, while Dante still held the Priorate, was suffered to return before the other exiles to Florence. This gave the watchful enemies and enviers of Dante occasion to pretend that he showed favour to the Cerchi and his friend. Dante himself, in a letter seen by his biographer, Bruni, asserts that all his misfortunes dated from his Priorate.

In 1301 the Neri returned to Florence and determined to establish themselves in power. In order to do so they appealed to Pope Boniface, and sought the aid of Charles of Valois (who was travelling to reconquer Sicily) complaining that the Cerchi were pure Ghibellines. The dread of French interference caused the Priors of August 1301 to send four ambassadors, one of whom was Dante, to Rome. Boniface temporized with them; and before they returned, Charles had entered Florence. Dante never saw his "bel San Giovanni" more.

Under cover of French power the Neri had it their own way in Florence. They drove the Cerchi to their towers; and for six days massacre and rapine held the town. A third part of the city was in flames. Meanwhile, new Priors, nominees of the Neri faction, were appointed, who condemned, exiled, and confiscated at pleasure. Dante was one of the proscribed persons. Charges were laid against him of embezzlement and unjust traffic while in office: it was also considered a crime that he had exiled the chiefs of the Donati, and endeavoured to keep Charles of Valois out of Florence. His sentence, tantamount to perpetual banishment with confiscation of property, was pronounced in January, 1302.

Dante's position was peculiarly trying. During his youth, true to the principles of his country and his blood, he had been a Guelf. While in office he had sought purely to extinguish faction, to preserve his country from foreign interference, and to separate the welfare of Florence from the interests of selfish parties. He now found himself, owing principally to his own patriotism, which had inflamed the hatred of the Neri, driven to herd with the Bianchi, and to make common cause with the Ghibellines. I have already tried to explain Dante's political position, and to show that he was really an idealist placed far above the strife of petty parties. Yet henceforth he had to call himself a Ghibelline, and, as far as Florence was concerned, to sign himself, "Exul immeritus," "Florentinus natione, non moribus."

The Florentine exiles assembled first at Gargonza, and thence betook themselves to Ghibelline Arezzo,* where they stayed till 1304. Dante was one of the twelve

---

* In 1304, on the night of July 21st, the Whites, under Baschiera Tosinghi, endeavoured to enter Florence by surprise. Petrarch was born in this night, his father being among the troops who marched to Florence.

counsellors appointed as a committee of management by the refugees. It was at Arezzo that he formed the friendship of Uguccione della Faggiuola, the illustrious Ghibelline chief, to whom he dedicated the first cantica of the *Divine Comedy*. This firm friend of his exile entertained Dante at Montefeltro, and afterwards at Lucca, and finally caused him to be honourably received by Can Grande at Verona. We shall see that Dante reposed great hopes in him as the deliverer of Italy. He does not, however, appear to have been particularly cordial to the Florentine Bianchi while they tarried at Arezzo. Finding all negotiations with the Neri useless, the exiles raised an army of 10,000 men, with the assistance of the Ghibellines of Arezzo, Romagna, Bologna, and Pistoja, and took the field in 1304. They were unsuccessful in this attempt to return with arms to their country. Dante seems to have been adverse to the display of force; but he could not impress his views upon the companions of his exile. They kept continually agitating and intriguing, until in 1306, disgusted with their base and trivial arts, Dante withdrew from them altogether and made a party for himself:

> E quel che più ti graverà le spalle,
>   Sarà la compagnia malvagia e scempia,
>   Con la qual tu cadrai in questa valle;
> Che tutta ingrata, tutta matta empia
>   Si farà contra te; ma poco appresso
>   Ella, non tu, n' avrà rotta la tempia.

His Solitude.

> Di sua bestialitate il suo processo
> Farà la pruova, sì ch' a te fia bello
> Averti fatta parte a te stesso.*

It is clear that Dante was a savage man to deal with, easily offended, not easily pleased, tenacious of his views, despotic in his will, requiring obedience when he had no claim to it but that of intellectual superiority. The austere, sarcastic, pregnant-witted, silent, acrid man must have cut a strange figure among giddy-pated party leaders, backstairs schemers, hot-headed young adventurers, and all the rabble of a discontented set of refugees. It was well for him and them that he seceded from them. For a long time after doing so he hoped that one or other of the factions would make overtures to win him back.

> La tua fortuna tanto onor ti serba,
> Che l' una parte e l' altra avranno fame
> Di te.†

But it does not appear that either of them were very desirous of the weight which his stern character and keen intellect would bring them.

The remainder of Dante's history is the record of

---

* *Paradiso*, xvii. 61. "And that which most will weigh upon your shoulders will be the vicious and vile company with whom you will fall into this vale. For ungrateful, mad, and impious, all will turn against you: yet soon they, and not you, will have brows broken thereby. Of their brutishness, their faring will be proof; so that it will become you well to have made for yourself a party for yourself alone."

† *Inferno*, xv. 70. "Thy fortune reserves such honour for thee, that both parties will have a hunger of thee."—CARLYLE's Translation.

his solitary wanderings and of his various writings. Occasionally in a letter or an anecdote that bears the stamp of truth, he emerges into distinctness. We see the darkness of his night dispelled at one time by the promise of Uguccione, at another by the advent of the Emperor; but these flashes of hope are brief, and end at last in total gloom. The brave strong spirit of the man supports him. His pride and courage never waver. In his poems and his letters he relaxes no strain of his grand and high-wrought style. Nay, so mighty is the source of strength within him, that, as the prospects of the present darken, the prophecy of the future grows more splendid in his soul; as earth sinks into shadow, heaven shines radiant around him.

II.

In August, 1306, we hear of Dante at Padua, witnessing a contract, and afterwards in Lunigiana, with Moroello de' Malaspini, Marquis of Villafranca. This prince entertained him generously and employed him in negotiations with the Bishop of Luni. It was to Moroello that Dante dedicated the *Purgatorio;* the prophecy which terminates the eighth canto refers to his magnificent and courteous hospitality. In the next year Dante was at Casentino, on the Arno, where he seems to have fallen in love with a lady, "a' miei principii, a' miei costumi, ed alla mia fortuna pienamente conforme."* In 1308 he was at Forli; and again in 1309 we find him in Lunigiana, on his way to Paris. It was during this visit to the Riviera, between Genoa and Leghorn, that Dante visited the Convent of Santa Croce, on the headland called Del Corvo, whence he sent a copy of the *Inferno* to his friend Uguccione. The letter of Frate Ilario,† who forwarded Dante's poem, is still extant: it gives so lively a picture of the poet's visit that I will translate a part:—" I say, then, that when this man (Dante) was on his way to lands beyond our mountains, and was passing through the diocese of Luni, whether the sacredness of the spot or some other reason moved him, he visited our convent. As soon as I perceived that he was unknown to myself and to my brethren, I questioned of him what he wanted; and seeing that he answered nought, again I asked him what he wanted. Thereat, he, looking round upon the brethren who were with me, answered—Peace. This making me the more eager to know of what condition was the man, I withdrew him from the rest, and after conversation with him knew that it was Dante. For though before that day I never saw him, his fame had reached me a long time since. When he noticed that my attention was wholly fixed upon him, and recognized how eagerly I waited for his words, he

---

* "Fully suited to my principles, my habits, and my fortune."
† The genuineness of this document has been called in question, but without sufficient reason, as it seems to me.

drew a little book from his breast and gave it to me frankly. 'Here,' he said, 'is one part of my work, which peradventure, you have never seen. This memento I leave you that you may the more firmly keep me in mind.' After he had showed the book, I took it with gratitude, and in his presence fixed my eyes on it attentively. Seeing that it was written in the vulgar dialect, I showed thereat some wonder, and he asked the reason of my doubt. I answered that I wondered at the language, seeing that it seemed not merely difficult, but quite impossible to explain in common speech such weighty matter, and also that a popular style appeared unsuited for the clothing of science so profound. To which, in reply, he said:—'You are doubtless reasonable in what you think; for when at first the seed, which, peradventure, dropped from heaven, was shooting up into the purpose of my work, I chose for it the due and customary speech; nor did I merely choose it, but, keeping to the usages of poetry, I began my labour thus:—

> Ultima regna canam, fluido conterminа mundo,
> Spiritibus quæ lata patent, quæ præmia solvunt
> Pro meritis cuicunque suis.*

Yet when I re-considered the circumstances of the present age, I saw that the songs of famous poets went almost for nought; wherefore, men of gentle blood, who

---

* "Of the furthest realms will I sing, conterminous with the world of waters, which spread abroad for souls, doomed each to the reward of his deserts."

wrote in better times, abandoned the liberal arts to the plebeian crowd. Accordingly, I laid aside the little lyre, to which at first I trusted, and tuned another, suited to the sense of modern men: for it is idle to set solid food before the lips of sucklings.'"

The picture of Dante among the monks in the loggia of their high-raised Camaldolese monastery, though rather theatrical, is striking. The Latin opening of the *Divine Comedy* as first designed is inestimably precious, since it shows in what a gulf of mere Virgilian mannerism Dante's genius would have sunk had he continued to place confidence in that poor imitative little lyre he strung.

By the choice of "common speech" which Dante made, he signalized his royal nature, and entered upon a domain as splendid as that discovered by Columbus. With the exception of a few lyrical poets he had no predecessor in Italian composition. Goethe's epigrammatic satire on modern versifiers, who forget how much of their so-called poetry is due to the mere use of a highly cultivated language, could not be applied to him. It was he who had to make the melodies of his native tongue. On the other hand he enjoyed the liberty of a first discoverer. Italian was a virgin soil,—

> A footfall there
> Suffices to upturn to the warm air
> Half-germinating spices.

The restrictive conditions under which the poet in

a formed language of literature (not to speak of a *dead* language) has to labour, did not oppress him. He was free to invent and to select without avoidance of stereotyped phrases or submission to conventional canons of what the critics call pure taste. Even the most natural and spontaneous expressions of the beautiful language he employed bore the stamp of his royalty, the superscription of his coinage.

III.

Dante continued his visit to Paris, and stayed there in the spring of 1309. Boccaccio, in a Latin poem addressed to Petrarch with a copy of the *Divine Comedy*, states that he even went so far as England:

Parisios dudum . . . . extremosque Britannos.

Giovanni da Serravalle, who lived a century after Dante, makes this tradition still more definite: "Anagogice dilexit theologiam sacram, in quâ diu studuit tam Oxoniis in regno Angliæ quam Parisiis in regno Franciæ." Dante's works unfortunately contain no reference to England, though he shows familiarity with Paris, and also with the Flemish towns.* It would have been curious to read some illustration drawn from the scenery of the High Street or the Isis in the midst of the *Inferno*.

Anyhow, Dante could not have long remained in

* *Inferno*, xv. 4.

the North;* the greatest political event of his lifetime was about to take place—the Emperor was coming once more to Italy; the Albert, to whom Dante had appealed so passionately in the 6th canto of the *Purgatorio*—

> O Alberto Tedesco, ch' abbandoni
> Costei, ch' è fatta indomita e selvaggia,
> E dovresti inforcar gli suoi arcioni—†

was dead. Henry, Count of Luxemburg, had succeeded him in 1308, and in the beginning of 1311 he assumed the iron crown at Milan. Dante hurried thither and threw himself at the foot of the Emperor, whom he regarded as the destined saviour of Italy. It was at this time that he addressed his triumphant and heart-thrilling Epistle to the Princes and Peoples of Italy, and put forth his *Treatise De Monarchiâ*, which had probably been written some years before. Perhaps this will be the best occasion to take notice of Dante's theory of the Universal Monarchy, for thus we shall be gradually building up our notion of his philosophy, and forming a basis for the consideration of his essentially political and philosophical poem.

The *De Monarchiâ* is written in Latin, and is divided

---

* It is worth mentioning that Boniface died in 1304, and was succeeded by Clement, the creature of Philip le Bel, who never set foot in Italy (see VILLANI, viii. 80.) Then began the Babylonian captivity of the Popes at Avignon. They became serfs of France, but not always obedient vassals; for on the death of Albert of Hapsburg, Philip could not get the Papal See to support the election of his brother Charles, in consequence of which Henry, Count of Luxemburg, was chosen.

† *Purgatorio*, vi. 97. "O Albert, the German, who desertest her who is grown unruly and wild, and oughtest to bestride her middle-bows!"

into three books. In the first of these Dante inquires whether an Universal Monarchy, which he defines as "a single principality supreme over all men in time, or in and over all things that are measured by time," is good for the world; in the second, whether the Roman people have a legitimate right to it; in the third, whether it is derived immediately from God or from his Vicar the Pope. The whole style of the book is wearisomely disputative, logic-chopping, and hair-splitting. Arguments of great pregnancy and weight are mingled with trivial quibblings upon words and idle superstitions. Fine thoughts are embedded in tiresome explanations or overloaded with scholastic pompousness of phrase. These are the common faults of Dante's prose works on philosophical subjects: the *Epistle to Can Grande*, in which he glosses the first few lines of his *Paradiso*, though shorter, is not less oppressively pedantic than the *De Monarchiâ*. He was not above the vices of the learning of his age. Indeed there was something in his own nature which inclined him to take pleasure in using the cumbrous mechanism of the logic of the schools, when he might have spoken plainly and directly. In spite, however, of defects of style, the *De Monarchiâ* is of first importance for the explanation of Dante's views. He settles the first* of his three questions affirmatively

---

* *De Monarchiâ*, L. 5—"Actuare semper totam potentiam intellectûs possibilis per prius ad speculandum et secundario propter hoc ad operandum per suam extensionem." "Pax universalis est optimum eorum quæ ad nostram beatitudinem ordinantur."

by defining the end of man to be his intellectual activity, contemplative and active, which can only exist unimpeded during profound peace. This view of human life is not a little remarkable in a theorist of the Middle Ages. Dante shows that a supreme monarchy would insure such peace, by establishing one moderator and justice-maker throughout the civilized world. Many other arguments he adduces from the Divine Nature to prove that such a monarchy as he intends would be the image of celestial order on the world. He also remarks that our Lord * consecrated monarchy by assuming humanity when monarchy was perfect and the world at peace beneath Augustus. The second book proves at length that Rome is the God-appointed seat of monarchy. The arguments are curious. Dante appeals to the Roman miracles recorded by Livy; † he describes the Roman people as most noble of all peoples; he asserts that Nature framed them for Empire, quoting Virgil's famous lines, "Excudent alii," &c., and that the Romans conquered the world for the world's good; he founds their right on their might; ‡ and finally points again to the fact that our Lord himself owned the sway of Augustus at his birth and of Tiberius at his death.

* Cf. Epistle to Henry, Section iii. ; *Ibid*, xviii. ; Cf. *Convito*, iv. 5. "E perocchè nella venuta," etc.

† *De Monarchiâ*, ii. 4.

‡ "Ille populus qui cunctis athletizantibus pro imperio mundi prævaluit, de divino jure prævaluit," li. 9. "Et quod per duellum acquiritur de jure acquiritur," li. 10.

Dante's veneration for Rome, based upon religious belief and strengthened by conviction, never wavered. Rome was the sacred, inviolable, God-created city in his eyes.

> Qualunque ruba quella, o quella schianta,
> Con bestemmia di fatto offende Dio,
> Che solo all' uso suo la creò santa.*

In the 3rd book Dante demonstrates that the Empire, which he has proved to be beneficial and to be of right Roman, is not dependent on "God's vicar or minister, by whom I mean the successor of Peter, who is in truth the keeper of the keys of the celestial realm." He meets all the Papal arguments from Scripture and from history, destroying them with skill, and adducing many passages of the Gospel in which the Empire as a separate power is recognized by Christ and His Apostle. The last chapter of the book, in which he winds up his argument, is of great value. It sets forth with precision the dualism of which we have already spoken. Man, he says, being by nature double, partaking of corruptibility and incorruptibility, has two ends to which he tends. In harmony with these two ends, he is subject to two orders, Temporal and Spiritual, the Empire and the Papacy; he has two guides, Reason and Faith, Philosophy and Revelation, the works of Sages and Poets, and the Gospel; he is fitted for two forms of beatitude, earthly and

---

* *Purgatorio*, xxxiii. 58.—"Whoso robs her or despoils her, with blasphemy of act offendeth God, who only for his own use made her holy."

celestial, to which the cardinal and theological virtues severally lead him. God alone is above the two chief rulers of mankind. Pope and Emperor* take their authority alike from Him; nor is either subject to the other. Their spheres are essentially different. In like manner the Sun and Moon rule the sky, and are distinct. Dante, however, adds:—"This truth must not be held so straitly but that the Roman Emperor should not in some point be inferior to the Roman Pontiff; seeing that the mortal felicity of man is, in some sort, subject to the immortal. Wherefore let Cæsar reverence Peter, even as a first-born son his father;† so that illumined by light of paternal grace he may with the more virtue shine upon the world, whereto he is appointed by that Sun who ruleth all things spiritual and temporal." These words close the treatise.

* Dante looked on Rome, the Holy City, as the seat of both:

> Soleva Roma, che 'l buon mondo feo,
> Duo Soli aver, che l' una e l' altra strada
> Facean vedere, e del mondo e di Deo.
> L' un l' altro ha spento, ed è giunta la spada
> Col pastorale ; e l' un coll' altro insieme
> Per viva forza, mal convien che vada.
> —*Purgatorio*, xvi. 106.

Compare the following sentence of Innocent IV.: "Two lights, the sun and the moon, illumine the globe; two powers, the papal and the royal, govern it; but as the moon receives her light from the more brilliant star, so kings reign by the chief of the Church who comes from God."

† Compare the end of the epistle to the Princes of Italy: "Hic est quem Petrus, Dei Vicarius, honorificare nos monet ; quem Clemens, nunc Petri successor, luce apostolicæ benedictionis illuminat ; ut ubi radius spiritualis non sufficit, ibi splendor minoris luminaris illustret."

IV.

While Dante was thus engaged in publishing and promulgating his political theories he did not forget his own countrymen, but addressed a letter, dated March, 1311, from the source of the Arno,—he was then residing at Casentino—which is truly notable for savage rancour. Headed with these words: "Dantes Allagherius florentinus et exul immeritus sceleratissimis Florentinis intrinsecis,"* it is sustained throughout on the same note of threatening and invective. This is how the proud exile inveighs against his civil foes:—"You, who transgress all laws, human and divine, you who are dragged by insatiable cupidity into all crime, quake you not to hear of the second death?" A little further on he taunts them with the coming of the Emperor:—"Hemmed in by a poor ditch do you put faith in your contemptible defences? What good will be your ditch, your bastions and towers, when the eagle, terrible with plumes of gold, comes flying, she, who over Pyrenee, or Caucasus, or Atlas, soaring, and supported by the breath of the celestial host, is wont, on her strong pinions, to look down on spreading ocean plains?" It was not a letter to put the Florentines in good humour: indeed, it led to another proclamation against Dante. Meanwhile,

* "Dante Alighieri, of Florence, an exile without blame, to those most wicked Florentines within the walls."

the poet, by the source of Arno, wondered why the Emperor delayed so long in Lombardy. Was he crushing factions there, pacifying Bergamo, besieging Cremona, attending to such trifles, when Florence shook her spear against him? Henry proved too slow a champion for the ardour of a prophet, for an exile's yearning eyes. Accordingly in April, 1311, Dante wrote him an epistle, which is extant. This letter is in many ways remarkable. Listen to its title: "To the most holy Triumpher and only Lord, Henry, by divine Providence King of the Romans, ever august, his most devoted servants, Dante Alighieri, of Florence, an exile without cause, and all the Tuscans in one band who wish for peace on earth, send salutation by the kissing of feet." Dante thus makes himself the Coryphaeus of his countrymen, of the faithful among them whom he recognized. He proceeds to greet the Emperor in terms of grandest flattery, comparing him to the much desired Sun-God, and applying to him the sacred words, "Behold the Lamb of God! Behold Him who taketh away the sins of the world!" Then he asks him why he tarries in the places of the north, seeking to extirpate the hydra which springs into life again as soon as slain. "Knowest thou not, most excellent of princes, nor from the watch-tower of thy supreme height markest thou, where the fox, from whom the stink ariseth, safe from hunters, hath her lair? Not of the headlong Po, nor of thy Tiber doth she slake her sinful thirst, but lo! her jaws envenom Arno's flowing tide, and Florence (canst thou now be ignorant) is the name of this dire pest. She is the viper preying on the vitals of her dam: she is the sick sheep that taints her master's flock: she is the impious and accursed Myrrha burning for her sire's embrace: she is that mad Amata, who, refused the marriage bond ordained by fate, and feared not to accept a son-in-law, by God denied, yea drove him by her fury into war, and, paying in the end the penalty of crime, suspended her own body by the noose." And so on, for several paragraphs of impassioned vituperation, biting as vitriol, vivid as Greek fire. It is necessary to keep some of these vindictive passages in mind, in order to comprehend the bitterness of Dante's gall, and to see why, exile as he was, without due cause, he made return to Florence for himself all but impossible. If Florence acted by him like a stepmother—which she did—he told her plainly of it, and recriminated as he best could.

But Henry did not respond to Dante's appeal, or turn his steps toward Florence. Passing by Genoa and Pisa southward, in the summer of 1312, he took the Imperial coronet at Rome in June. On his return he halted within a short distance of Florence; but, finding the forces of the Republic too powerful to engage, he made his way through Poggibonsi to Siena. There he caught a fever, and died, a year later, in August 1313, at Buonconvento. He was buried in the Campo Santo at Pisa. The solemn aisles and tranquil green turf of that cemetery, not yet adorned with Pisano's sculptures or Orcagna's frescoes, received the last and best of Dante's hopes. The death of Henry was the setting of the sun for him. In the first days of his bitter disappointment Dante fled for solitude to the mountains of Gubbio, where the convent of Santa Croce di Fonte Avellana* housed him. Much of the *Divine Comedy* is said to have been written there : if so, we marvel at the vigour of the man who lost no heart and uttered no complaints while singing in the midst of utter grief. About this time, too, Dante wrote his letter to the Cardinals of Italy, on the occasion of Clement's death, urging them to end the Babylonian exile of the Popes.

V.

Meanwhile both Pisa and Lucca had fallen into the hands of Dante's old friend the Ghibelline Uguccione. Dante, toward the end of 1314, joined him at the latter place. Here he wrote the last cantos of the *Purgatorio*. Here, too, we have a glimpse of a fair lady called Gentucca,† for whom Dante again felt love. Exile had still some flowers, it seems, for the stern poet of the deep and tender heart. For a moment,

* He describes this Convent in *Paradiso*, xxi. 106—111.
† *Purgatorio*, xxiv. 37.

too, his hopes of a return to Florence revived. Uguccione gained a great and bloody victory in August, 1315, over the Guelf party, headed by the Florentines, at Monte Catini. But he did not push his successes, or invade Florence. He used them for the consolidation of his own despotic power—vainly also, since in the spring of 1316, both Pisa and Lucca were lost to him by revolution and desire for changes in those fickle towns. Thus Dante was once more without a home, and disappointed of his expectations. Fortune, however, held him out a bait, which might have lured a less proud spirit. The Florentines offered their exiles safe return, provided they were willing to pay fines, undergo a short imprisonment, and walk in penitential raiment through the city streets. A friend of Dante wrote to tell him of this proclamation. We have Dante's answer—one of the noblest and most precious utterances of his unconquerable heart. "What!" he cries, "is this the glorious invitation which recals Dante, after an exile of three lustres to his home? Is this what innocence to every man apparent has deserved? Is this the meed of toil and ceaseless industry in study? . . . . This is not the way of coming home, my father: yet if you or others find one not beneath the fame of Dante and his honour, that will I pursue with no slack steps. But if none such give entrance to Florence, I will never enter Florence. How! Shall I not behold the sun and stars from every spot of earth?

Shall I not be free to meditate the sweetest truths in every place beneath the sky—unless I make myself ignoble, nay, ignominious to the people, and the State of Florence? Nor truly will bread fail." These words have in them the ring of Dante's voice, the flash of Dante's eyes, the quiver of Dante's nostril, the indignant blush on Dante's cheek, after the lapse of five centuries and a half. They are worthy to be bound like a phylactery, for strength and solace, round the brow of every "exile without crime," who sees the lustres passing over him, and yearns in vain for the horizons of his native land.

VI.

Dante now turned his steps to Verona. Can Grande, the greatest of the Scaligers, ruled there. At the time of Dante's coming in 1316 he was twenty-five years of age. He had survived his elder brothers, and held sway alone. Uguccione became the captain of Can Grande's forces, and Dante found an honourable asylum at his Court.[*] I can find no reason to credit the stories which are sometimes told of the young prince's want of courtesy to his great guest. On the contrary, the

---

[*] Sagacius Mucius Gazata, an historian of Reggio, received as an exile by Can Grande, describes his court thus:—"Different apartments, according to their condition, were assigned the exiles in the palace of the Scalas; each had his servants and his elegantly-appointed table. The rooms were marked by appropriate devices, by a figure of Victory for generals, of

dedication of the *Paradiso* to this patron, and the superb eulogy of him contained in its 17th canto,—unless we are to consider both deliberate pieces of flattery—seem to me to speak most plainly for themselves. That the bread of exile always tasted salt to Dante's lips; and that the stairs of the Scaligers were not less hard to tread than those of other patrons is of course true. But there seems to me no evidence that Can Grande was a brutal host, or that the poet suffered in his palace more than he had done at Lucca or in Lunigiana. Two sons of Dante, Jacopo and Pietro, joined him at Verona. The latter founded the family of Alighieri, which terminated in Ginevra, married to Count Antonio Sarego of Verona, in 1549.

Whatever was the reason of his wish to move, Dante transferred himself in 1319 from Verona to Ravenna, and became the guest of Guido da Polenta. There he finished his third cantica of the *Divine Comedy*. In the pine forest of Chiassi, which waves its mighty branches to the sea-wind on the spot where Roman navies anchored, men still point to Dante's avenue. He must have loved the place; for he thought

Hope for exiles, of Muses for poets, of Mercury for artists, of Paradise for preachers. During meals musicians, jesters, and jugglers passed through these apartments. The halls were decorated with pictures representing the vicissitudes of fortune. Cane often called certain of his guests to his own table, especially Guido da Castello di Reggio, called the Simple Lombard, and the Poet Dante."—SISMONDI, iii. 279. (Cf. *Purgatorio*, xvi. 125)—

E Guido da Castel, che me' si noma
Francescamente il semplice Lombardo.

of it while writing the most graceful passage of the *Purgatorio*; and it is pleasant to think that beneath those majestic aisles St. Bernard's prayer to Madonna—

> Virgine Madre, figlia del tuo Figlio,

ascending like the incense smoke of sweetest invocation, was composed. While at Ravenna Dante received an invitation from the poet Del Virgilio, to take the laurels at Bologna. We have his reply in a Latin eclogue:—

> Nonne triumphales melius pexare capillos,
> Et, patrio, redeam si quando, abscondere canos
> Fronde sub inserta, solitos flavescere, Sarno? *

He still thought of Florence, and would not crown his locks, now grey, except at her sweet shrine. This thought was often with him: it occurs at the beginning of the 25th canto of the *Paradiso*—

> Se mai continga che 'l poema sacro,
> Al quale ha posto mano e Cielo e Terra,
> Sì che m' ha fatto per molti' anni macro,
> Vinca la crudeltà, che fuor mi serra
> Del bello ovile, ov' io dormi' agnello
> Nimico a' lupi che gli danno guerra ;
> Con altra voce omai, con altro vello
> Ritornerò poeta, ed in sul fonte
> Del mio battesmo prenderò 'l cappello.†

---

* "Were it not better to adorn this head ; and if I should ever return, to veil grey hairs, which once were golden, by my native Arno neath the woven crown?"

† "If it ever happen that the sacred poem, to which both heaven and earth have lent a helping hand, in such wise that it hath made me lean these many years, subdue the cruelty that bars me out from that fair fold, where

But for Dante there remained another sort of coronation, and a restoration to another home. The prayer with which the *Vita Nuova* closes was soon about to be heard. Returning from a fruitless embassy to Venice, which he had undertaken on the part of Guido da Polenta, Dante caught a fever in the marshes. This ended his days, on the 14th of September, 1321. He was aged fifty-six years and four months. They buried * him at Ravenna, Count Guido purposing to raise a glorious tomb above his grave. But this was never done, and the bas-relief which we now visit is due to the piety of Bernardo Benbo, who caused it to be carved by Pietro Lombardo, and erected in 1483.

VII.

Before concluding the notice of Dante's life one point concerning his political idealism remains to be spoken of.

In the 1st canto of the *Inferno* (lines 100 — 106) there is a prophecy which has caused much trouble to the commentators. It runs thus:—

>Molti son gli animali, a cui s' ammoglia,
>E più saranno ancora, infin che 'l veltro
>Verrà, che la farà morir di doglia.

---

once I slept a lamb at enmity with the wolves that cause it woe; with altered voice, with altered hair, shall I return as poet, and above the fount of my baptism assume the crown."

* "Dante fu sepelito inhabito di Poeta."—VILLANI, ix. 33. What that habit was may be seen in Michelino's picture of Dante, robed and crowned with laurel, at the gate of Santa Maria del Fiore.

> Questi non ciberà terra, nè peltro,
> Ma sapienza ed amore e virtute,
> E sua nazion sarà tra Feltro e Feltro.
> Di quell' umile Italia fia salute.*

One thing is certain here: Dante predicts the advent of a Veltro, a hound, who shall purge Italy of the evil beasts that infest her, and shall be her salvation. Nor does this prediction stand alone. It continually reappears in the *Divine Comedy*—notably in *Purgatorio* xxxiii. and *Paradiso* xxvii. But who is the Veltro, and what is the meaning of his nation being between Feltro and Feltro? It is obvious that a great Ghibelline is prophesied: but who is he? The *Inferno* was in all probability written between 1302 and 1308; therefore Dante's lines cannot refer to Henry, who did not enter Italy till 1311. Nor for the same reason of dates, can they refer, as some critics have plausibly argued, to Can Grande. It is true that the name Cane singularly agrees with Veltro; it is true that the Scaliger in some sort dwelt between Feltro and Feltro, since the town of Feltre was capital of the Trevisan Marches to his north, and Montefeltro lay to the south; it is true that Can Grande, in his manhood, became general of the Ghibelline forces, and that Dante expressed the highest hopes of him in the 17th canto of the *Paradiso*. But when

---

* "The animals to which she weds herself are many, and will yet be more, until the greyhound comes, that will make her die with pain. He will not feed on land or pelf, but on wisdom, and love, and manfulness; and his nation shall be between Feltro and Feltro."—CARLYLE's Translation.

Dante published his *Inferno* Can Grande was but seventeen or eighteen years of age. He did not head the Ghibelline forces until ten years later. Dates agree better with the theory that Uguccione della Faggiuola was the Veltro. Those who adopt it explain the sentence about Feltro thus: "His race shall be in Montefeltro of Urbino, between Macerata Feltria and Sanleo Feltrio." Now seeing that Dante dedicated his *Inferno* to Uguccione, from whom he had received hospitality at Arezzo, and who was undoubtedly the most distinguished Ghibelline general of his day, I think that we may fairly suppose that he intended an allusion to him in these lines. That he continued to do so through the other Cantiche* is excessively unlikely. Dante, we have seen, in politics as well as love, was an idealist. According to his creed a great deliverer was to arrive for Italy. If he be Uguccione, well; if Henry the Emperor, better; if Can Grande, still the Scaliger will serve; if none be fit for the great quest, yet God in his good season will provide a man. I believe that thus his expectation of the Veltro, shadowy and prophetic from the first, may have fixed alternately on the three heroes we have named, and that it may have survived the proved incapacity of all. Thus, as the Jews in their hope of a Messiah were weaned from looking for a temporal saviour to the acceptation of a spiritual priest

* *Purgatorio*, xxxiii. 37—45, seems to identify the Veltro and the eagle of the Empire.

and king, Dante was forced, as time went by, to see his Veltro grow more visionary and ideal. That the Deliverer would appear, he never doubted: that the Desired should come to his temple was part of his political creed, part of his cherished doctrine, the cornerstone of his prophetic edifice. But the man destined to realize the idea appeared not. Thus we have completed Dante's circle of political beliefs, and have prepared the way for contemplating his poem from the point of view of his idealism.

VIII.

It remains to say something about the mortal envelope of Dante, which, between the years 1265 and 1321, might have been seen in Florentine streets, or glades of Casentino, or on the banks of the Adige, or among the forest avenues of Ravenna. After long communion with the soul of a man it is strange to fix attention firmly on the outward symbol and fleshly presentation of that soul which passes for the man himself. I have before me a cast [*] said to have been taken from a mould made on the face of Dante after death. About the forehead there is nothing overgrown or vacuous; it spreads no orb-like bubble-dome of bone such as the vulgar call a mighty brow. It is finely moulded, rather narrow, but long-drawn from the ear to the eyebrow, compact and firm. The brain within it must have filled those

[*] *See* Frontispiece.

walls with nerves most durable and hard. The eyes are half-closed, as in death. The nose is slightly aquiline, and depressed at the tip: perhaps the moulder's clay had weighed upon it there. The mouth is shut as though silence or paucity of words habitually dwelt upon the lips. The cheeks are hollow—hollowed with the care of the task of many years. The whole face is very calm and sad and grave, recalling to our minds the lines which Dante traced for his great spirits of the Pagan age:—

> Genti v' eran, con occhi tardi e gravi,
> Di grand' autorità ne' lor sembianti;
> Parlavan rado con voci soavi.*

Boccaccio describes the poet thus: "He was of middle stature; and when he reached manhood, he stooped somewhat, walking with a grave and measured gait. He always wore the most dignified raiment suited to his age. His face was long, his nose aquiline, his eyes rather large than small, his cheek-bones prominent, and his lower lip projected beyond the upper: his complexion was brown; his hair and beard thick, black and curling. His face was always full of serious and pensive thought." The tradition of Dante's hair being black and curly is curiously illustrated by an anecdote recorded by Filelfo: "They say that the women of Ravenna, looking at him after he had pub-

---

* *Inferno*, iv. 112.—"On it were people with eyes slow and grave, of great authority in their appearance. They spoke seldom with mild voices."—CARLYLE's Translation.

lished his *Inferno*, and wondering at the man who walked in Hell, exclaimed—see, the reason why his hair is so black and frizzled is that he could not have gone to Hell without returning with his hair a little singed." If the lines quoted above from Dante's *Eclogue to Del Virgilio* have a definite meaning, we should have gathered that his hair was light instead of black. Continuing Boccaccio's description, which I will compress: "In public and domestic manners he was wonderfully grave and orderly, and more than any other man both courteous and urbane. His appetite was extremely moderate; he commended delicate diet, but he usually lived on coarse food, blaming men who spent much time about the preparation of their dinners. He rarely spoke unless spoken to; yet when occasion called, he was most eloquent, with choice and ready utterance. In his studies he was diligent"—but here we will let Leonardo Bruni speak—"it was wonderful, considering his attention to study, that he never seemed to be engrossed in it, so graceful and so joyous was his company in youth." But it appears that Dante's studies sometimes made him very absent and indifferent to things around him, and also that his excessive absorption in them after Beatrice's death caused a temporary weak- of his eyesight. In brief, to use the phrase of Boccaccio, Dante was a man "sommamente composto, cortese, e civile," "sedate and courteous and urbane in the highest degree." Yet, since we must mix good report with bad, and since there is no doubt that Bruni and Boccaccio are panegyrists rather than historians, let us hear in the last place what Giovanni Villani says: "His knowledge made him somewhat arrogant and scornful, and haughty and, like philosophers who are deficient in good grace, he had not the art of conversing suitably with laymen." Filelfo adds that he was passionate at times, but never unless greatly stirred and with good reason. The explosion of his passion must have been volcanic, when it happened. The style of the Epistles to Henry and the Florentines betrays the central furnaces of angry fire which raged within.

Here I quit the vain attempt to gather from the past an image of what Dante really was. If we can feel his spirit, that suffices; and for this purpose the careful study of one canto of his great Epic is better than much pondering and comparing of Boccaccio, Bruni, Villani, Filelfo, and other more or less untrustworthy annalists, panegyrists, anecdote-mongers, and bookmakers. The *Divine Comedy* lies before us. Let us uncover our heads, therefore, and cry in the great words of Ennius:—

> Dantes poeta salve qui mortalibus
> Versus propinas flammeos medullitus! *

---

* I have tried, as I could not translate, to paraphrase this couplet thus:—

> Hail, Poet, who for mortal man dost pour
> Strong wine of words that burn and sense that sears,
> Drawn from thy bleeding bosom's fiery core,
> And tempered with the bitter fount of tears!

Hail, Dante!

This is the proper salutation for the man who fed his poem with the life-blood and the marrow of his soul through years which made him grey and gaunt.

CHAPTER IV.

THE SUBJECT AND SCHEME OF THE "DIVINE COMEDY."

(i.) Definition of the Epic. Dante's Comedy one of the Triad of Supreme Poems.—(ii.) Various Theories about its Subject.—(iii.) Dante's Account of his Poem in the Letter to Can Grande.—(iv.) Why he called it a Comedy.—(v.) Its Originality,—(vi.) An Apocalypse and not an Allegory.—(vii.) The Allegories of the Purgatory—(viii.) The Allegories of Virgil and Beatrice—(ix.) Dante's Names for Virgil and Beatrice.—(x.) The Frigidity of the Element of Symbolism in Virgil and Beatrice.

I.

"HOMER was the first and Dante the second epic poet: that is, the second poet, the series of whose creations bore a defined and intelligible relation to the knowledge and sentiment and religion of the age in which he lived, and of the ages which followed it." This is Shelley's verdict; and it is in many ways remarkable. It establishes a canon of the epic which excludes Virgil and every other so-called Epic Poet except Milton. It contradicts the ordinary definition by which an epic is said to be a national poem, reciting the deeds of a national hero, and by which such poems as the *Jerusalem* of Tasso, the *Orlando* of Ariosto, the *Henriade* of Voltaire, the *Shah Nameh* of Firdusi, and the *Lusiad* of Camoens, are indiscriminately admitted to the title. Whether it be not proper to restrict the term epic to a narrative poem of action may be questioned as a matter of convenience and prescription. But it cannot be doubted that Shelley's definition, although exclusive, does mark out and distinguish a supreme trinity of poems, which have summed up the experience and expressed the spirit of great eras of civilization, and have formed the education of succeeding centuries. If the *Divine Comedy* is to be received as an epic at all, we must accept some canon of this kind. For it cannot be properly termed a national narrative poem in the same sense as the *Iliad* and the *Odyssey*. What it has in common with the Homeric poems Shelley's definition states with accuracy. Homer represents pre-historic Hellas, with all its undeveloped germs and potentialities: Dante incarnates the spirit of Mediæval Christianity, so that we may study it in his poem as we interrogate the features of a face to learn the secrets of the soul beneath: Milton, in a narrower sphere, gives utterance to the conclusions of the reason and the imagination of man engaged upon the problem of the relation of God to the world and to his creatures. These conclusions, as far as Christianity is concerned, culminated and became the property of the understanding in the

Reformation of the eighteenth century. Milton gave them imperishable form, sculptured their metaphysics as enduringly as Homer carved the serene forms of the Hellenic Olympus and Dante painted the sublime visions of the mediæval faith.

Beside these three poets there is none who, in the form of a continuous work of art, has succeeded in fixing any moment so specific and representative in the history of thought as these. The mediæval romances, including the *Niebelungen* and the Carlovingian and Arthurian cycles, do indeed furnish us with a mass, as it were, of epical raw material " bearing a defined and intelligible relation to the knowledge and sentiment, and religion " of the feudal ages. But they are not a poem.* They never underwent that clarifying process of artistic genius by which a similar mass of epical raw material in Hellas was probably converted into the *Iliad* and the *Odyssey*. And when the minds of mighty poets like Ariosto were directed to them the moment for this alchemizing process had passed by. Were *Don Quixote* a poem, Cervantes might take his stand beside Homer, Dante, and Milton, with a better right than Ariosto.

It is upon these grounds that we are justified in asserting that the *Divine Comedy* has only two peers

* Had Sir Thomas Malory been a genius of the compass, calibre, and culture of a Shakspeare he might have given us a great Arthurian epic instead of his *Mort Arthur*. He had the moment, the right nick of time; but the faculty was wanting.

in the whole domain of literature, and that in the magnitude of its extent and the force of its vitality, it surpasses one at least of them—the Epic of Milton.

II.

Dante did not, like Homer and Milton, set forth the subject of his epic in the first lines* of the poem. This has been the source of much confusion and perplexity to critics. For when a poet of the quality of Dante, one of the supreme triad of epic singers, the interpreter of a chaotic middle age, the emerger from barbarian darkness and the babel of confounded dialects, the hierophant of novel mysteries and herald of a world's awakening, the voice that startled Europe from her somnambulism of a thousand years—when such a potent spirit sets himself to condense the whole political, religious, moral, and philosophical experience of his times into a work of art, the sense of which, in his own words, "is by no means simple, nay rather may be called polysensous, or of many senses," discoverable mainly by four methods of interpretation, "literal, allegorical, moral, anagogical," as is explained in the epistle to Can Grande—can we wonder that the critics are confounded? The cathedral

---

* This by itself would exclude it from the title of Epic in the opinion of critics like Coleridge, who maintain that the action of the Epic is foreseen from the first by the poet and his hearers.

of Dante's building is too vast for comprehension at a glance; and, as is the case with Gothic architecture, unwary observers easily mistake its efflorescences and decorations for the main design, not dreaming that a skeleton of solid structure underlies the whole. Boccaccio, staring at this mighty pile, when its masonry was new and its frescoes still unfaded, pronounced that Dante had erected it solely as a gallows for the better gibbeting of his political antagonists. With this verdict posterity cannot agree. We stand further off from the aisles and buttresses; we see what Boccaccio does not seem to have noticed, that the spire shoots upwards into bluest sky, taking the hues of evening and of dawn unheeded, when our fields beneath are dim with mists and dew. The ghastly decapitated limbs and grinning heads of Dante's victims do indeed make hideous gargoyles for the water-spouts and writhing corbels for the arches. But we know that these are details subordinate to some more universal plan. Else how should we be reading Dante's poem now? Positive philosophers, who get on well enough without a God or Gospel, study, it is said, these cantos daily, drawing spiritual sustenance from them. How should they do this, were the juices but the acid sap of envy, malice, and an exile's spite? No; it required the pur-blindness of a contemporary to accept this view of the *Divine Comedy.* But, says another interpreter, the poem is a huge political pamphlet, an allegorical attack on

Guelfism. Exclude all thoughts but this when you approach the three Cantiche, and you will find pitfalls of meaning hidden in each line, subtle disguises, labyrinths conducting to one centre. We have gained a step here. Dante, it is certain, had his Ghibelline antipathies for ever within view. Whatever else may occupy his mind, he never omits to gird at Florence, France, and the Papacy, the three heads of the Guelf faction. He breaks off his description of the celestial rose in order to exalt Henry and abuse Boniface:* he points an epigram against his country in the very presence chamber and before the throne of God.† But this interpretation by itself will not suffice. Something broader, of more universal human interest than that old strife of Pope and Emperor, must animate the *Comedy* and be the salt of its immortal life. Another critic might inform us that the poet had dissected the human soul, classifying its virtues and vices, and weighing the gravity of each so nicely in his moral balances as to form a graduated scale of ideal ethics.‡ Having performed so much by dry analysis, Dante, whose artist's thoughts took shape inevitably, next designed a picture of the destinies of man, clothing his universal science in strong individual types. This sounds plausible: are we not upon the verge of a full-formed and water-tight

---

* *Paradiso*, xxx. 136 to end. † *Ibid.*, xxxi. 39.

‡ Dante himself, in the epistle to Can Grande (section xvi.), says of his poem, "Genus philosophiæ est morale negotium, sive ethica."

hypothesis? But wait. Our next interpreter pronounces with a smile of bland superiority that Dante's poem is but St. Thomas Aquinas rhymed and set to music. The theology of mediævalism, with its fixed conditions of damnation, purgation, and beatification, with its minute and definite dogmas, with its rigour against heretics, and unbaptized just persons, with its sublime enthusiasms and puerile discussions, its scholasticism and its mystic poetry, stands there made beautiful, for all men to admire. What shall we reply? Has not the last interpreter carried the approval of the court? Certainly he has: but so has the last but one, and the one before him after his own fashion, while even Boccaccio, blundering in the background, is not without a shadow of applause. Let us then receive all these theories and hypotheses, and exegeses, admitting that they are all true in part, all true together simultaneously and in conjunction, but that over and above them all remains a mass of unexplained significances for which even Dante, at our bar, with all his apparatus of "literal, allegorical, moral, and anagogical" methods could not give account. If the *Divine Comedy* is, as we have said it is, the voice and ultimate articulation* of a whole æon of human culture—if it be the *logos*, the *verbum caro factum*, of the spirit of the Middle Ages,

---

* Le drame de l'autre vie, le jugement dernier et les trois états des âmes au delà de la tombe, étaient devenus le cadre de toutes les conceptions religieuses, philosophiques, poetiques, satiriques de l'Italie du moyen age.—*Renan, Averröes*, p. 302.

Dante's own Account. 99

then its vast and complex organism must remain in part at least an undecipherable puzzle. Works of art, like works of animate nature, are, thank heaven, beyond the reach of critical or chemical analysis. We can observe, investigate, describe, admire them. But we cannot, and their authors cannot, by the aid of test-tubes or alembics, solve the problem of their vital principle.

III.

Meanwhile, since we have the liberty to do so, let us hear what Dante, the most rigorous analyst of his own works, as the *Vita Nuova* and *Convito* prove, has to say about the plan of the *Divine Comedy*. "Let us consider," he writes, to Can Grande, "the subject of this work according to the letter first, and then according to the allegorical meaning. The subject of the whole work, then, taken literally, is the state of souls after death regarded as a matter of fact; for the action of the whole work deals with this, and is about this. But if the work be taken allegorically, its subject is Man, in so far as by merit or demerit in the exercise of free will he is exposed to the rewards or punishments of justice."* If I understand this passage rightly, Dante

---

* The inscription on the gate of Hell records: Giustizia mosse 'l mio alto Fattore.—*Inferno*, iii. 4. Compare *Inferno*, vii. 19. Ahi! Giustizia di Dio, etc.—*Inferno*, xxix. 55. La ministra dell' alto Sire, infallibil giustizia.—*Inferno*, xiv. 16; xxiv. 120—where the notion of vengeance is added.

means to say that the *Divine Comedy* not only relates a series of actual facts and undoubted truths concerning the local habitation and the condition of the soul after this life, but also unfolds a scheme of universal ethics based upon the conception of eternal justice, judging men according to their use of free will. Taken literally, the *Divine Comedy* is the account of an eye-witness of the spiritual world—a Marco Polo book of travels in the land which is more dim than Tartary or farthest Ind. Taken allegorically, it lays down the everlasting laws of morality, revealed no less by reason than by the Word of God. In other words the Dantesque account of Hell, Purgatory, and Paradise, is not an arbitrary or fantastic dream, but the vivid and substantial embodiment of a profound philosophy. Here the interpreter, who found in the *Divine Comedy* a transcendental treatise of ethics, may be heard clapping his hands and crying:—" O, upright judge! A second Daniel!" But the advocate of Catholicity steps up and calls attention to the fact that Dante was a child of his age; was, in a word, the puppet, mouthpiece, speaking-trumpet of the mediæval world; therefore, his profound philosophy and graduated scale of morals are but the expression and formulation of the faith of the Middle Ages. Even so: these two interpreters have now the field between them; nor need they quarrel, but rather join hands and strengthen each other by combining their hypotheses. The *Divine Comedy* is therefore the epic of Man, considered as a moral being, exercising free will under the eye of an inexorable judge, who punishes and rewards according to fixed laws. What these laws are Dante explains by the light of mediæval creeds. What these rewards and punishments are, he sets forth by the same light and describes them with minute particularity. The result is a drama of which humanity is the protagonist, of which the poet is spectator and historian; a drama in all essential respects eternal, though coloured with the prejudices and opinions of a single age. That which is mediæval and Catholic in Dante's poem may well pass away, except for antiquarian or artistic interest. But its ethical and human breath of life is immortal; it is as fresh as that of the *Iliad*, the *Antigone*, the *Republic*, the Epistle to the Romans, or *Othello*. For this, at least, is certain, that, however creeds and modes of thought change, the utterances of strong, clear-sighted spirits in all ages of the world, agree, and the conscience of humanity remains the same. Of this conscience Dante's poem is the epic.

IV.

With so mighty a burden of prophecy to bear, and with so grave a theme, how comes it that Dante's Epic is called a Comedy? This, too, he explains after his quaint pedantic fashion.* "The title of the book is:—*Incipit Comœdia Dantis Alagherii*

* *Epistle to Can Grande*, Section 2.

florentini natione non moribus. In order to understand this, one must know that *comædia* is named from κώμη *villa* and ᾠδή, which means *cantus*, so that *Comædia* is a sort of *villanus cantus*. It differs from tragedy in this, that tragedy in the commencement is full of admiration and calm, but in the end is stinking and horrible; whence it is named from τράγος, which is *hircus* and ᾠδή, as it were *cantus hircinus*, that is stinking like a goat, which appears through Seneca, his tragedies.* Whereas comedy begins with something harsh, but has a prosperous ending, as is seen in Terence, his comedies. In like manner the styles of tragedy and comedy are different: that of tragedy is heightened and sublime, that of comedy more lax and unpretending. Whence we see why my work is called *Comædia*. For if we regard the matter, in the commencement it is horrible and stinking, inasmuch as it begins with Hell; but in the conclusion it is prosperous, pleasant, and desirable, inasmuch as it ends with Paradise. If we look to the style, that is lax and unpretending, since it is written in the vulgar tongue,† in

---

* Averrhoes was of opinion that Tragedy is the art of praising, Comedy of blaming. Benvenuto d' Imola has reproduced this curious theory in his *Commentary on the Divine Comedy.*

† For Dante's reason for writing the *Divine Comedy* in Italian, and for the stiff commencement of the Latin poem he first designed, see Frate Ilario's letter, already quoted. In the first Treatise of the *Convito* (Chapters v.—xiii.) Dante explains his affection for his native language, and his indignation against those scholars who disparage it, and who, in order to secure their own reputation for science, neglect it for the Latin. Compare his answers to Del Virgilio's *Eclogues*.

which women and children speak." Such is Dante's dry account of the title of his poem. Posterity has added to Comedia the epithet Divina, and has placed the poem in a higher rank than that, " Alta Tragedia " of Virgil,* to which the Florentine dreamed never to aspire.

V.

In the structure of his poem, Dante was as original as in its conception. Critics have attempted to prove that the notion of a journey through the unseen world had occurred to predecessors, notably to one Guerino il Meschino, to the Provençal poet, Rodolph Houdan, to the author of a fabliau, entitled *Le Jongleur qui va en Enfer*, and to a Scandinavian bard. They also quote four lines from the *Tesoretto*,† written by Dante's tutor, Latini, in which there is some talk of an allegorical forest. But after due examination we find that Homer and Virgil are the

---

* *Inferno*, xx. 113.

† Pensando a capo chino
Perdei il gran cammino,
E tenni alla traversa
D' una selva diversa.—Cap. ii. 75.

Further on Ovid helps Brunetto out of a difficulty; but there is no connection between his interposition and the passage already quoted. The lines are these :—

Ma Ovidio per arte
Mi diede maestria
Sì ch' io trovai la via.—Cap. xix. 210.

Upon these two passages, separated by seventeen Capitoli, it is impossible to found a theory.

only poets who can be rightly said to have suggested the idea of the descent into Hell to Dante. The fabliaux are both below consideration, being clumsy attempts at turning into ridicule the hell that was so terrible to mediæval imaginations. The Italian version of Guerino's vision probably owes its most striking incidents to Dante's own poem. M. Ozanam must tell us how Dante could have become indebted to the Saga; and Professor Cantù, who seems to believe that Dante followed in Latini's wake, must show that losing one's way in a wood is so peculiar an incident in allegory as not to have occurred spontaneously to Dante's mind. Meanwhile, leaving the antiquarians to elucidate the pedigree of Dante's ideas, we may observe that from his earliest boyhood he was familiar with dreams and visions, and that he hints himself, at the end of the *Vita Nuova*, that the vision of the Comedy came to him as a revelation, while he was pondering on the thought of death, and upon the memory of Beatrice. An old story related by Boccaccio* makes it even probable that the *Divine Comedy* was sketched or partly written before Dante left Florence for exile—that is not very long after the death of Beatrice. We may feel sure that the scheme of the great work occurred to him spontaneously, and that, seeing its epical capacities, he devoted his lifetime to its elaboration, intending not

* FRATICELLI, pp. 168—172 of his *Life of Dante* discusses the details of this story.

only to glorify Beatrice with praise, such as no man hitherto had said or sung of any lady, but also to instruct the world in the philosophy of its true happiness. "The object of the whole work," he writes to Can Grande, "is to make those who live in this life leave their state of misery, and to lead them to a state of happiness." His purpose was both moral and political. The *status miseriæ* was the discord of divided Christendom as well as of the undegenerate will: the *status felicitatis* was the pacification of the world under the co-equal sway of Emperor and Pope in Rome, as well as the restoration of the human soul to faith.

VI.

Having shown what is the scope and subject of Dante's Epic, we may proceed to ask why it is called an Allegory. Dante's own use of the terms Literal and Allegorical resolves itself into this—that, besides the actual description of the spiritual world contained in his poem, there is a fixed philosophy and scheme of moral science underlying its vision. There is nothing here to lead us to suppose that he considered his Epic to be what we commonly mean by Allegory. At the risk of seeming to introduce a distinction where there is no difference, I should like to call the *Divine Comedy* an Apocalypse and not an Allegory.

Let us consider the meaning of these terms. An allegory, according to Quintilian, "aliud verbis, aliud sensu ostendit :" "its words convey one thing to our minds, its sense another." Now the object of Dante was to tell us as nearly as possible what the three unseen worlds veritably *are*, to reveal a certain well-defined and substantial truth of fact as he considered it. Dante never doubted that Hell, Purgatory, and Paradise existed. He believed, and sought to make us believe, that Brutus, Cassius, and Judas might be found within the jaws of Satan; Piccarda, among the lunar saints; Thomas of Aquino and Bonaventura, among the solar. This surely is of the nature of Apocalypse and not of allegory. The *Divine Comedy* resembles the Revelation of St. John, who saw heaven opened and told the world what he had seen, more than the allegory of Spenser, who veiled moral teaching in romance, or that of Bunyan, who described the perseverance of a Christian under the form of a story. The *Mythi* of Plato again are more akin to the *Divine Comedy*, while the Scripture parables belong to the same class as Spenser's and Bunyan's allegories. The *Platonic Mythus* and the *Dantesque Apocalypse* have this in common, that they give account of things unseen and spiritual, of the truth of which there is no doubt, but which need to be presented to mortal understandings in the form of pictures and narrations. The Scripture Parables and Bunyan's allegory have this in common, that they convey lessons of life and practice under the disguise of tales: dealing with matter of experience, and seeking to make their teaching attractive and impressive, they wrap it up in fables. The apocalyptic poet makes use of type and symbol because he cannot speak in plainer language. The allegorical poet chooses metaphor instead of precept, because he wishes to produce a certain definite effect. I do not deny that the *Divine Comedy* is full of allegories.* Virgil and Beatrice are both of them the personifications of abstract qualities. The Descent of Beatrice in the *Purgatorio* is one sustained symbolic pageant. The first canto of the *Inferno* contains a studied allegory. The punishments of Hell and Purgatory are for the most part allegorical. But what I maintain is, that these allegories are accidental, instrumental, or subservient to the poem, and not essential as is the case with Spenser's and Bunyan's fictions. The *Divine Comedy* is apocalyptic; but it often conveys its revelation in the form of allegory.

* Dante is himself constantly calling attention to this fact. Omitting the passage already quoted from the *Epistle to Can Grande* in which he calls his work "Polysemous" or "Polysenous" (for the text varies), we may cite two distinct appeals to the reader of the *Divine Comedy*:—

>O voi, ch' avete gl' intelletti sani,
>Mirate la dottrina, che s' asconde
>Sotto 'l velame degli versi strani.—*Inferno*, ix. 61.

And :—

>Aguzza qui, Lettor, ben gli occhi al vero;
>Che 'l velo è ora ben tanto sottile,
>Certo, che 'l trapassar dentro è leggiero.
>—*Purgatorio*, viii. 19.

We may remark that in both these places the allegory is not easy.

VII.

The taste of Dante's age inclined strongly to allegory. Intent on a few books, and seeking from their pages to extract the utmost meaning, mediæval students gladly found a double or a treble sense in poems and in histories. Theologians, obliged to express recondite doctrine to the understanding of the vulgar, called in the aid of metaphor and symbol. Moral qualities in masques and pageants were personified, dress and decoration helping the imagination through the eyesight. Then followed painting,[*] till in every church and cloister, frescoes taught the laity the mysteries of faith and doctrine, under the form of rude pictorial emblems. Allegory in the Middle Ages, like hieroglyphics in ancient Egypt, was a language read more easily by contemporaries than by posterity. Yet its inefficiency as a vehicle of thought was even then perceptible. This is proved by the early difficulty which critics felt about the meaning of the first canto of the *Inferno*. What was the wood

---

[*] The most important works of mural painting which illustrate the allegory of Dante are, the frescoes of Giotto, in the Lower Church at Assisi, representing the Virtues of St. Francis, those of Memmi and others in the Spanish Chapel of St. Maria Novella at Florence, those of the Palazzo Pubblico at Sienna, those of Orcagna in the Strozzi Chapel of Sta. Maria Novella, and those of the Campo Santo at Pisa. In these works the most abstract ideas and complex series of events are expressed to the eye through figures often very clumsy, almost always vague and artificial.

Allegory of Inferno I.

in which Dante lost his way? Some answered, youthful vice; others, exile; others, again, civil discord. What was the delightful mount he wished to gain? Some answered, virtue; others, his home; others, civil order. What were the lynx, the lion, and the wolf which frightened him from the right path? Some answered, envy, pride, and avarice; others found in them the vices of the three ages of man, youthful profligacy, mature pride, senile cupidity; others explained that they were Florence, France, and Rome. It is only after the lapse of many centuries, and the sifting of much chaff from the wheat, that we are pretty well satisfied about the matter, making up our minds that Dante intended to shadow forth in these images the confusion of politics and factions in which he found himself during his priorate of 1300; his vain attempts to regain the hill of civil order which his city had neglected, and the opposition on the part of Guelf Florence with her envy, of Guelf France with her pride, and of Guelf Rome with her avarice.* The vision awarded to him by Divine Grace, through the guidance of Virgil and Beatrice, or Human Science and Theology, restored him to the right point

---

* These three powers and the three vices they represented are Dante's pet antipathies.—Cf. *Inferno*, xv. 68.

Gente avara invidiosa e superba.'

Again,—*Inferno*, vi. 74.

Superbia invidia ed avarizia sono
Le tre faville che hanno i cuori accessi.

of view, and confirmed him in the faith of transcendental Ghibellinism.*

Having started this subject of Dante's use of allegory, let us investigate it a little more in detail, taking for our text the *Purgatorio*, which, as it happens, is more rich in this figure of poetry than either of the other cantiche. In Dante's allegory † we can discern four separate though interpenetrating kinds of symbolism. He either makes an arbitrary selection of natural objects to designate spiritual things; or he uses material metaphors, ‡ such as the roughness of the roadway of repentance, to signify the qualities of immaterial existences; or, again, he appeals immediately to the understanding, by taking some concrete person, animal,

---

* While adopting this political explanation of the allegory I cannot shut my eyes to *Purgatorio*, xxx. 136.

> Tanto giù cadde, che tutti argomenti
> Alla salute sua eran già corti,
> Fuor che mostrargli le perdute genti, etc.

It is here clear that Dante's own state of moral delinquency induced Beatrice to grant him the Vision. There is, therefore, a personal as well as political meaning in the allegory of *Inferno* 1. Compare *Purgatorio*, i. 58—66, where Virgil tells Cato about the cause of their journey.

† There is something pedantic in the parade and apparatus of these distinctions. Yet they will be of use if they do but fix the attention more closely upon the peculiarities of Dante's art.

‡ I have not included the punishments of Hell and Purgatory in this class—the carnal driven to and fro by ceaseless winds, the gluttons lashed by rain, homicides plunged in boiling blood, schismatics rending their own flesh, flatterers immersed in filth, hypocrites wearing cowls of gilded lead, pride sustaining heavy weights, the intemperate tantalized with fruit they cannot reach, &c.—because these, though figurative, seem intended to be real and retributive in kind, simply retaliative, in a word.

or object as the typical similitude of his thought; or, finally, he describes a pageant, in which long series of events are pictorially presented through the eye to the imagination. The mere statement of this classification is unintelligible. I must render it clear by copious illustrations.

To the first species belongs the symbolism* of the four visible stars in the hemisphere of the antipodes, which stand for the Cardinal Virtues, and of the three stars which represent the Theological Virtues. The former are stars of morning, because the Cardinal Virtues rule the soul in active life; the latter are evening stars, because the Theological Virtues preside over contemplation. Here it is obvious that Dante makes an arbitrary selection of natural objects, and attaches to them a peculiar meaning. The same may be said about the part which the sun plays in Purgatory. Without its light it is impossible to proceed a step:—

> Vedi, sola questa riga
> Non varcheresti dopo il Sol partito,†

Says Sordello, by which Dante wishes to signify that repentance and lustration are impossible without the grace of God.‡ The selection of the reed to symbolise humility is less arbitrary, and is more poetical,

---
* *Purgatorio*, i. 22—27, and *Ibid.*, viii. 89.
† *Purgatorio*, vii. 53.—"See: you could not cross even this line after the setting of the sun."
‡ *Purgatorio*, l. 95.

112 *The Subject and Scheme of the Divine Comedy.*

since there is perhaps no other plant so pliant beneath the double stress of wind and wave. It is also possible that Dante remembered the Greek legend of Prometheus, who, when reconciled with Zeus, put on his finger the ring of necessity, and on his brow the willow wand of submission.

The second species of symbolism is common enough in the *Purgatorio*. When Dante describes * the way of Purgatory as difficult at first, and easy afterwards, as tortuous, involved, and straitened, it is clear that he is using a strong material metaphor, such as Aristophanes was fond of in his Comedies, for illustrating the initial difficulties and the subsequent ease of the path of repentance. Of the same kind, but far more splendid in its imagery, is the passage which describes the door of Purgatory :—

> Là ne venimmo ; e lo scaglion primaio
> Bianco era marmo sì pulito e terso
> Ch' io mi specchiava in esso, quale i' paio.
> Era 'l secondo, tinto più che perso,
> D' una petrina ruvida ed arsiccia,
> Crepata per lo lungo, e per traverso.
> Lo terzo, che di sopra s' ammassiccia,
> Porfido mi parea sì fiammeggiante,
> Come sangue che fuor di vena spiccia.
> Sopra questo teneva ambo le piante
> L' Angel di Dio, sedendo in su la soglia,
> Che mi sembiava pietra di diamante. †

---

* *Purgatorio*, iv. 87 ; and x. 8.

† Thither we came : and the first mighty stair
Was marble white—so polished and so smooth
That I stood mirrored there as I appear.
The second, darker than the darkest blue,

The Steps of Purgatory.

In this grand passage every word tells, and the symbolism, once perceived, is of the most striking kind. The white and polished marble is purity and sincerity of soul, perfect candour, without which all penitence is vain. The dark slab, dry and rugged, represents a broken and a contrite heart: its rift is crosswise, indicating the length and breadth and depth of sorrow for past sin. The sanguine-coloured porphyry is love, red as heart's blood, and solid for the soul to stay thereon. These are the three "gradi di buona voglia." Upon the fourth step of adamant, which signifies the sure foundation of the Church, the angel stands. In his hands are two keys—the golden is said to mean the authority, the silver the science, of the confessor and absolver. It would be hard to find a finer allegory, combining, as this does, most perfect subtlety and fitness, with the dignity and splendour of a picture gorgeous to the eye.

To the third species belong many creations peculiar to Dante, or appropriated from history and old

> Was formed of a rough stone, rugged and dry,
> Cracked lengthwise and across through all its mass.
> The third, whose bulk completes the topmost stair,
> Seemed to my gaze of porphyry, that flamed
> Like blood forth bursting from a smitten vein.
> Thereon God's angel planting both his feet,
> Sat firmly stationed on the threshold floor,
> Which, as I thought, was solid diamond.
> *Purgatorio*, ix. 94—105.

mythology.* Such are the three beasts chosen in the 1st canto of the *Inferno* to represent three vices. Such is Geryon, the type of Fraud, and Cerberus the watch-dog of infernal violence. Such, too, but in a far finer and stronger sense, is Cato placed by Dante as the guardian of Purgatory. Cato of Utica was an unbaptized pagan; moreover, he ended his life by suicide. We should have expected to find him in the 13th canto of the *Inferno* rather than in the 1st of the *Purgatorio*. But, seeing that he illustrated in his lifetime the four virtues of the active life of man, and that in his death he sought to free himself from servitude to tyrants in whom evil passions raged, Dante selects him as the allegory of man made free by the annihilation of the carnal self for the exercise of virtue. This is the meaning of these lines:—

> Libertà va cercando, ch' è sì cara,
> Come sa chi per lei vita rifiuta.
> Tu 'l sai; chè non ti fu per lei amara
> In Utica la morte, ove lasciasti
> La veste, ch' al gran dì sarà sì chiara.†

The Countess Matilda, among the flowers of the earthly

---

* Are we to place here the statue of the four metals which seems to stand for the old mythus of the golden, brazen, and iron ages, adding, with characteristic Dantesque bitterness, a modern age of mud, and alluding also to the different forms of government, from pure monarchy to democratic anarchy?

† *Purgatorio*, l. 71—75. "He goes in search of freedom, the which how dear it is, he knows, who for it gives away his life. Thou knowest, for, for her sake, death to thee was not bitter in Utica, where thou didst quit the robe which at the last day will be so glorious."

Paradise, stands in like manner for the Love of Holy Church. And Virgil and Beatrice themselves, about whose symbolism I have much to say in another place, are, by a similar exercise of arbitrary fancy, chosen to represent the reason of man and the illumination of God.

The fourth kind of allegory takes the form of a triumphal show or pageant. Such shows were common enough in Italy, both in the Middle Age* and the Renaissance. We have all read how Lorenzo de' Medici paraded the streets of Florence with his comrades on a car of death, designed by Piero di Cosimo, and decorated by Granacci. Masques, moralities, and mysteries abounded in such acted allegories. The frescoes† of Simone Memmi and the Lorenzetti of Siena, show what

* See the account in VILLANI, viii. 70, of the Inferno, represented in the Arno, near the Ponte Alla Carraja on May-day, 1304, and in *Rolandino* of Padua of the allegorical assault upon the Camp of Honour, which took place in the Trevisan March in 1214 (*Muratori Dissert.* xxix.).

† In the fourteenth century the Italian artists allegorized Theology, Philosophy, and Sacred Legend. It is enough to call to mind (L) the frescoes of Giotto in the Church of St. Francis at Assisi, which represent the marriage of the saint with Poverty, and the Virtues of Chastity, Humility, &c. ; (ii.) the frescoes of Memmi and Gaddi in the Capella degli Spagnuoli of Sta. Maria Novella at Florence, which set forth the triumph of the Church Militant over Heresy, and the triumph of St. Domenic over Arius, Sabellius, and Averrhoes, together with an abstract of all the mediæval sciences ; (iii.) the picture in the Church of St. Catherine at Pisa, by Traini, which allegorizes the Inspiration of St. Thomas of Aquino, and his victory over infidelity in the form of Averrhoes ; (iv.) the Lorenzetti frescoes at Pisa, in the Campo Santo, which allegorize the mediæval conceptions of death, the vanity of life, and monastic meditation ; (v.) those in the Palazzo Pubblico of Sienna, which embody under allegorical forms the political philosophy of the Middle Ages.

triumphs were in days not far from those of Dante. They are not much to our taste: grim, symmetrical compositions, crowded with stiff figures, in which the painter has sacrificed beauty to meaning, giving Dissimulation, for example, two faces, and Prudence three eyes. Art struggles in the vain attempt to express complex thoughts and intricate actions through the medium of pictured forms; resigning her natural function of creating loveliness, she becomes the servile handmaid of the schools. It sufficed the artist that the style was fashionable, and afforded scope for ingenuity. He had his reward both in the appreciation of contemporaries, and in the careful study bestowed on his designs by antiquarian posterity. Dante, who, as we have before remarked, was the true child of his century, was not alive to the frigidity of these pictorial allegories. On the contrary, he taxed his genius to invent one and to describe it with all the splendour and distinctness of his unrivalled style. The five last cantos of the *Purgatorio* are nearly wholly devoted to the setting forth of the symbolic pageant. The theatre is the garden-grove of the Terrestrial Paradise: a car drawn by a griffin, and preceded by seven candlesticks, four beasts, and four-and-twenty elders first appears upon the scene. The chariot is the Apostolic Seat; the griffin is our Lord, whose human nature is aquiline, whose divinity is leonine; the four beasts are the Gospels, and the elders are the Books

of the Old Testament; the candles are the Seven
Gifts of the Spirit. By the right wheel walk Faith,
Hope, and Charity, attired in white and green and
red; by the left wheel Prudence, Justice, Temperance,
and Fortitude. Two old men,* Luke and Paul, follow
the car, and behind them come the four writers of
Canonical Epistles. The last old man, who sleeps
with eager countenance, is John. Such is the pageant
which appears between the trees of Paradise, and startles
Dante by its splendour. To a modern taste this
pageant is artistically a failure. The difficulty of
identifying all the personages who play parts in it,
and the dryness of the allegory, soon prove wearisome.
But the chariot stops. Angels appear amid a shower
of flowers; and above them all a lady, veiled with
white, mantled with green, and robed with Charity—
the colours of the three Theological Virtues—wearing
on her brow the olive wreath of wisdom, descends
into the car. This is Beatrice, the symbol of Divine
Theology, Dante's old love. The meeting of Beatrice
with Dante, and their colloquy, which occupy the
30th and 31st cantos, are justly celebrated for
their pathos and dramatic force. Beatrice reproves

* It will be observed that several personages figure more than once:
St. John, for instance, appears in three several places; it was necessary for
the allegory to regard him as evangelist, and as author of the *Epistle* and
the *Book of the Apocalypse*.

Dante for the disorder* of his life after her death. Meanwhile, the pageant waits, and in the sight of this august assembly Dante performs penance for his sins. In the 33rd canto the allegory is continued, and is made the vehicle of a condensed Church history. We hear how the griffin draws the car to a great tree, which tree is Rome, leafless and flowerless at first, as shorn of all its pagan virtues, but made glad again with verdure by the coming of the Church of Christ. Beatrice and the Seven Virtues take their seat beneath its branches, and the griffin ascends to heaven. Thus Christ left Theology and her attendant Virtues with his Church to gladden his chosen city, Rome.† What follows is a brief account of the troubles of the Holy See. The eagle which descends and breaks the boughs of the tree, is persecuting Rome; the fox is Novatianus; the eagle, who leaves his plumage in the car, is Con-

* Compare a Sonnet of Cavalcanti to the same purpose. *Rime di Guido Cavalcanti*, Firenze, 1813, p. 12; ROSSETTI's *Early Italian Poets*, p. 358.

† This seems to me the most rational interpretation of the Tree: but canto xxxii. 43.

> Beato se', grifon, che non discindi
> Col becco d' esto legno dolce al gusto
> Posciachè mal si torse 'l ventre quindi.

And canto xxxiii. 61 :—

> Per morder quella in pena ed in disio
> Cinque mille anni e più l' anima prima
> Bramò colui che 'l morso in sè punio.

point distinctly to the Tree being the old Tree of Eden. It is probable that Dante thought the Forbidden Tree of the garden was, itself, a type of Rome: lines 64—72 of canto xxxiii. seem to indicate this.

stantine, who gave the evil gift of temporality to the
Pope; the dragon is Photius and the Eastern schism; the
feathers which conceal the car are the overgrowth of
avarice and luxury consequent upon the donation of
Constantine; the seven heads which sprout upon the
car are the seven chief sins; the wheel signifies the
wanton Court of Papal Rome; the giant is Philip le
Bel; the stripes inflicted by him on his paramour are
Philip's injuries to Boniface; the dragging of the
chariot through the wood is the translation of the
Papal See to Avignon. In the 33rd canto Beatrice
continues the allegory in prophecy, foretelling a successor to the eagle, and the coming of a Dux or leader,
who will take vengeance on the giant and his paramour.

I have stripped this allegory of all its poetical
adornments, and analyzed it drily in order to make
Dante's use of symbolism clear. The whole passage is
one of the least interesting and least successful portions
of his poem. It is purely archaic, mediæval, obsolete in
style. Dante could have found no model for this
pageant in his classics. Yet he clearly thinks that it is
the highest flight of his imagination; for before engaging
with the arduous theme he summons to his aid Urania.
The example of the Hebrew prophets and the Book of
Revelations combined with the pictorial tendencies of
his age induced him to compose so vast and to our
taste so wearisome an allegory.

VIII.

In order to explain the semi-allegorical character of Beatrice and Virgil, I must revert to what I have before called Dante's dualism.* The central point of his

---

* Dante's ethical theory is based upon this dualism. Taking man as a being with two ends of earthly and heavenly felicity before him, Dante in the *Inferno* treats of those vices which obstruct the former end of man so utterly that there is no advance for him toward the latter. These, following Aristotle, he classifies (see *Inferno*, xi.) as Incontinence, Malice, and Bestiality (incontinentia, vitium, feritas; ἀκρασία, κακία, θηριότης). Incontinence comprehends sins of the flesh, gluttony, avarice, sloth, anger. Malice includes violence against our neighbours, ourselves, nature and God. Homicides, robbers, suicides, profligate persons, usurers, blasphemers and unnatural criminals, belong to this second class. Bestiality, an aggravated form of malice, is the vice of seducers, flatterers, simonists, wizards, traffickers in public offices, hypocrites, thieves, fraudulent advisers, breeders of civil and religious schism, falsifiers of truth in various fashions, and traitors of all species. As malice proceeds by violence, so bestiality, the anti-human vice *par excellence*, proceeds by fraud. It will be noticed that Dante's moral standard is wholly social. The worst crime is fraud, because it strikes at the root of society by undermining confidence and sapping the bonds of mutual loyalty. Next in the scale of evil is violence, less dangerous, because avowed and open. The most venial of the sins of hell is incontinence, which chiefly concerns the individual alone. Purgatory is allotted to the seven sins—pride, envy, anger, sloth, avarice, gluttony, carnal passion, corresponding to the subdivisions of incontinence in hell. Here, too, those which affect society are the worst: intemperate appetites in which the individual alone suffers, is held lightest. The purpose of Purgatory is to purify man from the vices incidental to his corruptible nature, and to leave him free for the exercise of that which is incorruptible in him. So far we are still within the limits of pagan morality: Dante is following Aristotle as a text-book. But now we pass over to the region of theology. The individual, purged of carnal grossness, and perfect in the human virtues of justice, temperance, fortitude, and prudence, begins to exercise his spiritual faculties, to be guided by the celestial virtues of faith, hope, and charity, and to expatiate in contemplation. In Paradise the active virtues are subordinate to the contemplative. St. Benedict is above Justinian and the Crusaders; St. Bernard is above St. Benedict. We have quitted

philosophy, we saw, was the conception of the two ends of man—mundane and celestial happiness. This conception determines his politics, so that he regarded the Empire and the Papacy as two independent systems appointed for the temporal and spiritual welfare of mankind respectively. The same conception ruled his view of history. He saw his temporal ideal realized in Pagan Rome, the spiritual kingdom perfected in the Catholic Church. This double thought is worked into the very substance of his poem. We have already noticed the opposition of the active and contemplative life symbolized in the * beautiful dream of Leah and Rachel —Leah, who decks herself and looks with joy upon her loveliness in the mirror; Rachel, who gazes only on her beautiful eyes in silent meditation. We have seen how the four Virtues of the Active Life are distinguished from the three Virtues of the Contemplative Life. We have now to trace the same deep-seated division in the

Aristotle for the teaching of the gospel as interpreted by the Church. Here let us notice that the just souls who had not the door of the Church opened to them either by baptism or by anticipatory faith in Christ, however much they may have fulfilled all righteousness of human morality, are excluded from Paradise. Nor is Purgatory possible for them ; since Purgatory is a place of passage prepared for such as are destined to celestial felicity. It will appear from this brief sketch how Dante combined the doctrines of moral philosophy and faith into one system—how he regarded human virtue, not as a title to Paradise, but as a necessary condition of the souls that were prepared for Paradise. Without faith and religion, righteousness and philosophy availed nothing. And in heaven the love of God transcended all knowledge of doctors in divinity, all justice of kings, all activity of champions of the faith.

* *Purgatorio*, xxvii.

mechanism and the structure of the Comedy. Needing an initiator into the eternal mysteries, Dante first receives the guidance of Virgil, who is the chosen type of Pagan art and science. Virgil is the symbol of human wisdom, of the Reason as distinct from Revelation, of Philosophy as separate from Scripture. But the province of these merely human powers is limited. They have no sway beyond the concerns of this world, beyond the destinies of man as a moral being unilluminated by the mysteries of faith. Therefore Virgil, whose power in Hell and Purgatory is complete, who, to use the words of Dante,* "conquers all things but the stubborn fiends," and leads the poet to the earthly Paradise, fails when the ascent to Heaven begins. There Dante needs a nobler mystagogue. He has selected Beatrice, the miracle of the most blessed Trinity, the mysterious Nine at whose birth all the influences of the spheres were favourable. Beatrice is the symbol of Divine Science, of Revelation as distinct from Reason, of Love superior to Skill. Fixing her eyes upon the face of God she grows more beautiful as she ascends the spheres, and as she grows in beauty Dante rises, so that Love and Adoration lead him to that heavenly Paradise or everlasting Rose of Bliss which is the final end of man. Virgil and Beatrice are therefore types and symbols of two separate faculties. Virgil is the grave accumulative intellect of man;

* *Inferno*, xiv. 43.

Virgil and Beatrice.   123

Beatrice is the ardent soul, that gazing upon God with love, is straightway rapt above the sun and stars. Virgil leads Dante with slow steps down circle after circle of Hell and up the Mountain of Purgation stair by stair; it is the tardy process of the understanding on its pathway of experience. Beatrice does but shine upon him with her radiance, and he rises to the very throne and Beatific Vision. Hers is the swift process of spiritual intuition, the faculty of faith and love which children have, in which the understanding finds no place. Not that Beatrice is deficient in knowledge: she includes Virgil, as it were, and goes beyond him, solving Dante's gravest doubts and embracing all the science of the things of God in an intuitive omniscience. But her science is not the essential point about her.

IX.

Dante's admiration and love of Virgil are pathetic. The eloquent surprise with which he greets him in the 1st *Inferno* — " Or se' tu quel Virgilio ! " " O anima cortese Mantovana ! "* — the rapture of Sordello in the *Purgatorio* when he learns his name: " O gloria de' Latin ! . . . O pregio eterno del luogo ond' io fui ! "† — the joy of

---

* *Inferno*, i. 79—87, ii. 59. "Art thou, then, that Virgil ?" "O courteous Mantuan spirit !"

† *Purgatorio*, vii. 16—20. "O glory of the Latin race. . . . . O eternal honour of my birth-place !"

Statius* in recognizing the poet who had taught him to be a Christian,—these are among the most exquisite and touching moments in the action of the Comedy. They realize the personality of Virgil, surrounding him with an atmosphere of sweetness, dignity, and grace. The very names and titles given by Dante to his guide are worth collecting. He addresses him in phrases like the following: "Tu duca, tu signore, e tu maestro;" or, "O tu, che onori ogni scienza ed arte;" or, "O virtù somma;" "O Sol, che sani ogni vista turbata!"† Again he calls him, "quel Savio gentil, che tutto seppe," "il mar di tutto 'l senno," "lo verace Duca," "il mio Conforto," "il dolce Pedagogo," "il mio Consiglio Saggio," "L' alto Dottore," "lo più che Padre," "nostra maggior Musa," "Virgilio dolcissimo Padre, Virgilio a cui per mia salute diémi."‡ Through all the prodigality of affection with which these terms are used we feel a double thought transpire—of Virgil as the poet and the man, of Virgil as the Reason. In the same way the double character of Beatrice, as Dante's lady, and as

---

* *Purgatorio*, xxi. and xxii.

† *Inferno*, ii. 140, iv. 73, x. 4, xi. 91. "Thou leader, thou lord, and thou master;" "Thou who art the honour of all science and all art;" "O height of Virtue;" "O sun that healest every troubled eye!"

‡ *Inferno*, vii. 3, viii. 7, xvi. 62.; *Purgatorio*, iii. 22, xii. 3, xiii. 75, xviii. 2, xxiii. 4; *Paradiso*, xv. 26; *Purgatorio*, xxx. 50. "That wise Gentile who knew all things;" "The sea of all wisdom;" "The true guide;" "My comfort;" "My sweet pedagogue;" "My wise counsellor;" "The exalted teacher;" "The more than father;" "Our chief Muse;" "Virgil, sweetest father, Virgil to whom for my salvation I gave myself."

The Allegory of Virgil and Beatrice. 125

Thelogy, eldest daughter of the grace of God, transpires through all her titles. Dante speaks thus of his celestial guide: "Ella, che mi vedea sì com' io;" "quella cui non potea mia cura essere ascosa;" "quel Sol che pria d' amor mi scaldò 'l petto;" "la dolce guida che sorridendo ardea negli occhi santi;" "il Sol degli occhi miei;" "quella Pia che guidò le penne delle miè ali;" "quella che imparadisa la mia mente;" "il segno di maggior disio;" "il mio conforto;" "O amanza del primo amante, O Diva."* It is worth noticing that while Virgil's titles turn upon his character of teacher, counsellor, and sage, those of Beatrice do not commemorate her science, but fix our attention upon her inspiration, on the miraculous virtue of her eyes by mere illumination to imparadise, inflame, and satisfy. So consistently anxious in all particulars is Dante to maintain his double thought.

X.

Unless we can regard Beatrice and Virgil both as real persons and also as allegories, we shall not have placed ourselves at Dante's point of view.

* *Paradiso,* l. 85, li. 26, lii. 1, iii. 23, xxx. 75, xxv. 49, xxviii. 3, iii. 136, xviii. 8, iv. 118. "She who saw me as I am;" "She from whom no care of mine could be hidden;" "That sun which first warmed my breast with love;" "The sweet guide who smiling burned;" "The sun of my eyes;" "That pious lady who guided the pinions of my wings;" "She who imparadises my soul;" "The object of surpassing desire;" "O love of the first lover, O goddess!"

Virgil,* though in one sense only the symbol of Philosophy and Reason, records the facts of his life, and receives the homage of Homer, Sordello, and Statius. So Beatrice, though taken as the type of Divine Science, is recognized by Dante as the Portinari who first stirred his soul to love, and who died at the age of twenty-four, leaving for his eyes "the ten years' thirst." I know not where in poetry to find anything more touching than the passages of the *Purgatorio* (canto xxvii. 19—54, and xxx. 40—54), in which the personalities of Virgil and Beatrice are brought into collision, the mild and melancholy radiance of the faithful guide of the *Inferno* paling before the rising splendour of the queen of Paradise, as the moon fades into the dawn and vanishes in silence. Dante drops some tears and quietly abandons his old friend for the new, the lesser for the greater love. We have to reconcile ourselves to Virgil's fate by reflecting that the understanding must give place to inspiration on the threshold of the mysteries of Heaven.

This mixture of symbolism with reality renders both Virgil and Beatrice frigid as persons. As soon as we have learned to sympathize with their humanity something always occurs to remind us that they are abstractions. It is right and proper that mere human

---

* This is clear from, *Inferno* xxx. 145, where Dante lifts the veil of allegory he is generally careful to keep drawn: E la' ragion ch' io ti sia sempre allato.

science should be excluded from Paradise and denied the sight of Beatrice. But who can help feeling sorrow for the good Virgil eternally condemned to Limbo? Who can forbear from tears while reading the grave sorrow of these hopeless lines?

> Tu non dimandi
> Che spiriti son questi, che tu vedi?
> Or vo' che sappi, innanzi che più andi,
> Ch' ei non peccaro: e s' egli hanno mercedi,
> Non basta, perch' e' non ebber battesmo,
> Ch' è porta della Fede che tu credi;
> E se furon dinanzi al Cristianesmo,
> Non adorâr debitamente Dio:
> E di questi cotal son lo medesmo.
> Per tai difetti, e non per altro rio,
> Semo perduti, e sol di tanto offesi,
> Che sanza speme vivemo in disio.*

Who can remember without rage that after Virgil has retired from the Terrestrial Paradise he must return to that:

> Luogo . . . . . non tristo da martìri,
> Ma di tenebre solo, ove i lamenti
> Non suonan come guai, ma son sospiri.

> * Thou askest not
> What spirits are these on whom thou gazest now?
> I would, before thou wendest, thou should'st know
> That these sinned not: and though they show good deeds,
> These nought avail for lack of baptism,
> Which is the portal of that faith thou holdest.
> And if they lived ere Christ on earth was born,
> They worshipped not God duly in right wise;
> And of these same behold even I am one!
> For faults like these, yea, for no other crime
> Lost are we; and our pain is this alone,
> That without hope we languish in desire.
> *Inferno*, iv. 31—42.

Compare *Purgatorio*, iii. 40—45.

Quivi sto lo co' parvoli innocenti,
  Da' denti morsi della morte, avante
  Che fosser dall' umana colpa esenti :
Quivi sto io con quei, che le tre sante
  Virtù non si vestiro, e senza vizio
  Conobber l' altre, e seguir tutte quante.*

Dante's theology and the inexorable system of his art alike require this. Divine Philosophy appears; human science is discarded. Dante dismisses Virgil with a facile tear. Had it not been for the chill comfort of the thought that Virgil was a symbol, could he have so parted from his "more than father," his "sweet father," his deliverer from the dreary wood?

A like confusion of the person and the symbol impairs the charm of Beatrice. In the *Vita Nuova* she interests us as a beautiful maiden, "the youngest of the angels." In *Purgatorio* xxx. 34—42, she revives this interest. But when she begins the sermon against Dante's sins (worthy of some Lady Ida before she felt the power of love), or when she is explaining the spots on the moon and smiling in sublime contempt of Dante's mortal grossness, our interest is considerably refrigerated.

* Place not terrible with torments,
But with gloom only ; where the lamentations
Sound not like wailings, but are simple sighs.
There is my station among innocent babes,
Smitten with death's fell tooth or e'er their flesh
From sin of frail humanity was purged.
There is my station among those who clad
Their soul with none of the three sacred virtues,
But guileless knew the rest, and kept their laws.
Purgatorio, vii. 28—36.

The Prosaic Element of the Poem. 129

She stands before us, in spite of all the poet's pains, as a pretentious preacher or a stiff automaton—pretentious if we still regard her as a woman, stiff and cold if we accommodate our minds to the allegory.

The attempt to combine incompatibilities, to interest us in persons who are allegorical, and to enliven abstractions by investing them with personality, is a radical defect in the *Divine Comedy*. The fusion cannot be complete. Hence there remains a prosy element in the very essence of the poem. It is not elastic and natural like Homer's *Iliad*, but artificial and mechanical. The same element of prose, the same sense of pressure and of artificiality, results from the determination of the three worlds. In this distinct division of human souls into the damned, the blest, the waiting to be blest, there is either an appalling tragic ἀνάγκη, or else a commonplace and prosy want of freedom. To the readers of Dante's own age it is probable that the tragedy of fate, freewill, and justice predominated. They shuddered to reflect how unalterable was the sentence, how slight a difference of mood in dying might determine æons of unmingled bliss or woe. But to us who have been schooled by centuries into a different conception of human destiny, there is something almost absurd in Dante's shutting people up in separate cells and ticketing them for all eternity. We know that all real life is fluid, subtle, changeful, active. None such is to be found in Hell or Paradise.

CHAPTER V.

THE HUMAN INTEREST OF THE "DIVINE COMEDY."

(i.) Dante's Personality, untainted by Symbolism, the main Interest of the *Divine Comedy*.—(ii.) Dante's Satire; the Cities of Italy.—(iii.) Dante's Animosity against Boniface.—(iv.) Filippo Argenti, Alberigo; the Severity of Dante.—(v.) Dante's Hatred of Treachery and Lukewarm Indifference.—(vi.) His Liberality; the Story of Manfred; Dante's Treatment of Lovers; his Boldness; Cacciaguida's Warning.—(vii.) Dante's Pride; Respect for Noble Ambition; Estimate of Fame.—(viii.) The gentler and more amiable Aspects of Dante's Character.—(ix.) Nature of the Human Interest of the Episodes of the *Divine Comedy*.—(x.) Hell; Farinata, Jason, Semiramis, Ulysses; Maestro Adamo; the Harpies' Forest; the Transformation of Men and Serpents.—(xi.) Purgatory; Difference of the Atmosphere of Hell and Purgatory.—(xii.) The Human Interest of the Purgatory; Casella, Buonconte, Sordello, Adrian, Statius, Forese Donati.—(xiii.) The Transition from Purgatory to Paradise; the State of the Saints; Light, Joy, and Love, the Triune Element of Paradise; their Charity and Contentment.—(xiv.) The Relation of the Spheres to the Celestial Rose explained.—(xv.) The Peculiarity of Dante's *Paradiso*, and the Faculties required for its Appreciation.—(xvi.) The Human Interest of the *Paradiso*; Piccarda, Donati, St. Francis and St. Dominic; Mars, Cacciaguida; Jupiter, the Eagle; Saturn; the Vision of Paradise itself; the Mystic Rose; St. Bernard's Prayer; the Beatific Vision.

I.

THE frigid symbolism which impairs the interest of Beatrice and Virgil does not affect Dante. In him the *Divine Comedy* centres: from him it derives its unity and life. There is but little in its action to arrest attention. No crisis of events occurs. Dante runs no dangers except when threatened by the Furies and pursued by the Malebranche among the Bolge. Purgatory is devoid of even this excitement, and Paradise is one prolonged ascent through spheres monotonous in splendid peace. Were we not held fascinated from the first line of the poem to the end by Dante's stern and vivid personality, as well as spell-bound by his marvellous style, few, perhaps, would read his epic. It would be impossible to find any work of art in the whole range of literature which so faithfully depicts a noble character in its mental strength and moral dignity. Who can say what sort of man the singer of the *Iliad* was? What notion, except a vague one, based on inference, have we of Sophocles or Shakspeare? If Goethe had left no writing but *Faust*, if all we knew of Milton had to be collected from the *Paradise*, how shadowy would be the picture in our memory of Goethe and of Milton compared with that of Dante, which is burned and stamped indelibly upon our mind by the perusal of his *Comedy!* So fascinating is the genuine portrait of a man of mark that we read the *Memoirs of Cellini* and the *Confessions of Rousseau*, with delight. But Cellini was a passionate savage and Rousseau a sentimental egotist: their biographies belong to the pathology of human nature. Whereas Dante, who has drawn himself as clearly in his verse as they in all their chapters, was a man eminent among men for the culture of his intellect and the nobility of his character.

II.

It has been well said that the *Divine Comedy* is not so much the work of immense learning—though that is in it—as of sublime and generous anger. We might adapt Swift's epitaph for Dante and write upon his tomb: "Sævissimâ indignatione cor dilaceratum." The fierce and fiery indignation of an injured heart is the first thing that strikes us when we reflect upon his personality. Hence Dante is pre-eminently a satirist—not in the ordinary sense in which we say that Juvenal, Horace, Regnier, and Dryden are satirists: Dante uses satire less for purposes of general invective than for the expression of intense personal feeling and matured opinion. His satire, like that of Archilochus, might well drive his foes—the mean and base and sordid of mankind—to hang themselves, so bitter is it, and so stinging in its brevity. When Michael Angelo painted his "Last Judgment" he placed the Pope's Master of the Ceremonies in Hell. The caricature was evident: the taunt was unendurable. Monsignore Biagio appealed to the Pope, but the Farnese answered wittily:—"I have the keys of Purgatory, but no man can deliver you from Hell." Dante has exercised this awful power which a great artist wields. He has dragged guilty souls forth from their skulking places, smiting and branding them upon the forehead, and setting the story of their infamy in his immortal verse for all posterity to read. No man

The Cities of Italy. 133

can deliver Ciacco and Argenti from his Hell—yet who would have heard of them if he had passed them by? The daughters of Lycambes and the Sculptor Bupalus of Ephesus, have not a sadder immortality. Nor was this Titanic rage spent merely upon individuals. Smarting with an exile's wrongs, and nursing a patriot's jealousy, he spared no city of his fatherland. Bologna * is full of pimps and pandars. The Genoese are men, "diversi d' ogni costume, e pien d' ogni magagna." † At Lucca, "ogni uom v' è barattier .... del no per li denar vi si fa ita." ‡ A citizen of Pistoja is made to say: "Son Vanni Fucci bestia, e Pistoja mi fu degna tana." § A comprehensive curse is uttered upon Pisa :—

> Ah! Pisa, vituperio delle genti
> Del bel paese, là dove il sì suona ;
> Poi chè i vicini a te punir son lenti,
> Muovasi la Capraia e la Gorgona,
> E faccian siepe ad Arno in su la foce,
> Sì ch' egli annieghi in te ogni persona.‖

---

* *Inferno,* xviii. 58—63.

† *Inferno,* xxxiii. 152. "Estranged from all morality, and full of all corruption."—CARLYLE.

‡ *Inferno,* xxi. 41. "Every man there is a barterer. .... There they make 'Ay' of 'No' for money."—CARLYLE.

§ *Inferno,* xxiv. 125. "I am Vanni Fucci, savage beast ; and Pistoja was a fitting den for me."—CARLYLE.

‖ *Inferno,* xxxiii. 79—84. "Ah, Pisa ! Scandal to the people of the beauteous land where 'Sì' is heard ! Since thy neighbours are slow to punish thee, let the Capraia and Gorgona move, and hedge up the Arno at its mouth, that it may drown in thee every living soul."—CARLYLE.

The vanity of the Sienese is ridiculed in an epigram which ricochets at France:

> Or fu giammai
> Gente sì vana, come la Sanese?
> Certo non la Francesca sì d' assai.*

But it is against Florence that Dante vents his bitterest indignation. The Florentines are "Gente avara, invidiosa e superba."† Pride, envy, avarice, are the three sparks which have inflamed them.‡ The mixture of their population, their greed for sudden gain, and their arrogance, so corrupt their blood § that—

> Virtù così per nimica si fuga
> Da tutti, come biscia.‖

In another place he calls Florence ¶ the pet plant of Lucifer, whose pride and envy caused his fall. Nor is he content with mere invective. He uses the more cutting weapon of irony against "La ben guidata,"** as he mockingly calls the misruled city of his birth. Can anything be more galling than the passages of prolonged and bitter sarcasm, beginning "Fiorenza mia, ben puoi

---

* *Inferno*, xxix. 121. "Now were there ever people vain as the Sienese? Certainly the French are not so vain by far."—CARLYLE.

† *Inferno*, xv. 68. "A people avaricious, envious, and proud."— CARLYLE.

‡ *Inferno*, vi. 74.

§ *Inferno*, xvi. 73.

‖ *Purgatorio*, xiv. 37. "Virtue like a foe is chased away by all as though she were a snake."

¶ *Paradiso*, x. 127.

** *Purgatorio*, xii. 102.

esser contenta!"* and "Godi, Fiorenza, poi che se' sì grande."† Again, in *Paradiso* itself, he uses his contempt for Florence to express astonishment:

> Io, ched'era al divino dall' umano,
> Ed all' eterno dal tempo venuto,
> E di Florenza in popol giusto e sano.‡

Dante knew the force of climax well. The third of these lines is, therefore, to be taken as a deliberate and carefully constructed sarcasm, carrying with it the full weight and solemnity of those which precede it. But the fiercest of all Dante's invectives against his native land, is the passage in which he describes the course of the Arno, rising meanly among "filthy swine, more fit for acorns than for human food;"§ next reaching the "snarling curs" of Arezzo; passing, "cursed and ill-starred ditch" that she is, from dogs to "wolves" in Florence; and finally descending to "foxes full of fraud" at Pisa. It is painful, but necessary, to fix one's mind upon these furious and bitter speeches. Without doing so we could not understand the temper of the man who trod the paths of Hell.

---

* *Purgatorio*, vi. 127. "My Florence, well mayest thou be contented."

† *Inferno*, xxvi. 1—12. "Joy, Florence, since thou art so great." —CARLYLE.

‡ *Paradiso*, xxxi. 35. "I who had passed from the human to the divine, from time to eternity, and from Florence to a people just and whole."

§ *Purgatorio*, xiv. 43—54.

III.

Dante displayed a like animosity against all distinguished persons whom he recognized as genuinely bad—pernicious to the world and hateful in the sight of God. I will take his treatment of Pope Boniface as an example. Not content with placing him head downwards in a red hot pit of Hell for simony, he calls [*] him "Lupo," "il principe de' nuovi farisei," "colui che siede e che traligna"—"wolf," "chief of the new Pharisees," "he who sits and swerves." After speaking with Niccolo in the fiery confessional, he bursts into a strain of denunciation so magnificent against his vice and that of Boniface, that I cannot refrain from quoting it :—

> Deh or mi di' quanto tesoro volle
> Nostro Signore in prima da san Pietro,
>   Che ponesse le chiavi in sua balìa?
>   Certo non chiese, se non : Viemmi dietro.
> Nè Pier, nè gli altri chiesero a Mattia
>   Oro od argento, quando fu sortito
>   Nel luogo, che perdè l' anima ria.
> Però ti sta, chè tu se' ben punito :
>   E guarda ben la mal tolta moneta,
>   Ch' esser ti fece contra Carlo ardito.
> E se non fosse, ch' ancor lo mi vieta
>   La reverenzia delle somme Chiavi
>   Che tu tenesti nella vita lieta,
> Io userei parole ancor più gravi ;
>   Chè la vostra avarizia il mondo attrista,
>   Calcando i buoni, e sollevando i pravi.

---

[*] *Paradiso*, ix. 132 ; *Inferno*, xxvii. 85 ; *Paradiso*, xii. 90.

> Di voi, Pastor, s' accorse 'l Vangelista,
> Quando colei, che siede sovra l' acque,
> Puttaneggiar co' regi a lui fu vista;
> Quella, che con le sette teste nacque
> E dalle diece corna ebbe argomento,
> Fin che virtude al suo marito piacque.
> Fatto v' avete Dio d' oro e d' argento:
> E che altro è da voi agl' idolatre,
> Se non ch' egli uno, e voi n' orate cento? *

This passage is one which must surely attach all generous and just souls to Dante. Was ever wrath more noble — breathing, as it does, a concentrated hatred of cupidity and baseness in high places? If only as a specimen of perfect oratory, this invective deserves everlasting recollection. Yet Dante has a still more splendid shaft of rhetoric against Boniface reserved in his quiver. Standing in the ninth sphere of

---

* *Inferno*, xix. 90—114. "Ah! Now tell me how much treasure our Lord required of St. Peter, before He put the keys into his keeping? Surely he demanded nought but 'Follow me!' Nor did Peter, nor the others, ask of Matthias gold or silver, when he was chosen for the office which the guilty soul had lost. Therefore stay thou here, for thou art justly punished; and keep well the ill-got money, which against Charles made thee be bold. And were it not that reverence for the great keys thou heldest in the glad life yet hinders me, I should use still heavier words; for your avarice grieves the world, trampling on the good and raising up the wicked. Shepherds such as ye the Evangelist perceived, when she that sitteth on the waters, was seen by him committing fornication with the kings; she that was born with seven heads, and in her ten horns had a witness so long as virtue pleased her spouse. Ye have made a god of gold and silver; and wherein do ye differ from the idolater, save that he worships one, and ye a hundred." — CARLYLE.

Paradise, above the fixed stars, St. Peter, flaming into sudden redness, cries,—

> Quegli, che usurpa in terra il luogo mio,
> Il luogo mio, il luogo mio, che vaca
> Nella presenza del figliuol di Dio,
> Fatto ha del cimiterio mio cloaca
> Del sangue e della puzza; onde 'l perverso,
> Che cadde di quassù, laggiù si placa.*

> *He who usurps on earth below my place—
> My place, my place, the which is void and empty
> Before the presence of the Son of God,
> Hath made my holy sepulchre a sink
> Of blood and stench; whence comes it that the rebel
> Who fell from hence is glad in hell and triumphs.
> *Paradiso*, xxvii. 22—36.

Boniface had got his place in the Holy See by a sort of simony. After causing Celestino V. to resign, Benedetto Gaetano of Anagni stipulated with Charles II. of Naples for the votes of twelve cardinals devoted to the House of Anjou, by means of which he wrought his election. See VILLANI, viii. 6. This Celestino may possibly be he whom Dante placed among the Vigliacchi:

> Guardai, e vidi l' ombra di colui
> Che fece, per viltate, il gran rifiuto.—*Inferno*, iii. 58.

Celestino preferred his religious leisure and his studies to the conduct of the Church in troublous times. He was, therefore, contemned by the fiery Dante, as he would have been by the faithful Milton. Dante, it must be remembered, while condemning the simony and avarice of Boniface, did not lose his respect for the Papal office, as these great lines about the sacrilege of Nogaret and the Colonnas attest:

> Veggio in Alagna entrar lo fiordaliso
> E nel Vicario suo Cristo esser catto.
> Veggiolo un' altra volta esser deriso:
> Veggio rinnovellar l' aceto e 'l fele
> E tra vivi ladroni essere anciso.—*Purgatorio*, xx. 86.

His attitude is like that of VILLANI's, viii. 64, "E non è da maravigliare della sentenzia di Dio, che contuttoche papa Bonifazio fosse più mondano che non richiedea alla sua dignità, e fatte avea assai delle cose a dispiacere

Was ever anger more tremendously expressed than by the ponderous repetition of the words "luogo mio!" Then, says Dante:—

> Di quel color, che per lo Sole avverso,
> Nube dipinge da sera e da mane,
> Vid' io allora tutto 'l Ciel cosperso.
> E come donna onesta, che permane
> Di sè sicura, e per l' altrui fallanza,
> Pure ascoltando, timida si fane:
> Cosi Beatrice trasmutò semblanza:
> E tale eclissi credo che in Ciel fue,
> Quando patì la suprema Possanza.*

Heaven grew red; the whole consistory of the saints blushed scarlet for the sordidness of Earth. Such eclipse, adds the poet, heaven suffered on the day of Calvary. This is one of Dante's sublime imaginations.

IV.

Well may we exclaim with Virgil, "Alma Sdegnosa!"—Spirit of noble wrath, well done! There are few readers, however, who will be wholly willing

di Dio, Iddio fece pulire lui per lo modo che detto avono, e poi l' offenditore di lui puli, non tanto per l' offesa della persona di papa Bonifazio, ma per lo peccato commesso contro alla maestà divina, il cui cospetto rappresentava in terra."

> * Even such colour as the smiling sun
> Doth paint on clouds of evening or of morn,
> I then beheld the whole of heaven o'erspread:
> And as a pure-souled lady who remains
> Whole in her virtue, for another's fault,
> Only to hear of it, is ta'en with fear;
> So Beatrice changed semblance where she stood.
> Eclipse like this, methinks, was once in heaven
> When the supreme Power suffered.

to echo the Latin poet's commendation in the place where it is uttered. Let us recall the scene.

While passing over the marsh of Styx, Dante and his guide meet a soul immersed in slimy waves: he swims toward the boat and addresses Dante savagely. "I replied: Remain to weep and wail, cursed spirit; for I know thee, foul though thou art. Thereat he stretched both hands to the bark, but my master seeing it repelled him with, Away, hence, with the other hounds!" Thereupon Virgil turns to Dante, clasps him in his arms with the eulogy of "Alma Sdegnosa!" I have quoted. Dante's answer is one that somewhat staggers modern feelings: "Master, I would very gladly see him soused in that broth ere we leave the lake." His wish is granted. The shriek of Argenti, at fearful odds among tormenting comrades, shrills across Styx. Whereat Dante pricks his ears and listens. His soul is satisfied. "Even now I yield praise and thanks to God therefore," he says.

What shall we say of this intensity of bitterness and scorn? Is not the man made of cast iron with adamantine entrails? Such, in fact, must be he who would tread the paths of Hell. Johnson moreover used to say that a man could not love well without being a good hater. So the spring of genuine tenderness and pity may be thought to flow from the hardest rock, even as granite yields the sweetest, purest water. What Dante's affection was we have already seen: and who shall read the *Purgatorio* and the *Paradiso* without marvelling at the exquisitely soft unfoldings of his heart, at the bright upward aspirations of his loving soul? These we must remember, when we follow him to the "thrilling regions of thick-ribbed ice," where traitors stick, like "straws in glass," in the cold crystal of Cocytus. Their hands and feet and trunk are cased in frozen chasms; the head alone emerges, and, as bitter tears flow down for very woe, they freeze. One of the sinners, unrecognized by Dante, cries to him—

> Levatemi dal viso i duri veli,
> Sì ch' io sfoghi 'l dolor, che 'l cuor m' impregna,
> Un poco, pria che 'l pianto si raggieli.*

For pity break the ice upon my face, that I may weep a little while before my fount of tears freeze up again!

---

* *Inferno*, xxxiii. 112. "Remove the hard veils from my face, that I may vent the grief, which stuffs my heart, a little ere the weeping freeze again."—CARLYLE. Dante's treatment of Bocca degli Abbati (*Inferno*, xxxii. 78—111) in Antenora, where traitors to their country are punished, is scarcely less typical of his stern implacability. Walking among the frozen heads that emerge above the ice he strikes one who cries out "Strikest thou me for more payment of my sin at Montaperti?" It is Bocca, who in the battle of Arbia, gained over to treason by the gold of the Ghibellines, struck the arm of Jacopo de' Pazzi the Guelf standard-bearer, next him in the ranks, so that the banner fell and the Guelfs were routed. Bocca here in hell refuses to yield his name to Dante: whereupon Dante seizes his head and pulls the hair out by handfuls, Bocca howling all the while with eyes turned downwards to the ice. A traitor close beside him cries with grim irony: "Bocca, is it not enough to clatter with your jaws in this hell frost? Must you be also barking?" Now Dante knows the name of him and cries:—

> Non vo' che più favelle
> Malvagio traditor; ch' alla tua onta
> Io porterò di te vere novelle.

Was ever prayer more piteous than this? Our blood is curdled as we read it. But Dante, colder, sharper than the ice, replies:—

> Se vuol ch' io ti sovvegna,
> Dimmi chi fosti, e s' io non ti disbrigo,
> Al fondo della ghiaccia ir mi convegna.*

Tell me who you are; then, if I help you not, may I go to the bottom of the glacier! By these words he gets all the information he desires. Alberigo tells his dolorous tale, and ends it thus:—

> Ma distendi oramai in qua la mano ;
> Aprimi gli occhi !†

Dante only adds:

> Ed Io non glieli apersi ;
> E cortesia fu lui esser villano.‡

There is no shrinking. The rhythm of the verse lays emphasis upon that awful *non*. Thus, it seems, that not only are tears frozen in this hideous place; but mercy, pity, and sweet human sympathies are stiffened into icicles that cut, and pierce, and sting. Nay, loyalty herself, who guards the brotherhood of men, has died. Thus does the will of God ordain. Dante would be vile had he relented here; well,

---

* "If thou would'st have me aid thee, tell me who thou art ; and if I do not extricate thee, may I have to go to the bottom of the ice."—CARLYLE.

† "But reach hither thy hand : open my eyes."—CARLYLE.

‡ "And I opened them not for him ; and to be rude to him was courtesy."—CARLYLE.

indeed, had he learned his Master's lesson and remembered his reproof:—

> Ancor se' tu degli altri sciocchi?
> Qui vive la pietà quand' è ben morta.
> Chi è più scellerato di colui,
> Ch' al giudicio di Dio passion porta?*

Art thou, then, also one of the fools? Here piety lives only in her death. Who is more base than he who pities the condemned of God?

V.

We have seen how Dante can hate and despise. There are two things which he abhors with all the intensity of his nature. They are treachery and lukewarm selfishness. Against these vices of the soul his heart turns adamant and glows red hot. His own sincerity leads him to exaggerate the latter fault. We understand his putting traitors in the lowest circle of Hell; nay, we approve of the cruel ingenuity which divides that pit of silent horror into its four regions of increasing torment, till the very claws and jaws of Lucifer himself, rending the three archtraitors,† are reached, and there is nothing left of woe in Hell to witness. But it is hard to comprehend that less

---

* *Inferno*, xx. 28. "Art thou, too, like the other fools? Here pity lives when it is rightly dead. Who more impious than he that sorrows at God's judgment?"—CARLYLE.

† Judas, Brutus, and Cassius were treasonable against Christ and the Empire.

malignant, but more subtle doom reserved for the indolent souls "who stood for themselves apart" in the wars of heaven and earth.* "Questi non hanno speranza di morte." Without even the grim hope of death as a refuge and respite from their torture, so low and sordid is their lot, that they are envious of the fiery beds and burning rain allotted to more manly sinners. Fameless on earth above, forgotten alike of mercy and of justice, hateful to God and to his foes, they roam, bitten by flies and wasps, and shedding blood and tears which turn to loathly worms. It was the rectitude of Dante's moral sense which made him estimate treason as the blackest of all crimes. The intensity of his political † sympathies led him to be so severe upon those other "Sciaurati che mai non fur vivi." The world accepts the former verdict; the latter may justly be deemed extravagant—we see it was provoked by the peculiar circumstances of the poet's life. Dante condemned wretches to this eternal misery and universal scorn, because they would not decide themselves for Guelf and Ghibelline, but preferred to keep quiet and trim

---

* *Inferno*, iii. 34—69.

† The same political-religious attitude of mind is found in Milton. See the grand passage at the close of his *Reformation in England*, where Milton sees for the true patriots and defenders of God's faith a double measure of celestial bliss and "supereminence of beatific vision," while the enslavers of their country, and self-exalters at the expense of their fellows, shall be thrust into "the darkest and deepest gulf of hell," to remain for all eternity "the basest, the lowermost, the most dejected, most underfoot and down-trodden vassals of perdition."

their sails. What would he have said to modern canons of nonintervention and neutrality for the good of trade?

VI.

Next to this generous heat and intensity of Dante's temper, we may notice his liberality of soul. He is free from false deference to authority and opinion. He has no respect for persons, no mean antipathies, no petty jealousies. This independence is strikingly exemplified by the story of Manfredi,* who died in contumacy of the Church. Therefore, Pope Clement caused his bones to be disinterred at Benevento and exposed to wind and rain upon the shores of the Garigliano. But, adds Manfredi:

> Per lor maladizion al non si perde,
> Che non possa tornar l' eterno amore,
> Mentre che la speranza ha fior del verde.†

---

* *Purgatorio*, iii. This Manfred is the great King of the Two Sicilies, who carried on the war against Pope Clement IV., and was finally killed by the army of Charles of Anjou, in the battle of Grandella, 1266. Treason of his own counts and officers lost him the day. He put his casque upon his head: the silver eagle of the House of Suabia fell from it upon his saddle-bow; whereupon he cried, "Hoc est signum Dei!" and went forth and perished. Charles refused to bury his body. The soldiers of the victorious army, honouring his valour, heaped stones upon it. But Pignatelli, Bishop of Cosenza, cleared away the stones, and gave the royal corpse to the river-bed of the Verde. Thus was the rancour of the Church against the House of Suabia carried beyond the grave.

† Their curse avails not so to damn the soul,
But that God's everlasting Love can turn,
Even while Hope shows yet one leaf alive.

This is a noble sentence, appealing to God's judgment seat from that of Peter, from mortal jealousy to the eternal love. The whole of Europe lay spellbound by superstition, dreading with undefined terror the ban of the Church. But Dante saw clearly and spoke boldly, as his reason and his faith in God's goodness prompted.

In connection with this liberality of judgment the Catholicity of Dante deserves record. He makes use of Pagan mythology and Christian legend indifferently. He appeals to the Bible miracles and Livy's portents as though they were on the same level of authority. Plato and Aristotle are quoted by him among the evidences of the faith. Aristotle, again, is cited as an exponent of the Divine scheme of Justice. Epicurus lies near Anastasius among the heresiarchs. Trajan and Rhiphæus shine in Jupiter side by side with Charlemagne and David. By Dante at least humanity was still regarded as one divinely-governed family.

Another instance of his liberality is his treatment of lovers. He is singularly lenient to them. The sweet planet Venus is full of lovers, some of whom, especially Cunizza, were less famous for their penitence than for their follies. Paolo and Francesca are placed as high in Hell as possible, and receive from Dante not merely the tribute of his profoundest sympathy, but also of his subtlest painting. "A thing," exclaims Carlyle, before this picture, "woven as out of rainbows, on a ground of eternal black. A small flute-voice of infinite wail speaks there, into our very heart of hearts." In Purgatory the carnal souls dwell immediately below the Earthly Paradise, almost within sight of that delicious garden. But the most notable instance of Dante's generosity toward sinners of the flesh is to be found in the 16th *Inferno*. Among Latini's comrades of guilt are the noble Florentines, Aldobrandi, Guidoguerra, and Rusticucci, valiant soldiers, tainted with one vice. Instead of shrinking from them with horror, as the modern Pharisee of conventional morality must do, Dante recalls their patriotic deeds, and longs to fall upon their necks.* "Had there been covert for me from the fire, I should have leaped down to embrace them, and I think my master would have suffered me. But fear conquered my good will." And again:—"Of

* *Inferno*, xvi. 46—60. Sismondi, in a note on the Count Guido Guerra, takes occasion to remark on the prevalence of Brunetto's sin as attested by the punishment of these illustrious Florentines, in a society so stern and moderate as that of Florence. Giovanni Villani's description of the Republic (*Storie Fiorentine*, vi. 70) represents a state of primitive simplicity and austere republican manners. Yet here is this vice of luxurious capitals and decadent civilizations in full bloom among the noblest, the most valiant, the most respected, the most learned citizens of Florence. "The crimes of Tegghiaio and of Rusticucci," says Sismondi, "like those of Œdipus and Orestes, seem like the effect of divine wrath; but, beneath the burden of this wrath, the men show themselves still great." The mediæval conscience was perhaps less developed on this point than ours is now. Sins of the flesh were included under one undiscriminating condemnation. It is true that Latini and his companions are placed lower in Hell than Paolo and Francesca; but in Purgatory one circle cleanses both classes of sinners together.

your land I am citizen; your deeds and honoured names have ever been with love related to me, and retained by me." I do not mean that Dante loved the sin of these men, or of Francesca and Cunizza. Far from it. The flesh had no dominion over him. But it was an essential part of his moral system to estimate vice not as a personal, but as a social evil. The sinner against human bonds and duties, the traitor or the falsifier, was the object of his deepest hatred.

The boldness with which Dante pronounces sentence, and attacks great criminals, deserves to be commemorated. He stands like Michaiah or Elijah in the presence of tyrants, preferring to risk life rather than to sacrifice his prophecy. Cacciaguida* warns him of the peril, but exhorts him to stand firm:—" A conscience, darkened by its own or by its neighbour's shame, will feel the harshness of thy words. Yet speak without concealment: publish thy vision: in the end thy lessons, bitter at first, will yield the juice of life. And this thy cry, like the wind, shall strike but the highest summits—no small honour to thee."

This audacity of speech was based upon a robust self-reliance which is one of Dante's most marked characteristics. We see it in the estimate which he, the first singer of the modern world, the creator of a new language, and a new style of art, forms of his own genius. The vaunt of Lucretius that he is "approaching

* *Paradiso*, xvii. 124—142.

untasted springs and culling flowers, which hitherto the Muse hath woven round no poet's brow," is far less justified than Dante's boast that "L'acqua ch' io prendo giammai non si corse," since Lucretius had the precedent of Parmenides, Empedocles, and other Greeks, while Dante had no predecessor. Yet he never doubts his vocation. "Follow thy star," says Latini: "thou canst not fail to reach a glorious haven." "Utter thy prophecy," adds Cacciaguida: "the world will listen." The five great poets of the elder age salute Dante with the name "che più onora e più dura." He accepts it modestly, but as a man born to sovereignty. He bids Apollo crown him with the noblest and most sacred laurels, since few are bold enough to seek the poet's or the victor's bays. Everywhere he assumes that his verdict will confer an immortality of shame or honour. This self-assurance has no alloy of vanity. It is the simple consciousness of greatness not to be concealed, compatible with true humility, and dignified by serene indifference to what a carping or a jealous world may say. The same confidence in his own powers made Dante leave the parties of the Blacks and Whites to stand alone. The same innate source of strength hardened his spirit, so that he became "Ben tetragono ai colpi di ventura"*—or to use the phrase of Marston "like sparkling steel, the strokes of chance made hard and firm."

* *Paradiso*, xvii. 24.

VII.

Dante's chief fault was one allied to the great qualities on which we have been dwelling—Pride. Like all proud people, he sometimes glories in the nobler and more generous aspects of this failing. He records the epithet "Sdegnoso" with approval, and dwells with complacency, in *Paradiso*, upon the long line of his honourable ancestry. Yet he was not insensible of this defect. There is a passage of the *Purgatorio* where he discusses the punishments which may be in store for him after this life. Standing among the envious, he cries:

> Gli occhi, mi fieno ancor qui tolti,
> Ma picciol tempo; chè poc' è l' offesa
> Fatta, per esser con invidia volti.
> Troppa è più la paura, ond' è sospesa
> L' anima mia, del tormento di sotto :
> Chè già lo carco di laggiù mi pesa.*

The penalty of pride was carrying heavy weights. This Dante dreaded more than the punishment of envy, which afflicted the eyesight with dense and acrid smoke.

Dignified ambition, Dante, with his masculine good

---

* *Purgatorio*, xiii. 133. "My eyes may yet be here taken from me, but for a little time: for small is the offence that they have caused by envious glances. Far greater is the dread that racks my soul of the torment down below; for even now the burden of that place weighs on me."

sense and health of intellect, prized as a virtue. The planet Mercury is thus described:

> Questa picciol stella si correda
> De' buoni spirti, che son stati attivi,
> Perchè onore e fama gli succeda.*

And fame is defined as that:

> Sanza la qual, chi sua vita consuma,
> Cotal vestigio in terra di sè lascia,
> Qual fummo in aere, od in acqua la schiuma.†

The vices so often confounded with ambition, and which sometimes deface the noblest fame, — envy, avarice, violence, cupidity — were hated by Dante. Nor did he fail to appreciate the brevity and valuelessness of mere reputation. What is Glory?‡ A mere breath. In a thousand years it matters not whether you have lived to be an old man or died a child: yet a thousand years in all eternity is but the twinkling of an eye:

> La vostra nominanza è color d' erba,
> Che viene e va; e quei la discolora,
> Per cui ell' esce della terra acerba.

---

* *Paradiso*, vi. 112. "This little star is furnished with good spirits who were spurred to action, that honour and fame might be their meed."

† *Inferno*, xxiv. 49. "Without which whoso consumes his life, leaves such vestige of himself on earth, as smoke in air or foam in water." — CARLYLE.

‡ *Purgatorio*, xi. 100—107, and 115—117. "Your glory is as the colour of grass which comes and goes again; and that destroys its hue which causes it to spring from the earth unripe."

VIII.

We have hitherto seen the harder qualities of Dante—his scorn, his wrath, his severity, his courage, his liberality, his pride, his ambition. These are prominent and easy to describe. But it would be no hard task to display his humility, his gentleness, his ecstasy of love and adoration—to set his yearning after Florence and his " bel San Giovanni" side by side with his invectives, to show the patience of his soul when condemned to eat a patron's bread and mount a benefactor's palace stairs. The whole *Purgatorio* is a monument to the beauty and tranquillity of Dante's soul. The whole *Paradiso* is a proof of its purity and radiance, and celestial love.* It is enough to mention the Confession of Charity in the 26th canto of the *Paradiso*, and the prayer which opens the last canto: let a man read these in silence, meditate upon them, and then try to estimate the height and the depth of the riches of the love of Dante's heart. How, moreover, can a poet describe the joy of the blest and the patience of the Saints, without having in his heart the fountain of that joy, without possessing the repose of that patience?

* "I know not in the world an affection equal to that of Dante."
—CARLYLE'S *Hero as Poet*.

IX.

The human interest of the *Divine Comedy*, though it centres in the personality of Dante, is not confined to him. The various individuals whom the poet passes in review, and who converse with him, preserve a running chain of ever new and varied incidents. Their histories, embedded like jewels in the gold of Dante's narration, add brilliance to the wrought work of his Art and point the lessons of his Science. They more than serve the ordinary purpose of episodes. Not only is the poem enlivened by them; it even owes to them its very life.

Nothing is more characteristic of Dante's method than the habit of presenting the concrete instead of the abstract. He does not talk to us of "Luctus et ultrices curæ, et metus, et malesuada fames, ac turpis egestas." He makes us hear the wailings of Hell in all their hideous variety;* we see the Furies on the battlements of Dis; the famine of Count Ugolino meets our eyes. Dante condenses aphorisms into pictures, and sums up chapters of morality in portraits. Therefore his Epic, which has for its subject the morality of Man, displays humanity piecemeal as it were in a succession of highly-finished miniatures—a panoramic gallery of representative human faces emerging from the darkness of

* Quivi sospiri, pianti ed alti guai. . . . .
Diverse lingue, orribili favelle,
Parole di dolore, accenti d' ira,
Voci alte e fioche, e suon di man con elle.

the background of that countless host which classical antiquity christened "the Majority." Each personage so summoned from the battalions of the dead is Coryphœus of an unnamed chorus. Through his particular experience the universal is expressed. At the same time what is specific to his lot is not omitted, and thus our interest is excited and sustained by a multitude of independently dramatic circumstances.

The various fortunes of the souls, who, after living widely different lives on earth, converge upon some single pit of hell, stripped of their accidents and huddled there in indiscriminate confusion of rank, age, race, sex, century, religion, affect our imagination with a deep and tragic sense of the eternal justice. The dead are a democracy. Their hierarchies are nought but different grades of vice and virtue. From the squadrons in which popes, peasants, captains, ladies, sages of the ancient world, and poets fill the ranks, Dante selects the more eminent personages.* Let us detach some of his portraits from each of the three Cantiche in order to estimate what amount of human interest there is in the *Divine Comedy*.

X.

To the majority of educated people Dante's name suggests two tales of pathos and of pity—that of Francesca da Rimini and that of the Count Ugolino.

* *Paradiso*, xvii. 133.

Those who know nothing else in Dante's poem know these episodes. It is therefore enough to mention what the universal verdict pronounces to be masterpieces. Rainbow-tinted on the background of fuliginous gloom, is the one picture; a Rembrandt study of faint rays revealing pallid horror between stony prison walls, is the other. Nor need we dwell on Farinata raising chest and forehead from his fiery grave, "as though he held Inferno in great scorn."* Let us, however, mark the tenor of his words. The great Ghibelline has laid thirty-six years in his sepulchre of flame. Yet the mere footfall of a Florentine and the sight of the familiar habit stir him to the interests of the upper world. "Chi fur gli maggior tui?" Undisturbed by Cavalcante's interruption,† unmoved by the pathos of the father's grief, Farinata stands erect, ready to resume his broken thread of speech:

> E se, continuando al primo detto,
> Egli han quell' arte, disse, male appresa,
> Ciò mi tormenta più che questo letto.‡

Farinata's§ tenacity is true to the spirit of Dante's

---

* *Inferno*, x. 55—60.

† This is noticeable, since Farinata's own daughter had married Cavalcante's son. It is also curious to notice how in Italian towns party spirit, after superseding patriotism, had been superseded by hereditary feuds. Dante is a Ghibelline, yet he taunts Farinata with the triumphs of his own Guelf Alighieri ancestry.

‡ "'And if,' continuing his former words, he said, 'they have learnt that art badly, it torments me more than this bed.'"—CARLYLE.

§ Farinata is placed among the heretics because of his devotion to the cause of Frederick II., and the house of Suabia, who were under the ban

age and to the genius of the poet. In no other period of history have politics raged so fiercely. Perhaps no other poet than Dante would have dared to paint a spirit triumphing in the potency of factious pride over Hell and the torments of "this bed."

Of all Dante's portraits those were perhaps the most admirable which are briefly sketched with the force of Velasquez, with the *sprezzatura* of Tintoretto, every line and deeply indented shadow telling. Here is Jason:

> Guarda quel grande, che viene,
> E per dolor non par lacrime spanda :
> Quanto aspetto reale ancor ritiene !
> Quegli è Giason. . . . *

Behold Achilles, with a commentary on the *Iliad* in a single line:

> Il grande Achille
> Che per amore al fine combatteo. †

The following character is also notable for its barbaric pomp and breadth of treatment:

> La prima di color, di cui novelle
> Tu vuoi saper . . . .
> Fu imperadrice di molte favelle.

---

of the Church, and who were reputed to have no care for the future life. They laughed at Papal interdicts and encouraged the Paterini schisms.

* *Inferno*, xviii. 83. "Look at that great soul who comes, and seems to shed no tear for pain. What a regal aspect he yet retains! That is Jason. . . ."—CARLYLE.

† *Inferno*, v. 65. "The great Achilles who for love's sake fought at last." Here I follow Fraticelli's reading "per amore;" Carlyle takes "con amore." According to Fraticelli's text the love of Achilles for Patroclus, which finally drove him from his tent to the field, is referred to.

Semiramis—Ulysses—Maestro Adamo.

> A vizio di lussuria fu sì rotta,
> Che libito fe' lecito in sua legge,
> Per tôrre il biasmo in che era condotta :
> Ell' è Semiramis.*

To these portraits of the antique dead we ought to add that of Ulysses †—one of the most finely and romantically conceived of all Dante's pictures. Ulysses and Diomede enclosed in one fire-pyramid with a double spire of flickering flame, approach Dante, and, like Greeks anxious for celebrity, show willingness to talk. The larger horn of fire vibrates; it tells how, setting forth from Ithaca in old age, the world-worn hero of the Odyssey took yet again the sea, stirring his companions to explore new regions and learn more of human vice and virtue. Storm came upon them in mid-ocean of the other hemisphere, and they were drowned. This speech ought to be familiar to English readers. One of Mr. Tennyson's most perfect pieces of classical work has been studied apparently from Dante's original.

Take a picture of another kind.‡ "Such pain as there would be, were all the hospitals of Valdichiana between July and September, and the diseases of Maremma and Sardinia enclosed in one ditch, was here; and such stench issued forth as comes from rotting

---

* *Inferno,* v. 52. "The first of these concerning whom thou seekest to know was empress of many tongues. With the vice of luxury she was so broken that she made lust and law alike in her decree, to take away the blame she has incurred. She is Semiramis."—CARLYLE.

† *Inferno,* xxvi.

‡ *Inferno,* xxix. 46—51, 58—62, 67 ; and xxx. 58—69.

limbs. ... Egina with her sickness of a nation when all living creatures to the very worms perished, showed not such dolorous sights. ... One lay upon the belly, one upon the shoulders, each of each; and one crawled toilsomely along the dismal road." It is thus that we are introduced to the valley of loathsome disease, wherein false coiners are heaped.* One of them, Adamo da Brescia, knows Dante. He lies dropsy-stricken, with swollen body and dry, gaping lips:

> O voi, che senza alcuna pene siete
> (E non so lo perchè) nel mondo gramo,
> Diss' egli a noi, guardate, ed attendete
> Alla miseria del Maestro Adamo :
> Io ebbi vivo assai di quel ch' i' volli ;
> Ed ora, lasso ! un gocciol d' acqua bramo.
> Li ruscelletti, che de' verdi colli
> Del Casentin descendon giuso in Arno,
> Facendo i lor canali e freddi e molli,
> Sempre mi stanno innanzi e non indarno ;
> Chè l' imagine lor vie più m' asciuga,
> Che 'l male, ond' lo nel volto mi discarno.†

---

* Dante's frequent allusions to the florin of Florence, implying the great disgrace which any depreciation of its quality was supposed to entail, are noticeable. This coin was first struck by the Florentines in 1252 to commemorate their growing power in Tuscany, which had been signalized by victories over the Pisans and Sienese. It was of gold of twenty-four carats, one-eighth of an ounce in weight. This piece has survived into the present century bearing the same stamp of a fleur-de-lys, the same value.

† "O ye! who are exempt from every punishment, and why I know not, in this grim world," said he to us, "look and attend to the misery of Master Adam. When alive, I had enough of what I wished; and now, alas ! I crave one little drop of water. The rivulets that from the verdant hills of Casentino descend into the Arno, making their channels cool and moist, stand constantly before me, and not in vain ; for the image of them dries me up far more than does the malady which from my visage wears the flesh."—CARLYLE.

I have introduced Master Adamo for the sake of the triplet about Casentino, which seems to me instinct with the truest poetry, coming as it does amid the ghastly lazaretto details of the scene. Lesser poets might have talked of Tantalus, or have imagined brooks and grassy meads; Dante pierces the soul with pathos by describing the cool dewy places of Adamo's home.

Shall we visit the grove of the Harpies?

> Non frondi verdi, ma di color fosco;
> Non rami schietti, ma nodosi e involti;
> Non pomi v' eran, ma stecchi con tosco.*

Break one of the gnarled, haggard, dull-hued poisonous twigs. It shrinks and spits forth blood; with the blood comes first a hissing bubble, then a shriek, then a clamorous lament—

> "Perchè mi schiante? . . .
> Perchè mi scerpi? . . .
> Non hai tu spirto di pietade alcuno?
> Uomini fummo ed or siam fatti sterpi!†

It is the soul of Piero delle Vigne‡ who cries; and his tale of injury and suicide is notable.

---

* *Inferno*, xiii. 4—6. "Not green the foliage, but brown in colour; not smooth the branches, but gnarled and warped; apples none were there, but withered sticks with poison."—CARLYLE.

† "Why dost thou rend me? . . . Why tearest thou me? Hast thou no breath of pity? Men we were, and now are turned to trees."—CARLYLE.

‡ Piero delle Vigne was born at Capua in indigence. He supported himself by begging in his youth at Bologna, where he acquired learning in law and literature remarkable for his times, and showed rare powers of eloquence and general ability. Frederick II., who admired talents and patronised letters, made him his secretary, his counsellor, and protonotary. Thus he came to hold both keys of Frederick's heart. Piero excelled in

Shall we venture to describe the Florentines entwined with serpents in the seventh pit of Malebolge—their hideous hissings, and hateful interchange of poisonous shapes; their mutual loathing and alternate wounds; their writhings and contortions on the burning sand? No. There is no strictly human interest here. As well dilate on Cerberus, with his three heads; the Centaurs, or Scarmiglione; or the tail of Minos; or Lucifer's three faces; or Geryon; or any other of Dante's grotesque phantasies. The demon world of Hell is not unnaturally peopled by him with grisly shapes. Humanity, sinking below bestiality, breeds monsters. The angel that fell from God's presence pierces the world, wormlike, even as the canker writhed through Eve's apple. Purgatory, the place of penitence and recreation, has no such deformity. All is human

letter-writing and in rhetoric; he was employed by Frederick to set forth his imperial policy in the most favourable light by both of these means; Piero's letters are still monuments of Frederick's history. When Frederick was excommunicated in 1239, Piero defended him at Padua in a set oration on the couplet of Ovid:

> Leniter ex merito quicquid patiare; ferendum est;
> Quæ venit indigne pœna dolenda venit.

This use of a couplet from *Ovid* as the text of a rhetorical oration is most characteristic of the manners of the times. At the council of Lyons in 1245, when Frederick was deposed by order of the Pope, Piero, though sent there to support his interests, held his tongue. He never regained Frederick's confidence, but was imprisoned in 1246 on a charge of conspiracy against the Emperor's life, which Villani and Dante both regarded as unjust, and soon ended his existence by dashing out his brains against the wall. Frederick was sensible of his loss: before condemning Piero he is said to have cried out, "Woe's me! what a man am I about to punish!" Piero was one of the earliest poets in the vulgar tongue.

there; even as all in Paradise is superhuman. So nicely does Dante preserve the rhythm of his worlds. Let us hasten to leave Hell, and pass "a riveder le stelle."

XI.

The portraits and landscapes of the *Inferno* detach themselves from a background, black and monotonous, illuminated only by the glare of flames and the red hue of blood. The sense of profound and pitchy gloom is conveyed to us by Dante less by means of actual description than by a systematic negation of light and colour. We are made to feel that we are walking in thick night. The impression, moreover, is a moral one. It is the despair of souls who have abandoned all hope at the gate of Hell, and who upon the shore of Acheron curse God, their parents, the seed from which they sprang, and the very day of their birth, which makes the caverns of that subterranean place of pain so black. As the souls in Paradise coruscate and scintillate the light of love, so those in Hell give forth an atmosphere of darkness:—

> Giù s' abbuia
> L' ombra di fuor, come la mente è trista.*

When we turn to the *Purgatorio* we find ourselves in

---

* *Paradiso*, ix. 72. "Down there the shade is murky outside even as the mind is saddened."

the free air of heaven. The dawn has begun, tinting the east with softest hues of Oriental sapphire, and trembling on the waves of the boundless sea of the antipodes. The holy mountain rears itself aloft into pure light of day, taking the sweet successions of morn, noon, and night upon its ample sides. The mountain and the ocean and the air are elements of health and purity, by which Dante, whether consciously or not, has symbolized the place of purgation and refreshment.

Charon, the demon, with eyes of burning coal, collected the damned upon the bank of Acheron. An angel radiant as the sun, "l' uccel divino," fanning with his wings the morning air, brings a freight of patient souls to Purgatory:—

> Ah! quanto son diverse quelle foci
> Dall' infernali! chè quivi per canti
> S' entra, e laggiù per lamenti feroci!*

These spirits are full of hope instead of despair. They come, as Dante says, "per farsi belle." Prayers and psalms are on their lips instead of curses. *In exitu Israel de Egypto*, sounds from the angelic bark: the gate of Purgatory turns upon its hinges to the murmur

---

* "Ah me! how diverse are these entrances
From those of Hell! for here with sound of singing
Souls pass; but there with savage lamentations."
Purgatorio, xii. 112.

of *Te Deum*. Morning begins with the Lord's Prayer, and evening is greeted with the Compline hymn:—

> Te lucis ante sì devotamente
> Le uscì di bocca, e con sì dolce note,
> Che fece me a me uscir di mente.*

Nor do prayers and praise ascend for the souls in torment merely. When one of the band is sent forth purged and fit for heaven, the mountain trembles from its summit to its base, the whole multitude chaunting "Gloria in excelsis Deo." Beneath their heavy weights, and in the midst of flames, they remember their brethren on earth, and pray that they, too, may be purged and shielded from temptation. Wherefore, says Dante:—

> Se di là sempre ben per noi si dice,
> Di qua che dire e far per lor si puote
> Da quel ch' hanno al voler buona radice?
> Ben si dè' loro aitar lavar le note,
> Che portàr quinci, sì che mondi e lievi
> Possano uscire alle stellate ruote.†

---

* "*Te lucis ante* with such pious passion
Fell from their lips, and with such melody,
That I was rapt from self and lost in listening."
Purgatorio, viii. 13—18.

† *Purgatorio*, xi. 31—36. "If *there* kind words for us are always being said, what can *here* be said and done for them by those whose will hath a good root? Verily we ought to help them wash away the stains they bore from earth, so that cleansed and light they may pass forth to the starry circles."

XII.

Critics have complained that the *Purgatorio* is dull. "Our sympathy," says Sismondi,* "for the persons introduced begins to languish. Their present state of existence is rendered indifferent to them by the vivacity of their hopes; their recollections of the past are absorbed in the future; and, experiencing no vehement emotions themselves, they have little power to excite them in us." This, pace tanti viri, is mistaken criticism. It is not true that the souls of Purgatory are indifferent to the past: they are keenly alive to the concerns of their relatives or descendants, being bound to them by mutual goodwill and interchange of prayers. "When thou hast crossed the broad waves tell my Giovanna that she pray for me where innocents are heard. I think not that her mother loves me since she left her widow's weeds," says Nino de' Visconti;† and this is the language of all the souls. Nor, again, is it a defect that Dante here ceases to excite our "vehement emotions." Francesca, Ugolino, Argenti, Delle Vigne, Alberigo, were assuredly sufficient. The unrelieved, unending torments of the prison-house tend to exhaust sympathy. The supremacy of hate and anguish becomes oppressive. It is a relief to find ourselves again surrounded by an atmosphere of peace, serenity,

* *Literature of Southern Europe*, by ROSCOE, Vol. I., p. 384.
† *Purgatorio*, viii. 70.

and goodness. Dante has adorned his *Purgatorio* with exquisite touches of natural description, with his finest similes and most elaborate allegories. He is aware that, lacking the stern tragedy of the *Inferno*, his *Purgatorio* must appeal to more delicate sensibilities and a subtler intelligence. Therefore the decorations of the second Cantica are studied and splendid: the human interest is fresh and healthy. He who cannot appreciate its peculiar beauties has a mind incapable of following the poet's plan. But who is there who fails to take an interest in Casella,* "wooed to sing" among these "milder shades," and detaining with his song the listening souls? Who is not arrested by the romance of Buonconte's † tale—the single tear which saved him from the fiend and gave his spirit to an angel's arms—the tempest and the flood of Arno? Sordello, too, how noble is his port, how dignified his repose!

> O anima Lombarda,
> Come ti stavi altera e disdegnosa,
> E nel muover degli occhi onesta e tarda !
> Ella non ci diceva alcuna cosa ;
> Ma lasciavane gir, solo guardando
> A guisa di leon, quando si posa.‡

---

* *Purgatorio*, ii. 75—132.   † *Purgatorio*, v. 94—129.

‡ "O Lombard soul
How proudly stoodst thou! how disdainfully !
And in thine eyes that moved, how grave and noble !
The shade said nought to us and made no sign,
But let us forward pass and only gazed
In semblance of a lion when he couches."—*Purgatorio*, vi. 61.

Adrian's complaint* of the fatigue of the great mantle of the Papacy forms a good counterpoise to the fierce heat of Boniface. The meeting, again, of Statius † with Virgil is exquisite in its simplicity and grace. Statius does not know the companion of Dante. He tells the poets, as they walk, how he lived in Rome under good Titus, and gained "the name which longest lasts, and honours most," by study of the divine Æneid :—

> La qual mamma
> Fummi, e fummi nutrice poetando:
> Sanz' essa non fermai peso di dramma. ‡

To this he adds: "willingly would I suffer one more year of Purgatory to have lived with Virgil." Then—

> Volser Virgilio a me queste parole
> Con viso, che tacendo dicea: Taci:
> Ma non può tutto la virtù che vuole.

Dante could not, if he would, keep silence.

> Chè riso e pianto son tanto seguaci
> Alla passion, da che ciascun si spicca,
> Che men seguon voler ne' più veraci. §

---

* *Purgatorio*, xix. 98—105.
† Cantos xxi. xxii.
‡ "Which gave me suck, and was my nurse in poesy; without it I dared not fix a drachm's weight"—that is, I suppose, he used Virgil's poem as the canon of all he wrote.
§ "These words made Virgil turn to me with a look that in silence said: Keep silence! But the might that wills cannot do all. For smiles and tears follow so suddenly the emotion from which either springs, that they less obey the will in the truthfullest natures."

Dante's smile leads Statius to question him; and at last the truth breaks forth:—

> Questi, che guida in alto gli occhi miei,
> E quel Virgilio, dal qual tu togliesti
> Forte a cantar degli uomini e de' Dei.[*]

Imagine the joy of the singer of the *Thebaid!* He falls at Virgil's feet; he questions him; he learns his hopeless fate in limbo; he asks news of the great men of his nation, of Terence, of Plautus, of Varro; but the sweetest and the strangest speech is this:—

> Tu prima m' inviasti
> Verso Parnaso a ber nelle sue grotte,
> E poscia appresso Dio m' alluminasti.
> Facesti, come quei, che va di notte,
> Che porta il lume dietro, e sé non giova;
> Ma dopo sè fa le persone dotte;
> Quando dicesti: Secol si rinnuova;
> Torna giustizia, e 'l primo tempo umano;
> E progenie discende dal Ciel nuova.
> Per te poeta fui, per te Cristiano.[†]

There is surely enough of human interest here. Alas! good Virgil. Statius is journeying to the starred spheres of heaven: thou must turn thy steps backward and descend through earth, treading the glaciers of

---

[*] "He who is guiding upward my eyes is that Virgil from whom thou didst take strength to sing of men and Gods.".

[†] *Purgatorio*, xxii. 64. "Thou first didst send me toward Parnassus, to drink in its grottoes; and afterwards in the ways of God didst give me light. Thou didst do as one who goes by night, who carries the light behind him, and helps not himself, but teaches those who come after, when thou saidest: 'The age begins anew; justice returns, and the first state of man; and a new race descends from heaven. By thee I was made poet, by thee Christian.'"

Cocytus, the fiery causeway of Phlegethon, crossing the black marsh of Styx, and piercing the thick gloom that encircles the sad quiet place of subdued radiance, where thy station is among the august good who died before they heard of Christ.

One more portrait: it is Forese Donati speaking:—

> Sì tosto m' ha condotto
> A ber lo dolce assenzio de' martiri
> La Nella mia col suo pianger dirotto.
> Con suo' prieghi devoti, e con sospiri
> Tratto m' ha della costa ove s' aspetta,
> E liberato m' ha degli altri giri.
> Tant' è più cara a Dio e più diletta
> La vedovella mia, che molto amai,
> Quanto in bene operare è più soletta.*

It is well to close the book of *Purgatorio* upon this passage. "The sweet bitterness of purging pain"— "My Nella—my widow, whom I greatly loved"— "with her earnest prayers and sighs, with her broken weeping"—"she has freed me from the place of waiting, and released me from the lower circles." It is thus that the patient souls endure affliction, and think upon their comrades of the other life. Neither in the *Inferno* nor in the *Paradiso* do we find humanity so complete, so delicate, so pure and true.

* *Purgatorio*, xxiii. 85. "Thus early to drink the sweet wormwood of pain was I brought by my Nella with her bitter tears. With her pious prayers and sighs she has drawn me from the shore of waiting and freed me from the other circles. So much the dearer to God and the better beloved is my widow, whom I greatly loved, the more she is unique in good deeds."

XIII.

It is difficult to describe the transition from Purgatory to Paradise.* Up to this point Dante, whether winding down the paths of Hell, or up the spiral slopes of the Holy mountain, has trodden earth. The sulphurous gusts of Malebolge, and the temperate airs of the world-encircling ocean, have successively parched and cooled his forehead. He now quits the ground, and soars from sphere to sphere, " of earthly grossness quit," ascending in the lightning of the eyes of Beatrice. With each assumption she becomes more beautiful. Celestial love so transfigures her that Dante is dazzled and struck blind with splendour. Yet strength is granted him, and still he rises.

Throughout these regions hope is swallowed in fruition, prayer is lost in praise. By heavenly alchemy the woes of earth are turned to gladness, and the whole world in the love of God seems beautiful. The light which was as darkness of the pit in Hell, which shone with temperate mildness on the mount of Purgatory, in Paradise is living, burning and consuming fire. The souls display their happiness by increase of radiance :—

> Per letiziar lassù fulgor s' acquista
> Sì come riso qui.

---

* Dante has prepared the way for it by his pageant in the last four cantos of the *Purgatorio*.

> E sì come ciascuno a noi venìa,
> Vedeasi l' ombra piena di letizia
> Nel folgor chiaro, che di lei uscìa.*

Here light and love and joy are one—a triune element of bliss in which the righteous spirits dance and sing :—

> Il ciel, ch' è pura luce ;
> Luce intellettual piena d' amore ;
> Amor di vero ben pien di letizia ;
> Letizia, che trascende ogni dolzore.†

The saints themselves appear to Dante in the form of stars and gems and coruscations. He calls them by fantastic names to image forth their attributes of love and light and joy. The angel Gabriel becomes a crown of flaming fire around Madonna's head. Cacciaguida is a "living topaz."‡ Another spirit is addressed as "blessed life that stayest hidden in thy joy!" "Precious and gleaming stones"—"pearls"—"rubies" —"multitudes of loves"—"bright conflagrations of the Holy Spirit"—"pious fires"—"the blessed flame"— "that radiant and precious joy"—"that ardent love"— "undying flowers"§—such are a few of the metaphors

---

* *Paradiso*, ix. 70, v. 106, and *passim*. "From joy in heaven splendour grows, like smiles on earth..... As each spirit came toward us we could see the shade to be full of gladness by the bright lightning that issued from it."

† "Heaven, which is full of light—
Light intellectual fulfilled of love ;
Love of true good fulfilled of perfect gladness ;
Gladness the which surpasses all sweet things."
Paradiso, xxx. 40.

‡ *Paradiso*, xv. 85.

§ *Paradiso*, xxi. 55 ; xx. 16 ; xxiii. 29 ; xix. 4 ; xix. 20 ; xix. 100 ; ix. 77 ; xii. 2 ; ix. 37 ; xxiv. 82 ; xix. 22.

used literally by Dante, to express the figure of the spirits that he saw. And of all these constellations, lightnings, spheres, and lamps of fire, not one is still or silent. Melody and movement are the life of Paradise, as light its element, and love its joy, and as its science is the sight of God's unclouded splendour. God himself is imagined by Dante as a point, infinitesimally small,* but infinitely luminous, pouring forth rays of light—light that undulates and palpitates through Paradise, throbbing in the life of all the animated spheres, circling through their orbits, and growing fainter as it spreads abroad through space. Upon this light of God the spirits gaze.† In it, as in a glass, they read past, present, and future. Towards it they move and burn. From it they take their love and joy.

The state of the saints is one of boundless love. There is no jealousy and no disparity in heaven. When a stranger comes they cry :—

<blockquote>Ecco chi crescerà li nostri amori.‡</blockquote>

Justice, which made the gate of Hell so strong, presides in Paradise : but here it takes the form of love : the saints rejoice in finding joy proportioned to deserts :—

<blockquote>Ma nel commensurar de' nostri gaggi
Col merto, è parte di nostra letizia,
Perchè non li vedem minor nè maggi :</blockquote>

---

* *Paradiso*, xxxiii. 85—90, xxx. 100.
† *Paradiso*, ix. 6—*et passim*.
‡ *Paradiso*, v. 105. "See one who will increase our loves."

> Quinci addolcisce la viva giustizia
> In noi l' affetto sì che non si puote
> Torcer giammai ad alcuna nequizia.*

As harmony on earth is made of notes combined, so here the different orders of the saints compose one bliss :—

> Diverse voci fanno dolci note :
> Così diversi scanni in nostra vita
> Rendon dolce armonia tra queste ruote.†

This harmony and contentment of the hierarchies of heaven is beautifully explained by Piccarda. Love fulfils them from the least saint to the highest seraph. Placed as they are, tier over tier, throughout the realm, they all are pleased, even as God is pleased. None desires a loftier station than his own : since each, according to his faculty, sees God and comprehends his will. Perfect concordance with the will of God itself is bliss :—

> In la sua volontade è nostra pace :
> Ella è quel mare, al qual tutto si muove
> Ciò, ch' ella cria, e che Natura face.
> Chiaro mi fu allor com' ogni dove
> In Cielo è Paradiso, e sì la grazia
> Del sommo Ben d' un modo non vi piove.‡

---

* *Paradiso*, vi. 118—123. "In measuring our rewards with our merits part of our joy consists, for we find them neither less nor more. Hence living justice so sweetens affection in us that it cannot ever turn to any wrongfulness."

† *Paradiso*, vi. 124. "Differing voices make up sweet chords : even so diverse stations in our life give out sweet harmony throughout these wheels."

‡ *Paradiso*, iii. 70—90. "In his will is our peace. It is that ocean towards which moves all that it creates or nature makes. Then was it clear to me how everywhere in heaven is Paradise, though the grace of the supreme good rains not there in one way only."

XIV.

It must be remembered, in following Dante through the spheres, that the saints themselves abide together in one Paradise, and form the pearl-white rose that opens to the rays of God's immediate glory.* The spirits shown to Dante in the several planets are not thereto allotted and confined: they are but mystically so displayed as in a pageant, shadowing forth to mortal sense the grades of the celestial hierarchies. This explanation is insisted on by Dante, in order to avoid the platonic heresy of astral influence and destinies, controlled by planetary powers. We need to remember it if we wish to understand the co-existence of the spheres, and of the rose which forms the last Apocalypse of Dante. The petals of that rose correspond to the wider and the narrower spheres of Heaven: the rose is the reality; the spirits of the spheres are figures of the truth.

XV.

It is a strange world—this Paradise conceived by Dante, unlike anything that earlier poet dreamed or seer saw in trance revealed to him. None but the clear and purged vision of a perfect spirit could have pierced its

* *Paradiso*, iv. 28—63.

infinite abyss of glory to that final fiery sphere sublimely figured as:

> Lo real manto di tutti i volumi
> Del mondo, che più ferve e più s' avviva
> Nell' alito di Dio e ne' costumi.*

None but the purest soul could have rejoiced to bathe itself in that illimitable sea of love. We are what we imagine. The "endless morn of light" which Milton dreamed of, Dante realized. His spirit, "shaping wings" for the eternal shore, in exile, age, and disappointment, sang these deathless songs of joy—so high, so piercing that the ear scarcely sustains their intense melody.

To appreciate the *Paradiso* rightly we require a portion of Shelley's or Beethoven's soul. It is only some "embodied joy," some spirit rapt by love above the vapours and the sounds of earth, that dares to soar or can breathe long in this ethereal rare atmosphere. Duller intelligences—purblind gropers, weak-winged Icari who dread the sun, clamour that the *Paradiso* is dull, grotesque, monotonous, devoid of action. What a man brings to Dante's poem, he will find there. Those to whom music, light, and love are elemental as the air they breathe, will be at home in Paradise. Discord, hate, and gloom, the passions of the flesh, the tempests

---

* *Paradiso*, xxiii. 112. "The royal robe of all the orbing circles of the whole world, which hath most heat and life even by the breath of God and by His presence."

of the heart, the toil of the understanding, are found to all satiety in the *Inferno*. Between them both, as we have seen, stands Purgatory, humane and mild, the temperate zone of that imagined world. Among all the marvels of Dante's poem, this perhaps remains the greatest— the gradations and the rhythm of its structure—the line of beauty, plastic in the poet's hand, which curves and is complete in the three Cantiche.

XVI.

In spite of the supernatural element which predominates in the *Paradiso*, it must not be thought that this part of the poem lacks human interest. The panegyrics of St. Francis and St. Dominic, which occupy the 12th and 13th cantos, Cacciaguida's prophecy of Dante's exile, and the history of the Roman empire uttered by Justinian, are among the longest and most interesting episodes, if I may use this term, of all the Comedy. No soul in Paradise is sweeter or more delicately painted than Piccarda Donati.* Dante finds her among the dream-like holy faces leaning toward him from the "cloud, lucent, thick, solid, and polished," "the eternal pearl," which is the moon. We fancy her, seen through that shining mist, like one of the white spring-lilies of the Alps, frail and faintly perfumed, exquisitely pure. Her very speech has in it a mild moony radiance, a

* Canto iii.

subdued and pearly lustre as of lilies dewy in twilight. How different are the dazzling spirits of the Doctors in Theology, Thomas Aquinas and Bonaventura. They blaze in the solar sphere, the light of which conquers all colour. It is from them that Dante hears the histories of St. Francis and St. Dominic—the Dominican of Aquino praising Francis, the Franciscan replying with a splendid eulogy of Dominic. It is thus that Dante inculcates a lesson of mutual respect and love on the two orders. What he has sung of these, undoubtedly the greatest men of the preceding age,* the renovators of the Church and arbiters of Catholicity for centuries, remains, after all verification or research, the best that could be said.†

* It may seem strange to call St. Francis and St. Dominic the greatest men of the age in which St. Louis, Henry Dandolo, Innocent III., Frederick II., and Piero delle Vigne lived; but I have written it advisedly. There was in them the force of a new life, expansive, energetic, aggressive, extinguishing all substances that could not be converted into its own aliment. What would have become of the Papacy, what new religious theories might have been developed in Italy, what destiny might have been in store for Provence and her literature at the expense of the Italian language, whether we should have had a Dante, and, if we had still had one, what he would have written, had Innocent not granted charters to the Dominican and Franciscan orders, who shall say? The most original men of their day perhaps they were not. But in them the greatest puissance of life lay.

† Compare GIOVANNI VILLANI, lib. v. xxiv. xxv., on the origin of the two orders patronized by Innocent III. and Honorius. Innocent saw in dreams these saints supporting the falling Lateran : "Che la chiesa di Dio cadea per molti errori e per molti dissoluti peccati, non temendo Iddio." It was the preaching and the Inquisition and the faggots of Dominic, the humble, holy life of Francis, which purged the Church. "E veramente la Sibilla Eritlea seguendo questi tempi, profetizzò di queste due sante ordini, dicendo, che due stelle orirebbono in allumiando il mondo." For Innocent's crusade against the Paterini and Albigenses, see SISMONDI, ii. 113.

He strikes their portraits off as sharply in his verse as though he were stamping medals in bronze:

> L' un fu tutto Serafico in ardore,
> L' altro per sapienza in terra fue
> Di Cherubica luce uno splendore.*

Francis is shown as rising like a sun:

> Nacque al mondo un Sole,
> Come fa questo tal volta di Gange.
> Però chi d' esso loco fa parole
> Non dica Ascesi, chè direbbe corto,
> Ma Oriente, se proprio dir vuole.†

Dominic is called with marvellous felicity:

> L' amoroso drudo
> Della fede Cristiana, il santo atleta
> Benigno a' suoi, ed a' nimici crudo—‡

"the amorous fere of Christian faith, the holy athlete, gentle to his friends and cruel to his foes."

After leaving the sun Dante finds himself in Mars. The planet is traversed and divided by a flaming cross, blood red, composed of myriads of glittering rubies. Each of these is the soul of martyr or confessor of the faith, crusader, champion, combatant for Christ. Among them are Joshua, Judas Maccabæus, Charlemagne, Robert Guiscard, William of Orange, Rinoardo,

---

* *Paradiso*, xi. 37. "The one was all seraphic in fervour; the other by his wisdom was upon earth a splendour of cherubic light."

† *Ibid.*, 50. "A sun was born to the world, as this sun rises at times from Ganges. Wherefore let him who speaks of that place, say not Assisi, for thus he would speak less than truth, but the East, if he is fain to speak aright."

‡ *Ibid.*, xii. 55.

Godfrey of Boullogne, and Orlando,*—an assembly of notables chosen by Dante with divine impartiality. But the soul that interests us most is Dante's ancestor, Cacciaguida, the Crusader. His discourse of the old prosperity of Florence and his prophecy of Dante's exile extend over three of the most personally interesting and important cantos of the poem.

> Tu lascerai ogni cosa diletta
> Più caramente; e questo è quello strale,
> Che l' arco dell' esilio pria saetta.
> Tu proverrai sì come sa di sale
> Lo pane altrui, e com' è duro calle
> Lo scendere e 'l salir per l' altrui scale. †

Memorable words, which cannot be too frequently transcribed!

The next planet is Jupiter. Here the marvels of Paradise begin in good earnest. Here, for the first time, we must confess that Dante's attempt to translate the

---

* Dante's references to mediæval romance are frequent:

> Dopo la dolorosa rotta, quando
> Carlo Magno perdè la santa gesta,
> Non sonò sì terribilmente Orlando.—*Inferno*, xxxi. 16.

Again:
> Non quegli a cui fu rotto il petto e l' ombra
> Con esso un colpo, per la man d' Artù.—*Ibid.*, xxxii. 61.

Again:
> Vidi Paris, Tristano.—*Ibid.*, v. 67.

Again:
> Noi leggevamo un giorno per diletto
> Di Lancillotto . . ., etc.—*Ibid.*, v. 128.

† *Paradiso*, xvii. 55. "Thou shalt leave everything most dearly loved; and this is that arrow which the bow of exile first shoots. Thou shalt experience how salt tastes the bread of another, and how hard a path it is to go up and down another's stairs."

invisible into form and symbol carries him into grotesqueness.* A troop of blessed spirits, wheeling in the air like multitudinous birds, spell out by mazy movements the sentence: "*Diligite justitiam qui judicatis terram.*" Upon the final letter M they rest; other saints beneath them, rising like sparks struck from a fire-brand, form the head and neck of an eagle. This eagle speaks with a single voice. First it inveighs against Pope Boniface. Then it points out to Dante the chief spirits that compose it. We must imagine them to be stationed in outline like a constellation of our skies, but clearer. Of these Trajan,† saved by Gregory's prayer from hell, because of his mercy to the widow, and Rhiphæus of Troy, called by Virgil *justissimus unus* sparkle on the eagle's eyelid. Dante's intense love of justice may be noticed. Jupiter, the sphere of royal spirits, is the planet of the just.

In Saturn ‡ new miracles are seen. A golden ladder reaches up to Heaven, on which are flames ascending and descending. Here the souls sing not; Beatrice dares not smile; because of Dante's frailty.§ The vision of Christ's triumph has yet to be granted to him. That will add celestial vigour to his mortal senses. Meanwhile, should he listen to the melodies and see the smile of the seventh sphere, nought would await

---
* Dante had not seen our modern illuminations by means of gas: else he might have dreaded a descent from the sublime to the ridiculous.
† Trajan's story is touchingly told in *Purgatorio* x. 73—93.
‡ *Paradiso*, xix. § *Ibid.*, xxlii.

him but the death of Semele. He discourses in this planet with Peter Damiano and St. Benedict—contemplative souls, who rank above the active spirits, since the life of contemplation is more heavenly than that of action.

Mars, Jupiter, and Saturn are full of wondrous pageants. What follows in the last twelve cantos of the *Paradiso* is one vision of continually increasing splendour. We climb from height to height of mysticism, interrupted only by the confession of faith,* which Dante makes St. Peter, by the exposition of hope† which St. James requires from him, and the profession of love which he yields St. John.‡ In these three cantos Dante sums up the doctrine of the Church upon the three so-called Theological Virtues, setting, as it were, to the music of his lyre the dogmas of the schools.

The 13th canto introduces us, at length, to very Paradise. The visions, or "ombriferi prefazii" in Dante's words, which form the prelude to the pageant of the mystic rose, are these :—

> E vidi lume in forma di riviera
> Fulvido di fulgori, intra duo rive
> Dipinte di mirabil primavera.
> Di tal fiumana uscian faville vive,
> E d' ogni parte si mescean ne' fiori,
> Quasi rubin, ch' oro circonscrive.

---

* Canto xxiv.   † Canto xxv.   ‡ Canto xxvi.

> Poi come inebriate dagli odori,
> Riprofondavan sè nel miro gurge;
> E s' una entrava, un' altra usciane fuori.*

The sparks are angels. The flowers are saints.

> Poi come gente stata sotto larve,
> Che pare altro che prima, se si sveste
> La sembianza non sua, in che disparve;
> Così mi si cambiaro in maggoir feste
> Li fiori e le faville, sì ch' io vidi
> Ambo le corti del ciel manifeste.†

But again the image changes. The courts of heaven this time assume the shape of a rose, expanding, leaf over leaf of candid lustre, spreading outwards from the heart of gold to God who is its sun. Within the petals fly innumerable bees, soaring sometimes to the sun, and thence, light-laden, diving to the flower again. These

---

* And I saw light in semblance of a river
Tawny with splendours in the midst of shores,
Painted with blossoms of a wondrous spring.
Forth from this stream there issued living sparks;
And on all sides they mingled with the flowers,
Like rubies that smooth bands of gold environ.
Then as though drunken with the fragrances,
They plunged again into the marvellous tide;
And as one sank, another issued forth.
                    Paradiso, xxx. 61—69.

† Then, like a band of maskers, who appear
Other than what they were, when they despoil
The borrowed semblance which had clothed their forms;
Even so the flowers and sparks before me changed
To greater gladness, so that I beheld
Both courts of heaven in splendour undisguised.
                    Paradiso, xxx. 91—96.

are angels, and the rose-leaves are the orders of the blest, fold within fold of glory and of love :—

> Le facce tutte avean di fiamma viva,
> E l' ale d' oro, e l' altro tanto bianco,
> Che nulla neve a quel termine arriva.*

The imagination is intoxicated with the wealth and perfume of this vision. But Dante must ascend a further step. Beatrice leaves him, taking her seat upon the highest tier of the celestial theatre, and fixing her eyes upon the face of God, to move them not again.† Theology has done her work. She hands her disciple over to the genius of mystic love. St. Bernard, "shining in the beauty of Mary, as the morning star in the sun's rays,"‡ takes him by the hand, and, gazing upwards to the throne, begins that prayer which is the very soul of supplication cadenced in words :—

> Vergine Madre, Figlia del tuo Figlio !

Mary listens. Then from within the light, that is the Holiest of Holies, the outline of a triune human form appears. The beatific vision of the Deity who made man in His image, is accorded to the poet. For a

---

* "Their faces were all of living fire, their wings of gold ; and the flower itself was so white that never snow approaches that perfection."

† Cosi orai; e quella sì lontana,
Come parea, sorrise, e riguardommi ;
Poi si tornò all' eterna fontana.

‡ *Paradiso*, xxxii. 107.

moment he gazes undestroyed. A thunderbolt then
falls upon his soul :—

All' alta fantasia qui mancò possa.

The apocalypse is ended. Words of strange simplicity,
attesting to the deep sincerity of Dante's vision, close
the Comedy :—

Ma già volgeva il mio disiro e '1 velle,
Sì come ruote che igualmente è mossa,
L' amor che muove il sole e l' altre stelle.*

This is what Dante gained by his apocalypse. This
union with God is what he wishes to teach by his poem.

There is something infinitely solemn in these final
visions and last words of Dante. What Dante fancied,
need not correspond in detail to the actual truth.
When the darkness of this life is dispelled, and the
wrestling with the flesh is past, the purged and dis-
embodied spirit may be destined to behold no snow-
white petals of the everlasting rose expand above it.
Yet the essence of this ultimate apocalypse—union of
the human soul with God—remains. It is in the firm-
ness only of this faith that we can find courage with
St. Francis to praise God for "our sister, death of
the body."

---

* " But now my every wish, my every will,
   Like to a wheel moved all ways in like wise,
   Obeyed that Love that moves the Sun and Stars."

Paradiso xxxiii. last lines.

CHAPTER VI.

THE QUALITIES OF DANTE'S GENIUS.

(i.) Definiteness, Intensity, Sincerity, Brevity.—(ii.) Mechanism of the *Divine Comedy*: its Cosmography: the Line traced by Dante in his Journey: the number of Days spent by him *en route*.—(iii.) The Geography of the *Inferno*.—(iv.) Smallness of Scale in Dante's World: Phlegethon, Nimrod, Lucifer, the Cornices of Purgatory.—(v.) Dante's Faculty of Vision: his Pictures: his Illustrations from Actual Scenes.—(vi.) Descriptions of Morning and Evening in Purgatory: View of the City of Dis.—(vii.) Dante's Similes.—(viii.) The Compression and Brevity of Dante's Thought.—(ix.) The Chief Faults of the *Divine Comedy* are Grotesqueness and Obscurity.

I.

AFTER our prolonged discussion of Dante's ideas and of the sources of interest in his Comedy it remains for us to consider the nature of his genius, and his special qualities as an artist. The task is difficult and discouraging. Dante is so comprehensive, so mysterious, so full of contradictions and brusque alternations, so unsubmissive to accepted rules of art,—at the same time so trenchant and uncompromising, so definite in purpose, swift in thought, direct in word, so clear in his obscurity, so sphinx-like under his limpidity of speech—that, like Proteus, when we seek to seize him, he assumes a thousand shapes, eluding and baffling analysis. Yet this analysis must be attempted.

The most obvious quality of Dante is definiteness. This gives a peculiar character to his sincerity, to his intensity, and to that wonderful faculty of vision for which he is unique among the poets of the world.

Dante's genius is like a wedge of steel — hard, narrow, fit for rending oaks. Smitten with sledge-hammer blows by his Titanic energy, it penetrates the toughest matter and pierces to the very core of things. The breadth of his thought is less remarkable than its depth. He goes straight to the essence of his subject, rejecting accidents, despising ornament; and having seized its truth, he grasps *that* with a grip of iron. Dante seems made to nullify the aphorism "not deep the poet sees, but wide:" he is so determined to be deep in insight and exact in detail that he narrows his subject, if need be, in order to secure the utmost definiteness. Nothing, again, can exceed the brevity of his speech. His words are like flowers and fruits upon a tree of silence—definite, precise, sincere. His pictures are painted with the strictest parsimony of description: yet no medal-striker ever made his outlines sharper or his shadows deeper. The salient and essential points of an object are selected and made visible with such vividness that we discern the whole. It would seem as if each line of Dante's poem, each simile, each aphorism, had been wrung from him with pain and struggle. He complains that the labour of it made him thin for many years, that the long theme pursued and hunted him. Nor were these pangs of parturition spasmodic: his poem has nothing of that quivering feverishness we find in works of men like Schiller, Shelley, or De Musset. Dante first dug deep for the crude ore; then smelted it at central furnaces of ash-white heat; then forged it on the anvil of incessant toil; then welded its formed parts into imperishable symmetry. Hence, every syllable of the Comedy is precious, vital with intensest feeling, instinct with sincerity of soul. Not a single sentence is improvised. It has all been framed by life-long meditation. What Dante calls the bridle of his art, "il fren dell' arte," curbs and limits him. Like his own Acheron, the burning river of his thought flows in prepared and well-constructed channels. The nature of his genius did not lead him to follow impulse or to rhapsodize. He loved to trace an elaborate network of dykes and ditches, to bank them up and bridge them over, to front them with carved stone, and pave them with well-seasoned brick, and then to open the sluices of his lava reservoir, and fill these labyrinths with streams of molten metal. The result is that art is everywhere apparent in his work. Art truly of so *bizarre* and extravagant a nature that La Harpe in his astonishment is almost justified in calling the Comedy "une rapsodie informe," while Voltaire's verdict, "une amplification stupidement barbare," provokes our sympathy with periwigged perplexity rather than indignation or contempt; yet art as vigorous as that of Sophocles, more conscious than that of Shakspeare, as complete and comprehensive as the art which gave its form to Chartres Cathedral. Force, depth, definiteness, brevity, sincerity, intensity, subordination to fixed purposes—these are the great qualities of Dante's genius.

II.

The determination of Dante's genius to the detailed, definite, and precise, is apparent at first sight in the mechanism of the *Divine Comedy*. There are three Cantiche, each of which contains thirty-three Cantos, exclusive of the first, which is regarded as a prelude to the whole. Each Cantica is terminated with the words *le stelle*. The 14,230 verses of the poem are so distributed that each Canto contains about 140 verses, and each Cantica about 4,700. The *Inferno* is shorter than the *Purgatorio* by thirty lines, than the *Paradiso* by twenty-four. Nor were these exact correspondences accidental. This is evident from the following passage in the *Purgatorio* :—

> Ma perchè piene son tutte le carte,
> Ordite a questa Cantica seconda,
> Non mi lascia più gir lo fren dell' arte.*

---

* xxxiii. 139.—"But because all the pages destined for this second Cantica are full, the bridle of art suffers me not to go further."

Nor is the structure of the poem only thus mechanically exact. The cosmography of Dante, if we may so designate his divisions of the three worlds, is just as accurate and symmetrical. There are nine circles in Hell, nine cornices in Purgatory, nine spheres in Paradise. Lucifer, "il gran vermo che 'l mondo fora," is stationed just below Jerusalem, in the centre of the globe; the mount of Purgatory rises in the other hemisphere, exactly opposite to Jerusalem; the apex of Paradise, again, is immediately above Jerusalem. Dante, setting out from the deserts near the Sacred City, completes the tour of Hell, Purgatory, and Paradise, by a spiral line of march, which brings him out at last above the point from which he started. All the astronomical conditions requisite for the execution of this journey are calculated by Dante, so that the utmost verisimilitude is given to his narrative. We are even able to estimate the days and hours employed. Dante begins his journey in the night of March 24, 1300, and ends it in the day of April 3, in the same year, having spent ten day's *en route*.

III.

Passing to matters of more detail, it would be easy enough to draw a map or plan of each of the three realms. The *Inferno* is the most complicated. Let us see how that is made. We have here no Miltonic vagueness. Dante does not say—

> Through many a dark and dreary vale
> They passed, and many a region dolorous,
> O'er many a frozen, many a fiery Alp,
> Rocks, caves, lakes, fens, bogs, dens, and shades of death.

His purpose was different from Milton's; his genius of another order. His Hell is a huge inverted funnel piercing to the centre of the globe.* It is divided into four chief regions, and subdivided into nine circles. After passing the gate of Hell Charon ferries us across the river Acheron. On its further shore is the Limbo of unbaptized souls—the first circle. The next four circles are occupied by the carnal, the gluttons, the avaricious and the prodigal, the angry and the indolent. So far the descent through Hell is gradual: we are moving downwards by a slow and ample slope, at the base of which Styx stagnates in a marsh. Having crossed it in the boat of Phlegyas, we enter the City of Dis—the worst and most contracted part of Hell. The first circle within its bastions is occupied by the heresiarchs. It is separated from the seventh circle by a crumbling precipice, over which we clamber till we reach the boiling lake of blood, the forest of the Harpies, and the burning plain through which flows

---

* We might divide the *Inferno* into the City of Dis, which includes the three regions in which the Violent, the Fraudulent, and the Traitorous souls are punished, and the milder region outside the City of Dis, in which is Limbo and the place of torment for the Incontinent.

Phlegethon. These three rings are compartments of the same circle, and are on the same level. They constitute the second grand region—the region of the violent. Between the seventh and eighth circle is a precipice of undefined depth, down which Geryon bears us on his back. At the foot of it yawns Malebolge, the eighth circle, a huge open bowl, partitioned into ten concentric rings, narrowing and inclining downwards to a well's mouth in their centre. This is the third grand region, devoted to the fraudulent. From the open mouth of the well which yawns in the centre of Malebolge, a shaft descends to the ninth circle, or fourth region, the uttermost abyss of Hell. This shaft does not exceed forty feet in depth. Giants lift us from the floor of Malebolge to the frozen basement, where the four chief classes of traitors are tortured in four belts of the glacier. Lucifer himself sits at the Nadir, blocking up with his huge bulk the bottom of the pit of Hell. Thus, it will be seen, that the successive circles are separated by very different obstacles and different distances, a sloping path in some cases leading almost imperceptibly from one to the other, a precipice occasionally intervening, or a river, which calls for special means of transit. Down to the minutest details Dante has contrived all in this subterranean world. Charon and his ferry; Minos judging with his nine times folded tail; Cerberus barking among the gluttons; Pluto ruling the avaricious; Styx with the ferry-boat of Phlegyas; the Furies on the wall of Dis; the Centaurs at the gate of Violence; the Minotaur, symbol of excessive lust; Geryon, the fraudful triform shape; the Giants, monstrous in humanity;—all these are patiently appointed to their several stations: all have a deep designed significance.

IV.

Akin to this precision of detail, or rather as its consequence, is the smallness of the scale of everything in Dante's world. Dante sees so accurately and distinctly that he measures all he sees; and with his measurements he introduces an element of limitation. His object is not to expand our imagination with a sense of vastness, but to force upon our understanding the fact of the reality of his journey. Phlegethon is described in the fourteenth canto as "a streamlet, the redness whereof still makes me shudder: its bottom, and both its banks, were made of stone, as well as the side copings; we walked on one of these hard margins: they were like the dykes which the Flemings raise between Ghent and Bruges as a defence against the sea, or like those with which the Paduans line the Brenta to protect their farms ere summer melts the Alpine snow—but not so lofty nor so thick." The precipice which divides the eighth from the ninth circle is measured with elaborate particularity by a comparison of the height of Nimrod with that of mortal men.* It is not deeper than about thirty-six feet, supposing the giant to have measured the same from the waist downwards as he did from the waist upwards.† Lucifer, the largest being imagined by Dante, is quite finite: when first seen, he looks like a windmill in the night; his wings are bigger than the sails of any ship; his arms bear the same proportion to a giant's whole height as that giant to Dante. The same precise information is given about Purgatory. We are told that the breadth of each balzo is equal to the height of three men—*i.e.*, that it measures about eighteen feet. The staircase leading from one cornice to the other is like that which goes up to the Church of Samminiato from the suburb of Florence. The sculptures on the floor are carved like tombstones or memorial brasses.

It is to the exactitude of these minutiæ that I call attention. Dante was in earnest about his poem. People were to know that he, with mortal feet, had

---

* This passage (*Inferno*, xxxi. 58—66) is so curiously illustrative of Dante's manner that I quote it :—

> La faccia sua mi parea lunga e grossa,
> Come la pina di San Pietro a Roma :
> E a sua proporzione eran l' altr' ossa.
> Sì che la ripa, ch' era perizoma
> Dal mezzo in giù, ne mostrava ben tanto
> Di sopra, che di giungere alla chioma
> Tre Frison s' averian dato mal vanto ;
> Perocch' io ne vedea trenta gran palmi
> Dal luogo in giù dov' uom s' affibbia il manto.

† *Inferno*, xxxiv. 1—30.

trodden Hell. Therefore he paints well-defined, conceivable facts; he leaves nothing vague or undetermined for the fancy to fill in. When he has something incredible to relate, he doubles the number of his touches, so as to invest the strangest circumstances with an air of prosaic realism. Virgil's descent by grasping the shaggy flanks of Lucifer, and turning round with a great effort at the centre in order to conquer the attraction of the earth, is a good instance of this determination to make the unseen and the non-existent real :—

> Di vello in vello giù discese poscia
> Tra 'l folto pelo, e le gelate crosse.
> Quando noi fummo là, dove la coscia
> Si volge appunto in sul grosso dell' anche,
> Lo duca con fatica e con angoscia
> Volse la testa ov' egli avea le zanche.*

By this unwearied exercise of his powerful and concrete imagination, Dante forces us to accept the marvels of his spiritual world—the transformation of men and serpents, the gyrations of Geryon, the souls that speak through hissing blood that drips from trees, the mutilated schismatics, the vocal flame that holds Ulysses, the games of Draghinazzo and his fiends, the Centaurs, and the Giants, and what not of terrible and strange.

* *Inferno*, xxxiv. 73. "When the wings were opened far, he applied him to the shaggy sides, and then from shag to shag descended down, between the tangled hair and frozen crusts. When we had come to where the thigh revolves, just on the swelling of the haunch, my guide with labour and with difficulty turned his head where he had had his feet before."
—CARLYLE.

V.

The definiteness which we have traced in the plan of Dante's poem, and in his descriptions of the scenery of Hell, determines the nature of his faculty of vision. In this he is unique—in the power of seeing things and presenting them before us visibly, so that they are indelibly impressed as images upon our memory. The brevity and intensity of his language help him here. There is some sort of occult power, some enchantment, in the mere collocation of his words. The alteration of an adjective, or the transposition of two syllables, is enough to break the spell. So definite was Dante's faculty of sight, so powerful the will with which he forced thought into language, so intense the labour of his brain, that a phrase of the *Divine Comedy*, though obscure and uncouth, will remain in our memory unbidden, and breed thoughts.

When Dante paints that which he has seen or fancied, he selects the most salient and striking point, and by vivid presentation of *that*, makes us see the whole. His pictures are forcible and concrete, never shadowy or general. Of course he sacrifices much by this method. Having a hundred things to say, he chooses only one; but he is unerring in his faculty of seizing on the essential property; and so skilful is his touch that he never fails to rouse the imagination of his reader to conceive of the remaining less important qualities he wishes to suggest. In the following two lines—

> La bocca sollevò dal fiero pasto
> Quel peccator, forbendola a' capelli—*

the words *forbendola*, gravely and simply introduced, as if there were no doubt about the action, bring the whole tragedy before our eyes. It is a triumph of supreme vision. The same may be said about the lines—

> Dal volto rimoven quell' aer grasso,
> Menando la sinistra innanzi spesso : †

by which Dante helps us to realize the disdainful, toilsome, onward movement of the angel over Styx. When it is necessary, not to fix the attention upon some special action or quality of the agent, but to stir our imagination with surprise, the strokes are just as definite and trenchant, the picture as complete.

> A noi venia la creatura bella
> Bianco vestita e uella faccia quale
> Par tremolando la mattutina stella. ‡

Who does not realize that moving radiance, whose face is as the trembling of the morning star?

---

* *Inferno*, xxxiii. 1. "From the fell repast that sinner raised his mouth, wiping it upon the hair."—CARLYLE.

† *Inferno*, ix. 82. "He waved the gross air from his countenance, often moving his left hand before him."—CARLYLE.

‡ *Purgatorio*, xii. 88. "Toward us came the beautiful creature, dressed in white, and in feature such as the morning-star which trembles."

Precision in description is sometimes achieved by Dante's referring to an actual scene. The sepulchres of the heresiarchs make the ground like the burying-place of Arles. The cliff leading to the seventh circle is like a *bergfall* on the Adige, near Rovoredo or Rivoli. The falls of Phlegethon resemble those of Acquacheta. The glacier of Cocytus is compared to the frozen Tanais or Danube. The crowd upon a bridge in Hell reminds the poet of the pilgrims at St. Angelo, in Rome, during the Jubilee. The hypocrites are like the monks of Cologne. The trees in the earthly paradise have a sound in them as of the pine wood at Chiassi. Antæus bends like the Garisenda tower at Bologna. The men who measure Nimrod are Frisians: the pilgrim who comes to see the handkerchief of St. Veronica, at Rome, is a Suevian. The pitch of Malebolge boils like that in the caulking-tubs of the Venetian arsenal. The pits of the Simonists are of the same size as the baptismal fonts at Florence. The face of Nimrod is as large as the bronze pine before the Vatican. All kinds of familiar incidents are laid under contribution to add reality to remote images. Latini's companions run like the Verona runners on the first Sunday in Lent. Dante, pressing through a crowd of souls in Purgatory, is like a man who has won at cards, and goes beset by multitudes. Wrestlers, stripped and oiled, help to realize the appearance of the souls in the

16th canto of *Inferno*. Historical events suggest other comparisons. The cavalry skirmishers of Campaldino, the exit of the garrison from Caprona, the plague of Ægina, the passage of Alexander's army across the Indian desert, render scenes of Hell more real and distinct. And who does not tremble when he hears the horn of Nimrod?

> Dopo la dolorosa rotta, quando
> Carlo Magno perdè la santa gesta,
> Non sonò sì terribilmente Orlando.*

I might multiply such examples indefinitely. I want, however, to set forth by copious instances the exquisite delicacy of Dante's pictures, the compression of his thought, and the aptitude of his similes, all flowing from his definiteness, and from the piercing faculty of vision which he had.

VI.

In Dante's pictures of natural scenery two things are noticeable—his earnest determination to make other people see exactly what he saw, and his extraordinary power of creating in their souls, by sympathy, the feelings which he had himself under the circumstances he describes. The following passage is almost prosaic in its minuteness; but it obliges us to think, and brings

---

* *Inferno*, xxxi. 16. "After the dolorous rout when Charlemain had lost the holy emprise Orlando did not sound so terribly."—CARLYLE.

the hour of early dew and chilly sunrise forcibly before our minds:—

> Quando noi fummo dove la rugiada
> Pugna col sole, e per essere in parte,
> Ove adorezza, poco si dirada.*

Shortly before, Dante has indulged in a description of the dawn upon the waters, no less definite, but infinitely more poetical, through its suggestion of an exquisitely fresh and tranquil scene:—

> L' alba vinceva l' ora mattutina
> Che fuggia innanzi, sì che di lontano
> Conobbi il tremolar della marina.†

Again still earlier in the canto, we hear that morning song of the cool air and sapphire sky preceding sunrise, when love's planet makes the whole East smile, and Dante re-ascends to breathe again beneath the vault of heaven.‡ "Dolce color d' Oriental zaffiro"—we see those lucent spaces of the light-irradiate east: we, too, ascend, quitting the gloom of Hell and night. The rhythm and the rapture of the poet's verse throbs through our soul and makes us one with him.

The description of evening which opens the 8th canto of the *Purgatorio* is so well known that we may merely allude to it in passing. Here, as in those

---

* *Purgatorio*, l. 121. "When we were at the place where the dew fights with the sun, and, from being in a part where the shade remains, yields but little."

† *Ibid.*, 115. "The dawn was conquering the morning air which fled before, so that from afar I recognized the trembling of the sea."

‡ *Ibid.*, 13—27.

pictures of the dawn, the poet paints not merely scenes but feelings. Who shall say by what strange alchemy of art those six lines have absorbed the very soul and substance of the melancholy sunset hour? The third line of my next quotation is hardly less wonderful :—

>	Noi andavam per lo vespero attenti
>	Oltre, quanto potean gli occhi allungarsi,
>	Contro i raggi serotini e lucenti.*

It is so simple and brief that no analysis will tell why it reveals to us the vast horizons of the radiant sea at sunset seen from some high mountain cornice.

The power of holding deep thoughts and delicate feelings in solution, and of connecting them with some well-defined scene, some accurately noted moment, is granted only to poetry of the very highest order. This power is eminent in the celebrated passage of the *Purgatorio*:

>	Nell' ora che comincia i tristi lai
>	La rondinella presso alla mattina,
>	Forse a memoria de' suoi primi guai ;
>	E che la mente nostra, pellegrina
>	Più dalla carne, e men da' pensier presa,
>	Alle sue vision quasi è divina ;
>	In sogno mi parea. . . . . †

---

* *Purgatorio*, xv. 139. "We walked through the evening air gazing intent onward as far as our eyes could reach, facing the last and lucent rays of day."

† *Ibid.*, ix. 13—18. "The hour in which the swallow begins to tune her sad complaint near morning, in memory perchance of her first sorrows, and when our soul, more a stranger to the flesh, and less a prisoner of thought, is, as it were, divinely free for her visions."

What is most noticeable in these lines is the mixture of accurate observation and description with profound reasoning, and the exquisite phrasing by which different thoughts are merged and made to form one element. "The earliest pipe of half awakened birds" is Tennyson's; Sir Thomas Browne has said: "We are somewhat more than ourselves in our sleeps, and the slumber of the body seems to be but the waking of the soul;" Theocritus tells us that "the flocks of morning dreams are true." But I know not where except in Dante's lines we shall find the perfume and the substance of all these thoughts combined. Their harmony, like some solemn strain of music, attunes us for the dream which is to follow.

The scenes of morning and of evening which I have quoted from the *Purgatorio* are bathed in lucent and placid beauty. Let us take one of an opposite character. I will choose for my example a picture which has always impressed my own imagination with the sense of deep and sinister reality. The poets in *Inferno* are crossing Styx, and Dante's mind is still full of the thoughts suggested by Argenti. Then, says Virgil:

> Omai figliuolo
> S' appressa la città ch' ha nome Dite,
> Co' gravi cittadin, col grande stuolo.
> Ed io ; Maestro già le sue meschite
> Là entro certo nella valle cerno
> Vermiglie, come se di fuoco uscite

Similes. 201

> Fossero : ed ei mi disse ; il fuoco eterno
> Ch' entro l' affoca le dimostra rosse,
> Come tu vedi, in questo basso Inferno.*

What is there, we ask, in the question and answer of this paragraph which gives such awful clearness to the flaming minarets and domes of Hell's city? What is the peculiar force of the simple phrases "Co' gravi cittadin," "in questo basso Inferno?" In some mysterious manner these lines, apparently dry and prosaic, stimulate our fancy so profoundly as to raise the infernal Babylon before our eyes in visible and livid pomp. We, too, are with Dante upon the blackness of the waters. We, too, behold those red-hot castle walls "with dreadful faces thronged and fiery arms."

VII.

I have reserved the similes of Dante for separate consideration. They form a class of pictures by themselves, chiefly remarkable for their aptness to the subjects illustrated ; Dante having shown the utmost skill in exactly suiting his similes to the matter in question, so that they never are merely ornamental or conventional (as is the case with some of Homer's), but are always to the point. Much of the grotesqueness of his

---

* *Inferno*, viii. 67. " 'Now, Son, the city that is named of Dis draws nigh, with the heavy citizens, with the great company.' And I : 'Master, already I discern its mosques, distinctly there within the valley, red as if they had come out of fire.' And to me he said : 'The eternal fire, that inward burns them, shows them red, as thou seest, in this low Hell.' "— CARLYLE.

imagery is due to his determination to make his subject definite by the use of any figure, however homely or even coarse, which will throw just the light upon it that it needs. But, as a rule, the most elegant and exquisite as well as the most spirited delineations to be found in Dante, are introduced by way of simile.

Here is one from the *Inferno* by which Virgil, saving Dante from the fiends, is compared to a mother rescuing her child from fire:

> Che prende il figlio, e fugge, e non s' arresta
> Avendo più di lui che di se cura
> Tanto che solo una camicia vesta.*

It is an episode from Raphael's Incendio de Borgo. In the *Paradiso* Beatrice is compared to a bird watching before the dawn for the first rays of light that she may fly abroad to get food for her little ones:

> Come l' augello, intra l' amate fronde,
> Posato al nido de' suoi dolci nati
> La notte che le cose ci nasconde,
> Che per veder gli aspetti desiati,
> E per trovar lo cibo onde gli pasca,
> In che i gravi labor gli sono grati,
> Previene 'l tempo in su l' aperta frasca,
> E con ardente affetto il Sole aspetta,
> Fiso guardando, pur che l' alba nasca.†

---

* xxiii. 37. "As a mother, that is awakened by the noise and near her sees the burning flames, who takes her child and flies, and caring more for him than for herself, pauses not so long as even to cast a shift about her."— CARLYLE.

* xxiii. 1—9. "As the bird, who, within the foliage she loves, has couched on the nest of her dear offspring through the night that hides all things from us, impatient to see their looks and to find food for them

The whole of this simile is beautiful, and many of its touches, especially those which describe the loving nature of the bird, have a modern charm beyond even the grace of Virgil, or Catullus, or Lucretius. Yet it is too long. The same fault, in a greater degree, impairs the picture of the rustic rising to find the earth white with rime.*

Country life supplies Dante with many of his most studied similes. The country fellow who sees fire-flies in the valley round the vineyard or the corn-field,† the goats gathered near their goatherd:

> Guardate dal pastor, che 'n su la verga
> Poggiato s' è, e lor poggiato serve : ‡

the sheep which:

> Escon del chiuso
> Ad una, a due, a tre ; e l' altre stanno
> Timidette atterrando l' occhi e 'l muso ;
> E ciò che fa la prima, e l' altre fanno,
> Addossandosi a lei, s' ella s' arresta,
> Semplici e quete, e lo perchè non sanno. §

All these reveal the most exact and delicate observation. The last four words show that Dante had studied and understood sheep nature.

(wherein the heavy toil is pleasant to her), anticipates day-time upon the open bough, and with fervent desire expects the sun, looking intently where first the dawn has birth."

* *Inferno*, xxiv. 1—15.
† *Inferno*, xxvi. 25—30.
‡ *Purgatorio*, xxvii. 76—87. "Watched by the herdsman, who upon his staff is stayed, and stayed thus keeps guard over them."
§ *Purgatorio*, iii. 79—84. "Issue from the fold by one, by two, by three ; and the others stand in timid wise, bending to earth their eyes and muzzle ; and what the first does, the others do, pressing from behind on it, if it halts, gentle and placid, and know not why."

The simile of the lark, borrowed and improved upon from a Provençal poet, has the same quality of perfect truth and delicacy:

> Qual lodoletta, che in aere si spazia
> Primà cantando, e poi tace contenta
> Dell' ultima dolcezza che la sazia.*

He who has observed the lark's flight on a spring morning will understand the peculiar delicacy of the word *ultima*. He too who has walked through Alpine woods or pastures on a misty morning will well remember the effect described in these lines:

> Ricorditi, lettor, se mai nell' alpe
> Ti colse nebbia, per la qual vedessi
> Non altrimenti, che per pelle talpe ;
> Come quando i vapori umidi e spessi
> A diradar cominciansi, la spera
> Del Sol debilemente entra per essi.†

It is characteristic of Dante, as in this instance, to help out one simile by another. The thick smoke of the fifth Balzo suggests vapour in the Alps, and that reminds him of the membrane over a mole's eyes. This piling of one simile upon another is admirably illustrated by the passage which describes the faces of the lunar saints:—

> Quali per vetri trasparenti e tersi,
> O ver per acque nitide e tranquille,
> Non si profonde che i fondi sien persi,

---

* *Paradiso*, xx. 73. "Like to a lark, which soars in mid air, singing at first, and then keeps silence satisfied with the last sweet note that sates her."

† *Purgatorio*, xvii. 1—6. "Remember, reader, if ever in the Alps a thick mist overtook thee, through which one sees just like a mole through its skin, how, when the moist and dense vapours begin to part, the sun's sphere feebly passes through them."

> Toman de' nostri visi le postille
> Debili sì, che perla in bianca fronte
> Non vien men forte alle nostre pupille.[*]

The images of reflections in pure water, *not deep enough to be dark beneath*, and of pearls upon a white brow, support each other and produce one effect of delicate transparency. It would be easy to draw any number of similes from the *Purgatorio*, which abounds in these ornaments. I will confine myself to three more. One is very brief:—

> ✓ A guisa di leon quando si posa.[†]

There stands Sordello. This is in Dante's grandest manner. Tasso, with greater taste perhaps than delicacy, has transferred this line bodily to the stanzas of his *Jerusalem*. Here is a simile describing the sweet sound of indistinct melody:—

> Tale imagine appunto mi rendea
> Ciò ch' I' udia, qual prender si suole,
> Quando a cantar con organi si stea;
> Ch' or sì, or no s' intendon le parole.[‡]

---

[*] *Paradiso*, iii. 10—15. "Just as through transparent and smooth glass, or through sparkling and clear water, not deep enough for the bottom to be dark, the images of our faces are reflected so faintly that a pearl on a white forehead strikes not our organ of sight less forcibly." Compare the description of Dante's entrance into the Moon, *Paradiso*, ii. 31—36.

[†] Canto vi. 64. "In semblance of a lion when he couches."

[‡] Canto ix. 142—145. "What I heard struck my sense exactly in the same way as when they sing to the sound of organs, and now the words are caught and now are lost."

The last is of a different order. Dante says to Florence:—

> Vedrai te simigliante a quella inferma,
> Che non può trovar posa in su le piume,
> Ma con dar volta suo dolore scherma.*

This is noticeable for its force and penetration more than for its beauty. It might have formed a transition to those images which are grotesque in Dante, had it been advisable to treat of them in this place. Dante had good precedents for coarseness in similes; Homer had compared the Trojans and Greeks wrestling for the body of Patroclus to tanners wringing the grease from a hide; Virgil had likened the mother of Lavinia to a whipping-top. These images are, neither of them, less grotesque than that of the frogs and water-snake which Dante uses to describe the flight of the fiends at the approach of the angel from heaven.

VIII.

The definiteness which we have traced in Dante's general conceptions, in the planning of his poem, in his imaginary geography, in his pictures, and in his similes, appears no less remarkably in the compression and exactitude of his thought. He condenses whole chapters and books into single sentences, brief, pregnant, trenchant, sharply outlined, unmistakeable in

---

* Canto vi. 149. "Thou wilt see that thou art like a sick woman who cannot find rest on the couch, but by turning seeks to ward her pain off."

meaning. Here is the mediæval theory of human life conveyed in a line:—

> A' vivi
> Del viver ch' è un correr alla morte.*

Here is the character of the true counsellor we all desire in times of difficulty:—

> Persona,
> Che vede, e vuol dirittamente, ed ama,†

A complete treatise of style is conveyed in the two lines which explain Dante's secret of composition and its superiority to that of other poets of his time:

> Io mi son un, che quando
> Amore spira, noto, e in quel modo
> Ch' ei detta dentro, vo significando.‡

With like force and brevity he brings before us complex psychological conditions:—

> Io era come quei che si riscote
> Di visione oblita, e che s' ingegna
> Indarno di ridurlasi alla mente.§

or,

> Contra miglior voler, voler mal pugna. ||

or,

> Sta come torre fermo che non crolla,
> Giammai la cima per soffiar de' venti;
> Che sempre l' uomo in cui pensier rampolla

---

* *Purgatorio* xxxiii. 54. "To those who live the life that is a race to death."

† *Paradiso* xvii. 103. "One who discerns, and wills aright, and loves."

‡ *Purgatorio* xxiv. 52. "I am one who, when love inspires, mark, and in such wise as he dictates within, give outward sign."

§ *Paradiso* xxiii. 49. "I was as one who is conscious of a forgotten dream, and who tries in vain to bring it back to his mind."

|| *Purgatorio* xx. 1. "Against a stouter will will fights badly."

> Sovra pensier, da se dilunga il segno,
> Perchè la foga l' un dell' altro insolla.*

Again, whole centuries of determinate existence are summed up in such lines as these:—

> Questi non hanno speranza di morte

or,

> Che senza speme viviamo in disio

or,

> Fitti nel limo dicon: Tristi fummo
> Nel' aer dolce che dal Sol s' allegra
> Portando dentro accidioso fummo.†

It is this intense force of definite expression—force as of some blowpipe compelling the most stubborn metal of strange thought to take the subtle shapes of poetry, which enables Dante to state the scholastic learning of his day often with the utmost elegance and perspicuity. One instance will suffice:—

> La contingenza, che fuor del quaderno
> Della vostra materia non si stende,
> Tutta è dipinta nel cospetto eterno:
> Necessità però quindi non prende,
> Se non come dal viso, in che si specchia
> Nave, che per corrente giù discende.‡

---

* *Purgatorio* v. 13. "Stand firm like a tower that bends not its summit for any winds that blow; since the man in whom thought germinates on thought ever removes from himself his aim, the one weakening the force of the other impulse."

† *Inferno* iii. 46. "These have no hope of death." *Ibid.* iv. 42. "That without hope we live in desire." *Ibid.* vii. 120. "Fixed in the slime they say: 'Sullen were we in the sweet air, that is gladdened by the sun, carrying lazy smoke within our hearts.'"—CARLYLE.

‡ *Paradiso* xvii. 37. "Contingency, of which your knowledge extends not beyond the limits of your material existence, is all depicted in the eternal vision; but derives not therefrom necessity, any more than a ship which is descending the current, receives motion from the sight in which it is mirrored." It is true that the first two lines are obscure and can scarcely be paraphrased without amplification. The last five are clear and beautiful.

It would be difficult to express more lucidly and briefly the quibble by which theologians reconcile the dogma of divine prescience with that of human liberty.

It must be admitted that Dante is often clumsy, obscure, and tedious in his expositions. The opening of the fourth canto of the *Purgatorio* contains a dissertation on the Unity of Consciousness, which is involved in the extreme. The *Paradiso* is interrupted by frequent pedantic discussions, wearisome in their minuteness and scholastic dryness. Dante, it must be remembered, had undertaken to treat in verse the questions of the pulpit and the schools: he had no model of didactic poetry to follow—he had to accommodate a new language to subjects hitherto discussed in Latin by his predecessors; the wonder consequently is, not that he should often be obscure and tedious, but that he should ever be exquisitely elegant and luminous and terse.

IX.

The chief faults of Dante's poem are grotesqueness and obscurity. His grotesqueness is the result of realism, rejecting nothing so long as it is suited to express an idea. His obscure circumlocutions are due partly to the difficulty of creating a style, partly to his determination to say out all he has to say in spite of obstacles, partly to a wilful love of conceits. Dante will be definite at any cost; he will be striking and pregnant; and if there is no way of expressing himself, except by roundabout dissertations and quaint ill-digested images, he does not avoid these thorny paths, but takes them with alacrity.

The instances of what appears grotesque to modern taste in Dante are numerous. But putting out of sight passages which are merely mediæval and quaint, we may find many which would be grotesque in any author, owing to the want of congruence between the form and substance of the thought expressed. Here is one:—

>A rotar cominciò la santa mola.*

The holy mill began to wheel. By these words Dante wishes to convey that St. Thomas Aquinas, and the doctors of the church, resumed their dance around him. To make the grave and reverend signiors encased in lamps of living flame, revolve at all is hazardous: to compare their movement to that of a mill is still more awkward. The epithet *santa*, by taking off all lightness, adds to the incongruous impression. The same species of quaintness occurs in the passage about Judas Maccabæus:—

>Ed al nome dell' alto Maccabeo
>Vidi muoversi un altro roteando;
>E letizia era ferza del paleo.†

---

* *Paradiso*, xii. 3. "The holy mill began to revolve."

† *Paradiso*, xviii. 40. "And at the name of noble Maccabæus I saw another move and wheel; and joy was whip to the top."

Here, as in the last instance, one of the blazing stars upon the blood-red cross is not merely compared to a top, but is actually *called* a top *sans ceremonie*. And, in order, as it were, to make the matter perfectly serious, the joy of the august spirit is said to whip him up to sudden movement. Another simile in the *Paradiso* exhibits the same grotesqueness. Adam, exalted to the highest heaven, when testifying his infinite joy by the palpitation of his veil of coruscating splendour, is compared to a quadruped burrowing about under a table-cloth :—

> Tal volta un animal coverto broglia
> Si, che l' affetto convien che si pala
> Per lo seguir che face a lui la 'nvoglia.*

It is the Pre-Raphaelite exactness of Dante which has brought him to this pass. He wanted a pungent illustration, and did not care whence he took it. Without quitting the *Paradiso* we may still find plenty of grotesqueness. The next piece I shall quote appears to me in every way intolerable. The metaphors are quaint and clumsy, and withal confused. Saints are called chests of richness and fatness to begin with, and next good oxherds for the purposes of sowing seed. The mixture of hinds, seedsmen and coffers, is

* *Paradiso*, xxvi. 97. "Sometimes an animal covered over wags so that its emotion is discernible through the movement of its coverlid."

unparalleled by even any of Pindar's conglomerated images :

> O quanta è l' ubertà che si soffolce
> In quell' arche ricchissime, che foro
> A seminar quaggiù buone bobolce ! *

Notice again, how Dante does not use these figures by way of simile, but applies them at once by way of metaphor to the Saints themselves.

Some of the grotesque passages of the *Paradiso* are rather to be called homely than ludicrous. When Dante talks thus :—

> Però secondo il color de' capelli
> Di cotal grazia, l' altissimo lume
> Degnamente convien che s' incappelli : †

we are startled by the connection between so common and trivial an accident as the colour of hair and so serious a matter as the special gifts of grace. St. Bernard again, while exhibiting the splendours of the *Rose of Paradise* to Dante, excuses the brevity of his remarks with this explanation :

> Ma perchè 'l tempo fugge che t' assonna,
> Qui farem punto, come buon sartore,
> Che com' egli ha del panno, fa la gonna.‡

It is somewhat startling to find St. Bernard, upon the threshold of the Beatific Vision, and with his prayer

---

* *Paradiso*, xxiii. 130. "Oh ! how great is the fruitfulness stored up in those most richly laden coffers, which were on earth good herdsmen for sowing."

† *Paradiso*, xxxii. 70. "Wherefore according to the colour of the hair of so great grace must the divine light be duly wreathed around the head of each."

‡ *Paradiso*, xxxii. 139. "But, since the time of thy vision flies, here will we break off, like a good tailor who cuts his coat according to the cloth."

to Madonna on his lips, talking of cutting his coat like a good tailor according to his cloth. In like manner the homely proverb:—

E lascia pur grattar dov' è la rogna: *

in the mouth of Cacciaguida, and a similar saying:—

Sì ch' è la muffa dov' era la gromma: †

in the speech of Bonaventura, savour too much of the market-place or workshop to be appropriate in Paradise.

It is easy to hold up these passages to ridicule—so easy that a clever journalist might make plenty of fun out of the *Divine Comedy*. But this is not my purpose. Having pointed out the coarseness and grotesqueness of Dante's images where they are most conspicuous, in his third cantica, enough has been done to satisfy the requirements of taste and criticism. It remains to give some examples of the obscurity which mars the beauty of too many passages in his poem.

The nature of Dante's subject rendered it necessary that he should often be obscure. A poet in the very dawn of his country's literature, composing in a metre so complicated as the Terza Rima, and dealing with all the science of his day, cannot be consistently perspicuous. When, furthermore, he undertakes to sing of unseen mysteries, and to describe the indescribable, and when the nature of his genius inclines on all

---

* *Paradiso*, xvii. 129. "And let them scratch who itch."
† *Ibid.* xii. 114. "So that mildew is now where the wine-crust used to be."

occasions to the minute, the detailed, and the scrupulously accurate, it is wholly impossible that he should not often fall into perplexed and laboured labyrinths of diction. The first instance I select is rather ponderous and intricate than difficult :—

> Ficca dirietro agli occhi tuoi la mente,
> E fa di quegli specchio alla figura,
> Che 'n questo specchio ti sarà parvente.*

Here you are warned to look attentively: Dante bids you fix your mind where your eyes are, and make your eyes mirrors of that figure which will appear before you in the mirror of the planet's disc. The circumlocution of the sentence is simply clumsy. Yet notice even here the accuracy and delicacy of the poet's thought: your eyes are to be *mirrors;* it might even seem as if Dante had observed that the retina reflects an image which the nerves translate into the language of the brain. Many of the obscurities of Dante result from a too patient use of scientific phrases. Another passage is obscure, less owing to its tortuousness of expression than to a deliberate inversion of language and conception:

> Chè l' immaginar nostro a cotai pieghe,
> Non che 'l parlare, è troppo color vivo.†

---

* *Paradiso*, xxi. 16. "Fix your mind in the direction of your eyes, and make of them a mirror for the figure which in this mirror will appear to you."

† *Paradiso*, xxiv. 26.

"For the painting of such folds our imagination itself is too bright a colour." He wants to give reason for not describing a melodious song. It would be natural to say that imagination has no hues bright enough : he chooses, instead, to say that the palette of the fancy has no colours subdued enough for the painting of such delicate shadows. Another species of obscurity, which is common enough in the *Divine Comedy*, consists simply in roundabout expression of ordinary circumstances :—

> Quando amboduo li figli di Latona
> Coperti del Montone e della Libra,
> Fanno dell' orizzonte insieme zona,
> Quant' è dal punto, che 'l zenit i libra,
> Infin che l' uno e l' altro da quel cinto,
> Cambiando l' emisperio, si dilibra.*

These six lines are devoted to describing a single moment of time. Dante selects the singular occasion on which both sun and moon are seen immediately above the horizon together, the one rising and the other setting, while each trembles on the verge, but does not sink beneath, or rise above, the line of the earth's surface. For an infinitesimal moment they appear equilibrated. By this display of astronomical science and accurate observation, Dante achieves somewhat. He gains a certain richness, fullness, and reality;

* *Paradiso*, xxix. 1—6. "When both the children of Latona, covered by the Ram and Libra, at the same moment make the horizon their belt,—such length of time as elapses from the point when the zenith holds them equally balanced, till that when each, changing its hemisphere, disengages itself from the poised circle."

but our attention is retarded and fatigued by the effort of overcoming the difficult sentence. When the riddle is read, we feel aggrieved at finding it so simple. In his attempt to be definite, Dante thus not unfrequently ends in wearisome analytical circumvolutions and entanglements of speech.

(217)

CHAPTER VII.

THE QUALITIES OF DANTE'S GENIUS.

(i.) The Sublimity of Dante: compared with Milton's: Fuseli and Blake: Orcagna and Michael Angelo: Dante's Sublimity not Pictorial but Moral: Dante and Shakspere: Milton and Æschylus.—(ii.) The relation of the *Divine Comedy* to the Plastic Art of Italy: *Purgatorio* Canto 12, and the Pavement of Sienna Cathedral: *Purgatorio* Canto 10, and the Bas-reliefs of the Tuscan Sculptors: Interdependence of the Fine Arts in Italy.—(iii.) The Metre of the *Divine Comedy*: compared with Homer's Hexameter and Milton's Blank Verse: Laws of the Terza Rima.—(iv.) Dante's Gift of a Voice and Language to Italy and Europe: the Study of Dante in Italy: the Conditions under which he will necessarily meet with Neglect and Attention.

I.

HITHERTO we have confined ourselves to the analysis of Dante's definiteness. Much in the course of that analysis has been suggested which will prove of service in our next inquiry. We have seen Dante minute, nay slavishly exact, in the mechanism of his poem, detailed in his visionary geography, distinct in his conception of the non-existent and unreal: we have shown that he makes the sacrifice of size and grandeur in order to secure definiteness; that precision is the chief quality of his delineation, that the same determination to be scientifically, minutely, accurate, betrays him into grotesqueness and obscurity of style. Yet in spite of all this, Dante, as a poet, is sublime. On this point I wish to fix attention now.

The term sublime, which Longinus was able to apply to Sappho's odes, has, in course of time, been gradually, unconsciously, limited to scenical sublimity. This is an instance of the mode in which language gets impoverished; and it is the duty of the critic to resist the process as far as in him lies. Yet it will not be otherwise than convenient to discuss the point of Dante's sublimity first upon the ground of scenical effect.

The sublimity of Dante does not, like that of Milton, consist in the breadth and vastness of his pictures.* Dante has no creation like the Sin and Death of Milton, formless and shadowy; no figure so majestic as Uriel, the angel of the Sun, or Azazel, the ensign-bearer of Pandemonium. He does not excite our imagination with such lines as the famous :—

> Like Teneriffe or Atlas unremoved.

His very giants are measured. We have seen how Nimrod and Lucifer are made. Antæus is compared to

---

* One kind of sublimity Dante and Milton share in common—the sublimity of lofty and solitary natures stooping to no meanness; incapable of a vile thought; firm, ardent, and imperious in their devotion to the cause of right. The passages in the Apology against Smectymnus, where Milton speaks of his poetic vocation, and of the generous zeal for truth which has dragged him from his studious repose, and the yet nobler passages in the Reason of Church Government, in which he describes the function of the poet and his own high aspirations, might have been written by Dante or for Dante.

nothing more mountainous than the dumpy Garisenda tower. Had Dante described Satan wallowing in hell, he would not have talked of "many a rood," but would have said:—"such space as there is at Verona between pillar and pillar of the amphitheatre, measured by a man, who, standing with his back to Trento, sees the sun ere noonday opposite his face, the demon covered." The cause of this difference between Milton and Dante, is that Dante rejoiced in the concrete and detailed— Milton in the abstract and indefinite. Milton was blind: his intellect behind his sightless eyes, ranged space unlimited, and filled with shadowy forms. Dante was as keen-eyed as a hawk, as observant of details in the objects he examined as a short-sighted man. While Milton is contented with sketching in an outline, and but faintly tinting it, Dante is not satisfied unless he finishes the shading of his picture down to its minutest details, and invests it with the greatest brilliancy of hue. When Dante is sublime, he wrings sublimity from his subject in spite of its detail and minuteness; Milton, whenever he descends to details, ceases to be sublime: —witness the wars in heaven, the dialogues of the eternal Father and the Son, Raphael's repast, and the connubial felicities of Eden.

Considered from this point of view, Dante and Milton may be taken as the type of two opposite qualities of genius—breadth and detail, extension and intensity. Descending to a lower level of genius, and seeking an illustration from the sister art of painting, we might compare them respectively to Fuseli and Blake.* What strikes us in Fuseli's best work is the largeness of his conception, the broad mysterious force of his imagination. Blake attracts us by the pregnancy of meaning he conveys, by the intensity and compression of his thought. The absence of vagueness in Blake prevents our calling his designs sublime in the highest sense †: they startle our imagination, rather than dilate it. On the other hand the vagueness of Fuseli is excessive: it degenerates into feebleness. A sort of grand vacuity is the fault of the one master: grotesqueness, smallness, and a tendency to confusing detail are the blemishes upon the other's work. This illustration may help to explain what I want to establish about Dante and Milton. In Dante we have nothing so grandiose as Pandemonium: his fiends are "cabined, cribbed, confined" in petty cells. But the Bolge are full of action, variety and interest. We do not wonder what the demons find to do to drive away their sulphurous ennui.

Dante's definiteness was partly idiosyncratic, partly mediæval. He belonged to an age of subtle questions, of mechanical art, of party politics, of intense individuality, of distinct beliefs, of crude and overmastering

* It is noticeable by the way that Fuseli illustrated Milton and Blake Dante—both very badly, but very characteristically.
† The designs of God appearing in the whirlwind to Job, and of Job's vision in the night are vague enough to be sublime.

passions. Again, his mediævalism was Italian: it had nothing in it of the Germanic element, that *sentiment de l'infini*, which was the most precious legacy to modern times of the dark ages. Dante has not the mediæval qualities of the Gothic cathedral in all its vastness, but of the Gothic shrine in all its wealth of patient thought, and laborious and powerful invention. As the Duomo of Siena differs from the Cathedral of Strasburg, so does the Italian mediævalism of Dante differ from that of the Germanic races. Milton, on the contrary, was a northern giant of the Renaissance—cultivated in the classics, and inheriting from his Teutonic ancestry the sense of an infinity obscurely felt, rather than prominently apparent in his works.

The painter of the "Triumph of Death" and the "Last Judgment" at Pisa, is the proper parallel in painting to Dante; Michael Angelo to Milton. The concrete details of Orcagna's[*] work correspond to the same quality in the *Divine Comedy:* the shadowy vastness of Michael Angelo's designs is the counterpart to the conceptions of the *Paradise Lost.* Orcagna's "Last Judgment" makes us shudder and suffer more than Michael Angelo's: in the latter there is no such figure as the

[*] I use the familiar name of Orcagna, as the representative of a whole order of painting, though it has been clearly shown by Crowe and Cavalcaselle that he had no hand in the Campo Santo frescoes. The frescoes of Judgment, Paradise, and Hell, especially the last, by Orcagna in the Strozzi Chapel of Santa Maria Novella are undoubtedly inspired by Dante. The *Inferno* is a distinct effort to represent a vertical section of the Dantesque Hell with all its regions and Bolge and presiding genii of evil.

crouching Archangel of Humanity, who veils his face beneath the throne. The actual event is realized without exaggeration, but without attempt at idealization. A court of Justice is not more full of daily details and natural anxieties. Michael Angelo, on the other hand, elevates and expands our imagination in a far higher degree. Leaving us free from intense emotions and keen sympathies, he unrolls before our intellect the abstract spectacle of Judgment. In a word, he belongs, like Milton, to the era of the Classical Renaissance; whereas Orcagna, like Dante, is a child of the Middle Ages.

Definiteness, as I have already hinted, interferes with *pictorial* sublimity. Vastness and vagueness, it will hardly be denied, are essential to the true sublimity of a scene. A poet so minute in his proportions as Dante can scarcely produce the necessary sense of vastness; a painter so precise in details has little scope for mysterious obscurity. Yet we may observe that his grandest effects are those which have in them these elements of vastness and vagueness. When Dante crosses the threshold of Hell, he is immediately astounded by the confused roar of cries, and groans, and curses, of beaten breasts, and sobs, and shrieks, resounding through the air that has no stars. This is indubitably sublime. *Mi mise dentro alle segrete cose*, is all our preface: and Hell, under one of its most awful aspects, the place of utter darkness, where there is wailing and gnashing of teeth, appears before us suddenly in undetermined largeness. So is the first sight of the City of Dis: the landscape is broad—the scene indefinite: we are upon the waters under clouds of murky night: far off rise battlements and turrets glowing with a hidden fire. More, as yet, we know not of its grave citizens, its great host. We are approaching it, and it is fraught with mysteries to be disclosed. Sublime, again, is the thunder of the falls of Phlegethon down precipices of unknown depth—the fiery torrent hurling and howling through eternal night from ledge to ledge of invisible crags. Still more magnificent is the passage of the angel, dryshod, over Styx. Every incident enhances the sublimity of this scene — the furies on the battlements, the cry for Medusa, the chafing of the sullen sea, the fear of Dante, the pallor of Virgil, the suspense that broods before the dreadful gate of Dis. Then, suddenly, the alien splendour comes, passing irresistibly, heeding nought, scattering the fiends like frogs, waving from before his face the turbid mist, touching with a rod the gate, working swift deliverance, and sailing back again unmoved to regions of beatitude and light. Here the elements of vastness and mystery are blended with distinctness in a fusion of supreme soul-shaking majesty.

But the real sublimity of Dante is not pictorial. It is moral. The personality of the seer himself, and the tremendous destinies of his characters in the three realms, make up the grandeur of his poem. Dante, in describing all human passion and emotion, all moral states and qualities, is truly sublime. He is tragic, piercing, thrilling, touching, intense, as no other poet, except Shakspere, ever has been. Like Shakspere, too, he has the faculty of alchemizing our emotions as we read, of compelling them to take the tone of his own mood.

Concerning this quality of moral sublimity, which is eminent in Dante, some distinctions have to be made. I have mentioned Shakspere's name—not that Shakspere and Dante belong to the same order of poets, for Shakspere is like a mirror, reflecting everything in human nature, while Dante has rather the properties of some universally applicable chemical test paper, analyzing and pronouncing judgment upon everything it touches—but because there is a species of sublimity common to the works of both. Both are always human : they do not pass the limits of humanity ; and therefore they are in one sense finite : they rarely call the vague and abstract and illimitable to their aid. Milton and Æschylus, whose moral sublimity is of the highest order, deal in Titanic ideas, and superhuman conceptions. The *Eumenides* of Æschylus, the *Death* of Milton, appeal to our sense of mystery, and raise a supernatural awe. They are the personifications of abstract qualities, common, indeed, to all humanity, but in a sphere of being beyond our world. Shadowy terrors environ them. They rise before us like Brocken spectres of the soul projected on the mists of the unknown and terrible. In Shakspere, on the contrary, it is the tragic passion of Lear supporting the dead body of Cordelia; of Macbeth hearing the news of the queen's death; of Hamlet wrestling with Laertes in Ophelia's grave— in Dante it is the anguish of Ugolino; the stubborn defiance of Farinata; the sentence pronounced upon Ciacco, which we point to as sublime. Æschylus and Milton keep us within the circle of conceptions sublime by reason of their hugeness and imposing mystery. Shakspere and Dante confine us to παθήματα sublime by reason of their tragic intensity. Æschylus and Milton overawe our imaginations, and leave our sympathies comparatively untouched. Shakspere and Dante excite our emotions and overwhelm our sympathies.

Since, therefore, Dante's sublimity is moral and not scenic—human and not abstract—since it is to be sought for in the passions of the Soul itself, it follows that his definiteness does not impair its potency. The situation of Francesca and Paolo is enhanced by all the brief though detailed touches which present it vividly to our imaginations. But that species of the sublime which distinguishes Isaiah, Job, St. Paul, St. John, Æschylus, Lucretius, Milton, Pindar, which owes its effect to the width rather than to the profundity of the seer's vision, to the vastness rather than to the distinctness of his images, to the comprehensiveness rather than to the intensity of his genius, is not to be found in Dante.

II.

In comparing Dante with Milton I said that his mediævalism was Italian. This reminds me of one very important point about the *Divine Comedy*—its relation to the plastic arts of the fourteenth century. Dante, like all the greatest men of genius in Italy,[*] was sensitive to every form of art. We have seen that to some extent, at least, he practised both painting and music. We have also seen that the Allegorical Pageant of the *Purgatorio* is composed in the spirit of one of Memmi's or Lorenzetti's frescoes. In such a poem as the *Divine Comedy* there are multitudes of passages, and these the finest, which cannot be translated into the language of painting; but so true is Dante as a painter to the spirit of his time, that those which are susceptible of illustration ask rather for the brush of Giotto, than for the pen of Michael Angelo,[†] or the chiaroscuro of Doré. Yet it was not merely the painting of his age that Dante absorbed into himself and vocalized. What strikes us even more than his anticipations of the Giottesque

[*] It is enough to mention Leonardo, Michael Angelo, Orcagna, Giotto, Raphael. Francia and Cellini were no mean poets. Salvator Rosa is well known as a satirist and musical composer.

[†] A book of Michael Angelo's designs for the *Divine Comedy* is said, on good authority, to have been lost in the Gulf of Lyons, on ship-board during a storm.

and Sienese schools of allegorical design, is the deep intuition into the future of Italian sculpture which the *Purgatorio* contains. Passing over the pavement of the Cathedral of Sienna, where Beccafumi's tarsia-work of marble tells the Bible history afresh in living form, we seem to be treading the first parapet of Purgatory:

> Mostrava ancor lo duro pavimento,
> Come Almeone a sua madre fe' caro
> Parer lo sventurato adornamento.
> Mostrava, come i figli si gittaro
> Sovra Sennacherib dentro dal tempio,
> E come morto lui quivi 'l lasciaro.
>
> . . . . .
>
> Mostrava, come in rotta si fuggiro
> Gli Assiri, poi che fu morto Oloferne;
> E anche le reliquie del martiro.
>
> . . . . .
>
> O Saul, come 'n su la propria spada,
> Quivi parevi morto in Gelboè,
> Che poi non sentì pioggia nè rugiada.
>
> . . . . .
>
> Morti li morti, e i vivi parean vivi:
> Non vide me' di me, chi vide 'l vero,
> Quant' io calcai fin che chinato givi.*

Yet even the façade of the Duomo was not finished

---

* *Purgatorio*, xii. 49—54; 58—60; 40—43; 67—69. "The solid pavement also showed how Alcmæon made the disastrous ornament appear precious to his mother. It showed how his sons fell upon Sennacherib inside the temple, and how they left him there a corpse. . . . . It showed how the Assyrians fled in rout after Holofernes was slain, and the relics of the carnage as well. . . . . O Saul! how, fallen on thy own sword, didst thou there seem dead upon Gilboa, which thereafter felt neither rain nor dew. . . . . The dead seemed dead, the living alive; he who saw the reality, saw not more truly than I did, all that I passed over with my feet, walking with down-turned eyes."

until 1290; and it is certain that Dante could not have borrowed his conception from that pictured floor.[*]

The wall which bounds the staircase leading from the door of Purgatory to the region where pride is punished, carries us with the same force to the façade of Orvieto—or better, since the poet's vision surpasses the first stiff products of Tuscan sculpture, to the reliefs of Rosellini, da Majano, della Quercia, Donatello, and Ghiberti.

> Lassù non eran mossi i piè nostri anco,
>   Quand' io conobbi quella ripa intorno,
>   Che dritto di salita aveva manco,
> Esser di marmo candido, ed adorno
>   D' intagli sì, che non pur Policleto,
>   Ma la natura gli averebbe scorno.
> L' Angel, che venne in terra col decreto
>   Della molt' anni lagrimata pace,
>   Ch' aperse 'l Ciel dal suo lungo divieto,
> Dinanzi a noi pareva sì verace,
>   Quivi intagliato in un atto soave,
>   Che non sembiava immagine, che tace.
> Giurato si saria, ch' el dicesse *Ave;*
>   Perchè quivi era immaginata quella,
>   Ch' ad aprir l' alto amor volse la chiave.
> Ed avea in atto impressa esta favella:
>   *Ecce Ancilla Dei* sì propriamente
>   Come figura in cera si suggella.[†]

---

[*] Duccio's part in the work of the pavement has been disproved.

[†] *Purgatorio*, x. Esp. 28—45. "Our feet had not yet moved upon that upper path, when I perceived the bank around which hemmed us in, to be of white marble, and adorned with sculptured forms, that might have put not merely Polycletus but even nature herself to shame. The angel who came to earth to announce the peace wept-for through so many years, which unlocked heaven from its ancient interdict, before our eyes appeared so lively wrought and with so sweet a gesture that it seemed not a mere silent image. One might have sworn that he said: Ave! For there was

It is impossible while reading these lines, and the following fifty, which describe the bas-reliefs of Trajan's story and of David dancing before the ark, not to feel that here we have in poetry what the hands of those pure Tuscan sculptors wrought in stone. The spirit of devotion is the same. The union of grace and naïveté is the same. Dante anticipates the development of two centuries. Beyond Ghiberti there is no forecast in this canto of the *Purgatorio*. The change which passed over Italian art, when classical study had opened new horizons for the sculptor, and the painter, and the architect, was not foreseen by Dante. But all that is chaste, natural, sincere, and delicate in the originality of the earlier period, he has expressed— and that so faithfully that, given the passage just quoted from the 10th canto of the *Purgatorio*, together with a Madonna of Pisano, or a Saint in Paradise of Orcagna, we must pronounce them all to be the manifestations of one genius, of one age of culture. Dante's manner of conceiving pictures, both in painting and sculpture, bears as definite a relation to the art of the Trecento and the Quattrocento as Ariosto's to the glowing splendour of Venetian Paganism, and Tasso's to the sentimentalism of Guercino and the masters of the late Renaissance. These correspondences between

---

she portrayed who turned the key that opened Divine love: and in her attitude was written that word, *Ecce Ancilla Domini*, as sensibly as a figure sealed on wax."

poetry and the plastic arts of Italy are always noticeable. It is characteristic of the abundant and prolific life of Southern art that, as in the Athens of Pericles, so in the Florence of Dante and the Rome of Leo, the interpenetrations of the sister arts have been appreciated, and the incarnation of a new spirit has been signalised by novel forms in poetry, painting and sculpture simultaneously.

III.

It would be impossible to quit the *Divine Comedy* without a word about its verse—the *canto fermo* of its metre, which made Carlyle protest that the whole poem is one prolonged song. The Terza Rima of the *Divine Comedy* has, indeed, a powerful continuity of rhythm. In reading the hexameters of Homer we seem to be sailing buoyantly over the crests of Atlantic waves: Milton's blank verse is like a fugue voluminously full upon an organ of many stops: Dante's *Rime*, terse, definite, restrained within precise limits, has no Homeric ocean-roll, no surges and subsidences of Miltonic cadence, but, instead, a forceful onward march as of serried troops in burnished coats of glittering steel. His lines support each other, gathering weight by discipline, and by the strict precision of their movement. Or, to use another metaphor, they are closely welded and interlinked like chain armour, so that the texture of the whole is durable and supple, combining the utmost elasticity with adamantine hardness. Here we may remark how truly the form of a poem is the product of the poet's genius. Dante definite, distinct, and crystalline; Homer large, liberal, and myriad-murmuring as the sea; Milton with spirit attuned to the everlasting symphonies of unheard angels' songs—each surely and inevitably suits his cadence to his soul.

How Terza Rima was invented we need not inquire. Like all severe Italian metre it is Hendecasyllabic. That is to say, the normal line consists of nine syllables in addition to the rhyme, which, according to Italian prosody, is generally disyllabic; so that there are, as a rule, eleven syllables altogether. Thus:—

<blockquote>
O Niobe con che occhi dolenti. . . . .
Mo su mo giù e mo ricirculando. . . . .
</blockquote>

when the lines are so formed, they are called *Versi piani*. When the rhyme is trisyllable as thus:—

<blockquote>
Pagando di moneta senza conio :
</blockquote>

the line is called *Sdrucciolo*. When the rhyme is mono-syllabic, as in the following instance:—

<blockquote>
Dell' opera che mal per te si fe :
</blockquote>

the line is said to be *Tronco*, or mutilated.

Of course a large number of Dante's lines cannot be scanned without elision or slur. As in our blank verse, so in the Terza Rima, much license is allowed; and the scansion of the verse is determined less by feet than by accent and emphasis, more than two syllables rapidly pronounced being accepted as equivalents for a single foot. Milton writes:—

> Submiss: he reared me; and whom thou seekest I am.

Dante writes:—

> Bestemmiavano Iddio e i lor parenti.

Yet no sensible critic will complain because Milton has not conformed to the regularity of his own line:—

> His constant lamp and waves his purple wing:

or Dante to that of the evenly balanced:—

> Mo su, mo giù, e mo ricirculando.

Plasticity of metre in the hands of a great master is the secret of variety and beauty.

IV.

To Italy the *Divine Comedy* gave a voice and language. Silent since Claudian, the muse of Europe awoke on Dante's lips; and since his day her song in Italy and elsewhere has never ceased. Dante achieved for the modern world what Homer did for Greece. "Dante," to use the words of Shelley, "was the first awakener of entranced Europe; he created a language, in itself music and persuasion, out of a chaos of inharmonious barbarisms. He was the congregator of those great spirits who presided over the resurrection of learning; the Lucifer of that starry flock, which, in the

13th century, shone forth from republican Italy, as from a heaven, into the darkness of the benighted world." But, more than this, Dante bequeathed to his own nation, a Bible, a Testament, a Book of Prophecy, which cannot be mute. Generations may rise and pass away. New creeds and polities may rule and perish. But the speech of Dante will still be fresh, for it is human—it proclaims immutable laws, which Zeus made not, but which stand for ever firm in the conscience and the soul of man. "The years straying towards infidelity, he withholds by his steady faith." Wherever, throughout Europe, but most of all upon the sacred soil of Italy, there breathes a patriot who groans because of the divisions of his nation, but who, in spite of darkness and the vice and greed of governors, believes and hopes and knows that liberty and unity and peace and justice must prevail, there Dante lives. His words for such men are imperishable. His gospel, as visionary, perhaps, as the peace preached by the Apostles, is still, because of its ideality, eternal. The heavenly Jerusalem of seers and of poets hovers like a dream above our eyes, to cherish in our hearts the seed of immortality which finds no form on earth.

After Dante's death Florence founded a chair for the exposition of his poem in the Duomo. Michelino painted his portrait on the wall, where it still looms, bedimmed with age, by the great door. Boccaccio was the first to lecture on the *Comedy*. This example of

Florence was followed by Bologna, Pisa, Piacenza, Venice. A kind of college for the commentating of the poem was formed at Milan by the Prince Archbishop Giovanni Visconti. Dante's fame spread through Europe. The Bishops of Bath and Salisbury desired to read his Comedy; and at their instance, Serravalle, Bishop of Fermo, translated it into Latin. Twenty-one editions of the *Divine Comedy* were printed in the 16th, forty-two in the 17th, four in the 18th, and how many in the 19th century? When Batines counted its translators in 1843, he found nineteen Latin, twenty-five French, twenty English, twenty German, two Spanish. This list has lately received numerous additions. The names of Dante's commentators would fill a book. The published catalogue of Dantesque Bibliography consists of three octavo volumes.

A complete review of Dantesque literature would prove satisfactorily that but little of the attention which the *Divine Comedy* has received has been intelligent. At first Dante was valued for his scholastic learning and abstruse meanings. Next, when his style became old fashioned, and his theology had grown out of date, the world affected to forget him. Castiglione, for example, celebrates Petrarch and Boccaccio as the fathers of Italian literature, while he never mentions Dante. Ficino, though in his Italian version of the De Monarchia, he speaks of "Dante Alighieri per patria celeste, per abitazione fiorentino, di stirpe angelica," yet chiefly cared for the few traces of Platonism to be found in him. In the corruption of the 18th century the very name of Dante became obsolete. A nation of slaves and *cicisbei* had no appetite for his strong meat. But even then the dawn of better things began to be apparent. The French Revolution, and the agitation of ideas which had preceded it, stirred men to nobler purposes. Alfieri, in whom the flame of patriotism burned more brightly even than the fire of poetry, transcribed a volume of the finest passages of the *Comedy*, and wrote upon the first page of his MS. that were the work to do again, he should not omit one line—the faults of Dante being of more value than the beauties of other poets. Ugo Foscolo, soon after, by his manly criticism, relieved the study of Dante from Della Cruscan frivolities and dissertations upon phrases. Parini and Monti, Giusti, the poet of patriotism, and Leopardi, the melancholy spirit of a nobler age astray on modern seas of doubt, drank in the spirit of the master's style. The commentaries lastly of Bianchi and Fraticelli, threw real illumination on the sense of the *Divine Comedy*.

Thus Dante had the double honour of being neglected in the degradation of his country, and studied with enthusiasm in her hour of resurrection. As love, liberty, and the moral dignity of man are immortal, so Dante, the prophet of these things, cannot die. When the ages, lapsing to infidelity, and wallowing in the slough of materialism, forget them, Dante will be forgotten. But when, in the revolution of time, they surely and inevitably resume their sway, then Dante's star will rise again like Phosphor washed in Orient waves heralding the dawn.

CHAPTER VIII.

THE POETRY OF CHIVALROUS LOVE.

(i.) Difference between Classical and Mediæval Conceptions of Love.—(ii.) Chivalry and Feudalism.—(iii.) Platonic Love.—(iv.) Prose Romances and Provençal Poetry.—(v.) Italian Lyrists.—(vi.) Depth of Thought and Feeling introduced into the Poetry of Love in Italy.—(vii.) Dante and Guido Cavalcanti : Cino da Pistoja and Petrarch : Guido Guinicelli.—(viii.) Dante and Petrarch.

I.

HAVING touched more than once incidentally upon the *Vita Nuova* without going into detailed criticism, I must, in conclusion, deal separately with the subject-matter of the Poetry of Love as it was cultivated by the earliest Italian authors. In this field Dante won his first laurels. It is on this ground that Petrarch comes into competition with him. Here, alone, if anywhere, can the poet of *Vaucluse* and *Laura* be said to have borne away the palm from the poet of *Florence* and of *Beatrice*.

It was in the midst of a warlike, jealous, scheming, turbulent, restless society that the first notes of song were heard in Italy. But the song itself was not a

Marseillaise—on the contrary, the melodies with which Italy awoke to her artistic priesthood were love-ditties. The ancient world had heard nothing at all like these lyrics. They were quite fresh and modern. The spirit of Christianity, the spirit of chivalry; German feudalism, and crusading zeal ; Arabic imagination, and the Provençal Gai Saber, had all contributed their quota to the growth of new poetical ideas. New languages formed from the debris of Latin, rhymes borrowed from the prosody of Eastern poets, metres based upon the principle of accent, and not of quantity, had sprung into existence simultaneously with novel thoughts and modes of feeling since the voice of Claudian, who closed the Roman age of literature, had ceased. A few scholars still perused what remnants of Latin poetry survived the ruin of the Empire. But the real life of the modern world was not in these studies. Classical taste and erudition had little to do with the revival of art and letters in the thirteenth century. For the new conceptions of every kind which had started into being from the chaos which followed on the wreck of pagan civilization, spontaneous and natural expression was found in the vulgar tongues of modern Europe, and in forms of art, original though rude.

II.

In that interval which had elapsed between the days when Claudian, about 400 years after Christ, was singing the praises of Honorius in the last strains of pure and living Latin that the world has heard, to the year 1250, when at the death of Frederick II., the seed of modern literature had been already sown in Italy—an interval of about 850 years—Love, destined to inspire the first singers of the new era, had assumed a totally new character. In the ancient world the poetry of sensual passion prevailed. The poetry of sentiment was unknown to all the amorists of Greece and Rome, from Sappho down to Ovid and the latest writers of erotic epigrams. Classical poetry, though sometimes tender and affectionate, though splendid in its force and radiance and many-hued intensity, always treated the passion of Love as a physical emotion. There was nothing mysterious or respectful in the adoration of a lover for his mistress at Athens or at Rome. He might, indeed, spend sleepless hours beneath her window, watering the wreaths of roses with which he crowned her doorposts with his tears; like Sappho, he might tremble at the sight of her, and show the signs of overmastering emotion. But he never treated Aspasia or Delia like a deity; never served her for years in silence and estrangement; never sought to elevate his amorous devotion to the height of a religious worship, or by the contemplation of her beauty to raise his soul above the sordid cares and sensualities of life. The phrase of Dante, " Love that withdraws my thought from all vile things," would have been unintelligible to Catullus. This new aspect of Love the modern world owed to Chivalry, to Christianity, to the Germanic reverence for women, in which religious awe seems to have been blended with the service of the weaker by the stronger.

III.

Chivalry is not to be confounded with feudalism. Feudalism was a form of social organization based upon military principles. Chivalry was an ideal binding men together by participation in potent spiritual enthusiasms. Feudalism was the bare reality of mediæval life. Chivalry was the golden dream of possibilities which hovered above the eyes of mediæval men and women, ennobling their lives, but finding its truest expression less in actual existence than in legend and literature. The pages of feudal history tell a dismal tale of warfare, cruelty, oppression, and ill-regulated passions. The chivalrous romances present sunny pictures of courtesy and generosity and self-subordination to exalted aims. It is always thus. The spirit wars against the flesh, the idea against the fact, in the lives of nations as well as of individuals. Christianity, for example, in theory, is far different from the practice of the Christian Commonwealths. Yet, who shall say that the spirit in this warfare is not real, or that the idea is impotent? that Christianity, though never practised in its whole integrity, is not the very salt and essence of the life of modern nations? Even so Chivalry, though rarely realized in its pure beauty, though scarcely to be seized outside the songs of poets, and the fictions of romancers, was the force which gave its value to the institutions and the deeds of feudalism. Whatever was most noble in the self-devotion of Crusaders, most beneficial to the world in the foundation of the knightly orders, most brilliant in the lives of Richard, the Edwards, Tancred, Godfrey of Bullogne, most enthusiastic in the lives of Rudel, Dante, Petrarch; most humane in the courtesy of the Black Prince; most splendid in the courage of Bayard; in the gallantry of Gaston de Foix; in the constancy of Sir Walter Manny; in the loyalty of Blondel; in the piety of St. Louis—may be claimed by the evanescent and impalpable yet potent spirit which we call Chivalry.

Regarding Chivalry, not as an actual fact of history, but as a spiritual force, tending to take form and substance in the world at a particular period, we find that its very essence was enthusiasm of an unselfish kind. The true knight gave up all thought of himself. At the moment of investiture he swore to renounce all greed and gain of every kind; to do nobly for the mere love of nobleness; to be generous of his goods; to be courteous to the vanquished; to redress wrongs; to draw his sword in no quarrel but a just one; to keep his word; to respect oaths; and, above all things, to protect the helpless and to serve women. The investiture of a knight was no less truly a consecration to high unselfish aim for life, than was the ordination of a priest. In the enthusiasm which inspired the knight, two main, and at first sight, very different influences mingled—the one was zeal for the faith, the other zeal for love. His motto was: "Dieu et ma Dame." Of the one enthusiasm Percival, "in whom the very faith stood most;" and Galahad, the achiever of the Holy Grail, were the ideal champions; the other was represented by Lancelot, lover of Guinevere, and Tristram, lover of Iseult. Some antagonism naturally existed between the chivalry of Religion and the chivalry of Love. That may be clearly traced in the old romances, especially in the Legend of the Grail, as condensed by our Sir Thomas Malory. The Crusades, by developing a deeply religious spirit and setting martyrdom in Holy Land before the souls of knights and warriors as an object to be devoutly desired, put a sword between the Love of God and the Love of the Lady. Orders of knighthood were formed like those of Malta and the Temple, which enforced celibacy and monastic chastity of life. In less ascetic minds, however, and when the influence of the Crusade was not so paramount, the twofold enthusiasm which had for its motto, "Mon Dieu et ma Dame," blended and produced a peculiar worship of the Lady as the living symbol of purity and holiness. God was the ultimate object of the worship of the chivalrous lover; but the lady stood between his soul and God as the visible image and perpetual reminder of the heaven to which he ardently aspired. Thus Petrarch and Dante both constantly repeat that it was the thought of their lady which had ennobled them, and turned their souls to God. The state of feeling generated by this love was called by the Provençals, Joie. The word is curiously significant of the ecstacy which filled the heart of the true lover with delight, and made him feel in his exalted mood capable of almost more than mortal deeds. This Joie was less an emotion than a permanent state of being. To use the language of the schools, it was not an affection ($\pi\acute{a}\vartheta\eta\mu a$), but a habit ($\H{\epsilon}\xi\iota\varsigma$.) It is particularly to be noticed that the love of chivalry in which it realized itself, never ended in marriage; and the lady who inspired it was not unusually a wife. Thus it existed wholly independent of the marriage-tie upon the one side, and of sensuality upon the other, forming the source of noble and exhilarating enthusiasms in the lover's soul, and exalting him above his meaner impulses of every kind. At the same time it did not in actual life exclude other and less spiritual passions. Cino da Pistoja, in spite of his love for the beautiful Selvaggia, was the father of several children by an honoured and noble wife. Petrarch, while adoring Laura, became the parent of a son and daughter by another woman. Dante himself, who is the most luminous example in literature of the chivalrous ecstacy of love, suffered Beatrice to become the wife of another, and married his own wife, Ginevra Donati, without for a moment ceasing to adore in Beatrice the mistress of his soul. His emphatic assertion that she had revealed to him all wisdom and virtue, the conclusion of the *Vita Nuova*, and the whole tenor of the *Divine Comedy*, are undoubted proofs of the existence of a chivalrous passion, side by side with other affections, in the heart of the greatest, truest, sincerest man of modern Europe.

IV.

We are led irresistibly from the contemplation of chivalrous love to think of Plato. The mania of love described by Plato in the *Phædrus* is the only parallel which exists to the mediæval Joie which I have been describing. It is not a little curious that these two enthusiastic words should have been instinctively chosen at different ages of the world for the denomination of a state of the soul so similar. The mania of Plato was a permanent ecstasy of the spirit, in which love led the way to heaven, and raised a man above himself. The love of Plato was equally removed from civil affection and from sensual passion. Therefore it is not to be wondered at that as soon as Plato began to attract the notice of modern students, they should have claimed him as their master in the mysteries of a passion which had received so splendid an illustration in modern history from the poets of Provence and Italy. But between the chivalry of the middle ages, and the enthusiasm described by Plato, there was really a great difference. Plato believed that the lover is the inspirer of high thoughts, the begetter of beauty in the soul of the beloved. Modern chivalry reversed this, making, as we have seen, the beloved person the source of inspiration, revelation, elevation to celestial heights. Still the differences between modern Joie and ancient Mania are superficial, and such as proceed from different national conventionalities. The points of similarity are permanent. Both set forth an ideal of love, pure from the grossness of the flesh, not to be confounded with matrimonial affection or sensual passion, by means of which the spirit of man is rendered capable of self-devotion and high deeds. It was the recognition of this similarity which caused the modern Italians to talk and write so much of what is called Platonic love—a love, which, owing to the frailty of human nature, has fallen into much and well-deserved discredit.

V.

Returning from this digression, we may proceed to the literature of chivalry, which preceded the Canzonieri of the Italian poets, and prepared the way for their artistic treatment of La Joie des Amants. This literature consisted of two great masses—the prose romances of Charlemagne and Arthur, and the poems of the Provençal Troubadours. In order to understand the relation of the prose fictions to the whole subject of chivalrous love, it must be borne in mind that chivalry had absorbed and organized not only much of the Christian but also a large portion of the old Teutonic spirit. The unselfishness, humility, forgiveness of injuries, indifference to worldly wealth, the chastity and purity of love which formed ingredients of the chivalrous ideal, were Christian. The adoration of woman, the love of battles and of feats of arms for their own sake, the scrupulous sense of honour, the obedience to laws, the truthfulness and loyalty to persons, the respect of knighthood as a form of consecration,—all these no less essential elements of chivalry, were Teutonic. It is curious to trace the blending of these two diverse influences in the cycles of mediæval romance. In the legends of Charlemagne the Teutonic spirit, as yet semi-barbarous and unsoftened by Christianity, appears in all its savage heroism. Love finds but little place in the ideal of knighthood, and the warrior's faith is scarcely better than a fierce and superstitious animosity against the foes of Christendom. But in the romances of Arthur we meet with a complete fusion of the martial and the amorous elements of chivalry, together with refined religious sentiment. The Arthurian cycle has no real basis of history.* It professes to deal with times far more remote than those of Charlemagne; yet it represents a much softer and more organized society. It is, in fact, a mythical structure, representative of knighthood as ideally conceived about the period of the 12th and 13th centuries. The creators of the Arthurian tales, starting with the chief ideas of mediæval knighthood, embodied them freely in a series of legends. For their patrons, the lords and ladies of our Norman Court, and of Provence, they framed romantic stories of knightly prowess and devoted love; in the legend of the Holy Grail, they allegorized the spirit of the religious orders; in the histories of Guinevere and Iseult they beautified the ideal of chivalrous love: Lancelot's Castle was called by them La Joyous Garde —the Keep of Joy. The fierce passions of Roland and

* I do not enter into the question of its mythical basis—whether solar or not. Achilles and Arthur may both of them be Sun-gods, existing in the imagination of Gauls and Britons as heroes long after their divinity had been forgotten. Solar mythology is not devoid of antiquarian interest. But the students of literature and nationalities are concerned not with the decay of language and the metamorphosis of mythology so much as with the living embodiments of the thoughts and emotions of races in their popular heroes, their ideals of humanity set forth by the greatest of their poets.

his peers are softened in the heroes of the Table Round. Lancelot, Galahad, Percival, Gawaine, Bors, Tristram, Beaumains and Sir Kay, are portraits of the noblest knighthood, delicately traced with firmly marked and characteristic differences. There was not a Crusader, not a knight of France or Italy, who would not have desired to win like fame with one of them. Thus it came to pass that a body of epical material was gathered together which contained the whole ideal of the knightly character, setting forth in fairest lineaments the nature of chivalrous love. Lancelot and Tristram were not happy in their passion; but it made them what they were—the first and bravest and most tender-souled of feudal heroes. Reflecting the sentiments of the age which gave them birth, and in return reacting on their period and on the spirit of succeeding centuries, these romances were of the first importance in forming that theory of chivalrous love which first the Provençal, and then the Italian poets, expressed in verse. What nation can claim for its own the romances of Arthur, still remains doubtful. Northern antiquarians stand firm for the undisputed right of Walter Mapes and other Englishmen or Normans at the English Court. Fauriel, the great French historian, believes them to have been a product of Provençal literature. Be that as it may, it is certainly in Provence that lyrical expression is first given to the sentiments with which the prose romance abounds. The new element which the troubadours contributed to the knightly ideal, and which M. Fauriel thinks he can trace in the Arthurian cycle, was partly the natural growth of their own beautiful country, partly the result of contact with Arabic civilization. The Christian and Mahommedan chivalries came twice into collision during the 11th century—at Toledo and in Palestine. It is impossible to doubt that the consequence of this collision was the addition of a certain Oriental perfume to the sterner ideal of knighthood, rooted already in Teutonic Christianity. The extravagant warmth of feeling which we find in Troubadour poetry is Eastern. The worship of women, which was something almost religious in the North, loses much of its mystery, and acquires a new voluptuousness in Southern Europe. We feel ourselves, in reading the Provençal lyrics, to be in contact with a nation that retained something of classical luxury, and had imbibed a portion of Moorish sensuality.

VI.

After this long preamble we are, at length, approaching the Italian lyrics of love. The chivalry, which we have seen emerging from the mists of German paganism, acquiring Christianity, and developing the graces of courtesy and love, has now at last, at the beginning of the 12th century, found lyrical expression in Provence. For one century and a half it flourished there.

During this period the language of Provence continued to be the medium of civilizing culture to the south of Europe. Through the singers of Toulouse and Aix and Arles, the spirit of the modern world found vocal utterance. Then, suddenly, amid corruption from within, and persecution from without, the literature of Provence perished; not, however, before the mantle of the troubadours had fallen upon a nobler race of poets, upon Piero delle Vigne, upon Guido Cavalcanti, upon Cino da Pistoja, upon Dante, and on Petrarch, all of whom were confessedly and obviously scions of the old Provençal stem, though bearing a more splendid wealth of blossom, and a more enduring fruitage of sustained and solid thought. The sceptre had been transferred from Provence to Italy—from Provence incomplete in language, immature in culture, unfavoured in territory, to Italy possessed of a mighty voice, fitted by nature for magnificent development, prepared by long struggles for a progressive civilization. Let us not forget to pay our tribute of respect to the almost obsolete predecessors of the great Italian poets. Had it not been for those generations of ineffective, but most fruitful lyrists of Provence, the first age of Italian letters would have been far other, and less splendid, than it was.

Of the extent to which Provençal poetry was cultivated in Europe before Italian had become a language of literature, the following names are the best evidence.

Frederick the Emperor, Richard Cœur de Lion, Alfonso the Second and Peter the Third of Aragon, Frederick the Third of Sicily, the Dauphin of Auvergne, the Count of Foix, the Prince of Orange, the Marquis of Montferrat, each and all crowned sovereigns, were composers of better or worse poems in this tongue. The greatest kings and warriors, the chiefs of the most illustrious nations of the South and North, the generals of crusading armies, the princes of Italy, agreed to use one language, and to sing of love and arms in the same strains. The culture of Provence united Europe, and gave a single voice to chivalry. But it is not among royal authors — in spite of Frederick's poem on the beauties of all nations, and of Richard's nobler lament from the Tower Tenebrous—that we find the purest burst of lyric song. The leonine Sordello of Mantua, who fought, so runs the tale, with Eccelin, and who called the craven peers of Christendom to banquet on the heart of the heroic Blacas; Geoffrey de Rudel, who loved the lady of Tripoli, and sought her far across the sea, and died when he beheld her face; Bertrand de Born, the evil-hearted counsellor, whom Dante saw in hell; Pierre Vidal, that Don Quixote of real life, who styled himself Greek Emperor, and for his lady's sake went clad in wolf-skin on all fours, to the great peril of his limbs; Peyrols, who sang of the contention between love and the crusades; Arnaud Daniel, praised alike by Dante and Petrarch, as the sweetest singer of gentle love; Arnaud de Marveil, called by Petrarch "the less famous Arnald," who loved his master's wife, the Countess Adelaide of Beziers; Folquet, Bishop of Toulouse, the murderous counsellor of Montfort in his fierce crusade, whom Petrarch praised and Dante met in Paradise—these are some of the most famous singers of Provence, the teachers of the coming age in art and love. The two Arnolds, Folquet, Sordello, and Pierre Vidal, deserve especial mention, as the troubadours who seem to have had most influence over Dante and Petrarch. In the *Divine Comedy*, and the *Trionfo dell' Amore*, of Petrarch, their names frequently occur.

As specimens of their poetry, and in order to illustrate the extent of their influence in forming the Italian style of love-song, I will select three pieces. The first is Rudel's "Song of Far away," written when he was languishing in love for the fair lady of Tripoli, whom he had never seen, and whom he was destined only to see upon the threshold of death:—

>Angry and sad from hence I go,
> Unless I see my love afar:
>When we may meet I do not know,
> Our lands are placed apart so far:
>God, who hast made all things that grow,
> And framed for me this love afar,
>Give strength unto my heart that so
> Still hopes to see my love afar;
>Ah, Lord! I believe 'tis truth I show
> In loving her who dwells afar,
>Seeing that for one joy of woe
> A thousand-fold I reap afar!

> All other loves I here forego
> Except the love of her afar;
> For none more beautiful I know
> In any land or near or far.*

The second is "Peyrol's Contention with Love." This poem bears a marked resemblance to pieces of Cino and Petrarch. At the same time it illustrates the division between the amorous and religious impulses in chivalry:—

> Love! I long have been your slave
> Till my heart is broken;
> What is the reward I have?
> Where my duty's token?
>
> Peyrols! can you then forget
> That same blooming Beauty,
> Whom with such delight you met,
> Swearing love and duty?
> That's the way I paid the debt!
> Let me tell you your light heart
> Tender thoughts disperses;
> When you act the lover's part
> You falsify your verses.
>
> Love! I've still been true to you,
> And, if now I leave you,
> 'Tis what I am forced to do;
> Do not let it grieve you.
> Heaven will see me safely through!
> Heaven, too, make the kings agree!
> Keep them both from fighting!
> Lest Saladin their folly see
> Which he'll take delight in.
>
> Peyrols! do the best you will,
> You alone can't save it;
> Every Turk you cannot kill,
> That storms the Tower of David;
> Here remain and sing your fill!

---
* In this translation I have kept the monotony of rhyme which occurs in the original.

You're not wanted by the kings;
　Stay then and amuse you;
They're so fond of quarrellings,
　They can well excuse you.

Love! I've felt your power depart;
　Though my fair one's beauty
Lingers still about my heart,
　Yet I'll do my duty.
Many a lover now must part;
Many hearts must now begin
　To feel their sad griefs springing,
Which but for cruel Saladin
　Had joyously been singing.*

The third is "Vidal's Vision of his Master Love." This I have versified from the prose abstract given of the poem by Sismondi. It cannot, therefore, pretend to much accuracy; but I have preferred to give it a metrical form as being more suited to the expression of such thoughts:—

It was the season when sweet May
　Makes wood and meadows green again;
I sought the fields at break of day
　To sooth my solitary pain:
What there I saw for your delight,
Even as my heart dictates, I write.

A youth as fair as morning, tall,
　But slender, with a smiling mouth,
And laughing eyes and musical
　Low voice that murmured like the South,
What time the winds of April blow
On banks of moss where violets grow,

---

* From SISMONDI's *Literature of the South of Europe*. Translated by ROSCOE, Vol. i, p. 146.

> Attired in armour clean and white,
>   With flower-emblazoned robe and wreath
> Of roses on his helm so bright,
>   Bestrode a stéed milk-white beneath
> The saddle-bows embossed with blaze
> Of jasper and of chrysoprase.
>
> Bending, the Knight with gracious mien,
>   Cried to me: "Vidal! I am Love!
> These ladies that I ride between
>   Are Mercy, whose embroidered glove
> You see upon my casque, and she
> Whose name is maiden Modesty.".
>
> Thereat two damsels I espied,
>   Meek, gentle, clad in white and red,
> Who rode with Love on either side;
>   But as I gazed, my master said,
> Like one who loves exceedingly:
> "Behold my Squire, Sir Loyalty!"
>
> A goodly youth he was, I trow,
>   Like one who dares with single might
> Oppose a myriad-handed foe
>   In battle for his lady's right,
> Or for the faith of Christ who trod
> Our sinful earth a suffering God.

The importance of this vision cannot be exaggerated. Chivalrous Love is presented to us here as in a mythus. He is a very distinct personage, very different from the fiery youth described by Sappho and Anacreon, or from the wayward boy of later classical imagination; or, again, from the parrot-winged wild spirit of Arabian tales. A youthful knight, in the bloom of beauty, among the fields of May, riding a snow-white steed, attended by Loyalty for squire, and by Modesty and

Mercy for handmaidens — what could be a better portrait than this of the chivalrous passion?

The point of transition from Provençal to Italian poetry is clearly marked. Dante was born about thirty years after the death of Folquet, the fanatic troubadour, who helped de Montfort to destroy the cities and great houses of his native land. Between Folquet and Dante no eminent singer of Provence arose; but many minor poets in Sicily and in Tuscany adapted the new language of Italian to the old themes of love. Among these the most notable were Ciullo d' Alcamo, Piero delle Vigne, Frederick the Second, the king Enzo his son, Guittone of Arezzo, Guido Guinicelli, and Guido Cavalcanti, whose poetical career began earlier than that of his friend Dante. I mention these names to show how the interval was bridged over between the last singers of Provence, and the great master-singer of modern Europe.

VII.

The really notable point in the transition from Provence to Italy is that we get the same subject of chivalrous love treated in a more masculine style, with far more intellectual depth of meaning, with frequent recurrence to allegory, and in a language more capable of expressing profound thought and elevated passion. The studies of philosophy and science, conducted in the Universities of Bologna and Naples, told immediately on poetry by introducing a grave and metaphysical turn of thought. The vehement political struggles which had so long occupied the very heart of Italy, deepened the feelings and strengthened the characters of poets, who were at the same time politicians. The religious enthusiasm, resuscitated by the preaching of St. Dominic, and by the fraternity of St. Francis, impressed a more spiritual seriousness on art. The Italians were not children like the Troubadours, but men, awaking from the lethargy of years to find an instrument of music ready to their fingers, and with impulses within their souls for singing. How they used that lute of the Troubadours; how they strung it with fresh chords, and made it answer to the virile thoughts and passions of their breasts, can only be understood by the profound study of Cino, Guido, Dante, Petrarch.

In order to show how far more deeply and intensely the Italian poets treated the same thoughts as those developed by the Troubadours, we may take this beautiful sonnet of Jacopo da Lentino, translated by Rossetti: (page 41.)—

> I have it in my heart to serve God so
> That into Paradise I shall repair—
> The holy place through the which everywhere
> I have heard say that joy and solace flow.
> Without my lady I were loth to go,—
> She who has the bright face and the bright hair;
> Because if she were absent, I being there,

> My pleasure would be less than nought, I know.
> Look you, I say not this to such intent
>   As that I there would deal in any sin :
>   I only would behold her gracious mien,
>   And beautiful soft eyes, and lovely face,
>   That so it should be my complete content
>   To see my lady joyful in her place.

Two of the Troubadours, Bernard de Ventadour and Boniface Calvo, had used the same extravagant hyperboles of passion—the one speaking of his mistress exclaims: "Paradise without thee is imperfect"; the other thinks it unnecessary to pray God to take his lady to heaven, seeing that heaven would be nothing without her courtesy and gentleness. The artless crudity of the Provençal thought is at once refined by the delicate and balanced beauty of its Italian setting. Notice again what exquisite dignity has been added to the same order of thought by Dante in the *Vita Nuova*.—(Rossetti's Translation, p. 289-293).

> Beatrice is gone up into high Heaven,
>   The kingdom where the angels are at peace ;
>   And lives with them ; and to her friends is dead.
> Not by the frost of winter was she driven
>   Away, like others ; nor by Summer-heats ;
>   But through a perfect gentleness instead.
> For from the lamp of her meek lowlihead
> Such an exceeding glory went up hence
>   That it woke wonder in the Eternal Sire,
>   Until a sweet desire
> Entered Him for that lovely excellence,
>   So that He bade her to Himself aspire :
> Counting this weary and most evil place
> Unworthy of a thing so full of grace.

and again :

> But from the height of woman's fairness, she,
> Going up from us with the joy we had,
> Grew perfectly and spiritually fair;
> That so she spreads even there
> A light of Love which makes the angels glad,
> And even unto their subtle minds can bring
> A certain awe of profound marvelling.*

The following translation from a sonnet by Piero delle Vigne, one of the earliest compositions in pure Italian, will serve to illustrate what has been said about the increase of philosophical depth in the Italian treatment of chivalrous love :—

> Since Love hath ne'er of any man been seen,
> Nor touched by mortal fingers bodily,
> Many there are who led by folly lean
> To think that Love is a nonentity;
> But forasmuch as Love hath power within
> The heart of men to prove his mastery,
> Greater must be the worth of him, I ween,
> Than if he were beholden visibly.
> Lo ! how the magnet by its secret might
> Doth draw the steel, and still with strong control
> Unto itself compels it powerfully !
> This thing doth bid me to believe aright
> That love exists, and fortifies my soul
> To trust the common folk's credulity.

This sonnet forms a fitting prelude to Guido Guinicelli's canzone of the "Gentle Heart," to Guido Cavalcanti's pedantic canzone "Donna mi priega," and to those

---

* This is, perhaps, a fitting place to pay some tribute of gratitude to Mr. D. G. ROSSETTI for the services he has rendered to all students of Early Italian Poetry by his translations, and of admiration for the exquisite perfection of style with which he has given a fitting English dress to these subtly beautiful compositions.

allegorical canzoni of Dante, which are so elaborately commented upon by him in the *Convito*. It must be remembered that whereas the lyrists of Provence were simple knights, those of Italy were learned men. Dante calls them "doctores" or teachers, as well as "trovatores" or inventors. One other sonnet preparatory to the great period of Italian composition may be quoted. It is from Guittone of Arezzo, translated by Rossetti. Of the whole of Guittone's voluminous collection, this perhaps alone deserves to be remembered. It is deeply religious, and sublime in its simplicity:—

> Lady of Heaven, the mother glorified
>   Of glory, which is Jesus,—He whose death
>   Us from the gates of hell delivereth
> And our first parents' error sets aside:
> Behold this earthly Love, how his darts glide—
>   How sharpened—to what fate—throughout this earth!
>   Pitiful mother, partner of our birth,
> Win these from following where his flight doth guide.
> And O, inspire in me that holy love
>   Which leads the soul back to its origin,
>   Till of all other love the link do fall.
> This water only can this fire reprove,—
>   Only such cure suffice for such like sin;
>   As nail from out a plank is struck by nail.*

---

* It is not perhaps undeserving of notice that the last line of this sonnet:

Come d'asse si trae chiodo con chiodo:

has been transferred by Petrarch, word by word, into his Trionfo d'Amore. (Cap. iii. 66).

VIII.

I have now attempted to prove, partly by analysis, and partly by examples, that the Provençal poetry of chivalrous love became ennobled in the hands of the Italians. The Italian poets continued to write of love; but they contrived, while doing so, to make their amorous lyrics the vehicle of thought. In the *Vita Nuova* Dante says,—" The reason why certain of a very mean sort obtained at the first some fame as poets is, that before them no man had written verses in the language of Si; and of these the first was moved to the writing of such verses by the wish to make himself understood by a certain lady, unto whom Latin poetry was difficult. This thing is against such as rhyme concerning other matters than love; that mode of speech having been first used for the expression of love alone." This clearly proves that at that time Dante was convinced that all Italian poetry ought, in form at least, to treat of love. Of himself too, he says, in the *Purgatorio*,—" I am he who writes as love dictates," alluding, I fancy, in a covert way to other poets who wrote less spontaneously— less immediately under the enthusiastic influence of some passion of the soul, of love in its widest significance.

Since then it was the invariable custom to use the vulgar tongue for amorous poetry, and since at the same time poets felt the need of expressing more than mere sentiment in their verses, it followed that many of the Italian lyrists, while professedly singing of their mistress, were really hinting at metaphysical or political questions. To mean one thing when you spoke another was quite consistent with the mediæval taste for allegory. To this class of poets belonged Guido Cavalcanti, celebrated as Dante's friend, and also as one of the most singular and richly-gifted poets of his time. Guido, it will be remembered, was exiled by Dante, with the party of the ultra-Guelfs, to Serrezzano, in 1300. He married a daughter of Farinato degli Uberti; and of him old Cavalcanti asked the touching question which interrupts Dante's colloquy with the great Ghibelline general in hell among the fiery tombs. In the treatise on the vulgar tongue Dante praises him, together with Cino, as "those who have most sweetly and subtly written poems in Italian." Cino da Pistoja was a poet of a different type, less profound, more fluent, less gifted, but more capable of using his gifts. His love for the beautiful Selvaggia, daughter of Vergiolesi, the chief of the Pistojan Bianchi at his time; his poems on the death of the Emperor Henry, and his immense learning as a jurist, have contributed to render him conspicuous among the Italian men of letters of his day. As a poet he was the predecessor of Petrarch. Indeed, Guido Cavalcanti and Dante, Cino and Petrarch, mark two very different qualities of poetry. Dante and Guido are obscure and intricate, audacious in imagination, potent, and at the same time somewhat pedantic in thought. Cino and Petrarch are fluent and full of facile grace, expressing elegant ideas and harmonious sentiments in lucid language. In Cino and in Petrarch we are less struck by the profundity of thought and feeling than by the limpidity of its expression. The head illuminates the heart. In Dante we feel that the heart always inflames the brain, and that thoughts and feelings are forced by vehement enthusiasm into their proper mould of speech. With Guido the enthusiasm is less fervid; the heart has less to say, but the brain works with a Titanic energy of its own. Another Guido—Guido Guinicelli,—from whose poem on the gentle heart Dante has deigned to borrow phrases and ideas—resembles the master-poet in the quality of writing as love dictates, obeying the spontaneous impulses of an enthusiastic soul. Meeting this Guido in the *Purgatorio*, Dante calls him "father of myself and of others, my betters, who have practised sweet and graceful love-verse." Again, in the *Convito*, he distinguishes him as "quel nobile Guido." But Guido Guinicelli lacked the energy, concision, depth, and fine which his great pupil displayed so eminently, and which the other Guido shared in a great measure. Dante, in fact, combined the gifts, with who shall say how great an over measure of poetic faculty, of both the Guidi. Guido Cavalcanti and Guido Guinicelli are poets whose types of genius combined and culminated in Dante. Cino da Pistoja was the forerunner of Petrarch, who was destined to surpass him.

IX.

Let us, therefore, in conclusion, briefly set Dante and Petrarch, as the two culminating poets of chivalrous passion, in contrast.

Arthur Hallam, in his *Oration on the Influence of Italian Works of Imagination*, writes as follows:— " Petrarch appears to me a corollary from Dante ; the same spirit in a different mould of individual character, and that a weaker mould ; yet better adapted, by the circumstances of his position, to diffuse the great thought which possessed them both, and to call into existence so great a number of inferior recipients of it, as might affect insensibly, but surely, the course of general feeling." This sentence, which treats of the relative position of Dante and Petrarch as Italian patriots more than as Italian poets, will yet serve as a good starting-point for our comparison. Consider for a moment the different temperaments and circumstances of these two men. Dante, a citizen of Florence, holding the highest post of honour in the State, is exiled in the prime of life. Petrarch, an exile from his earliest infancy, nay, born in exile, lives at Avignon upon the patronage of foreign nobles. Dante from the first, severe, sedate, modest, slow to speak, austere of habit —Petrarch, gay, fond of company, fluent of speech, and fit for all the purposes of elegant society. Compare the picture of Dante at Siena in the druggist's shop, so immersed in reading a new book that all the bustle of the town engaged in a public festivity could not make him lift his eyes from its pages, with that of Petrarch and his brother, neatly attired in their new clothes, picking their way daintily through the muddy streets of Avignon, sheltering their freshly-combed and curled hair from the wind, on their way to a polite entertainment. In Petrarch there was nothing tragic. In Dante everything was tragic. Petrarch amused himself in the palaces of the Visconti and the Colonnas —made friends of princes whom he stooped to flatter. Dante spoke of the salt bread and steep stairs of the Scaligers. Petrarch received the laurel-crown on the Capitol, not without some previous negociations by which he had smoothed his way to this honour. Petrarch, when weary with the bustle of the world, or worn out with paying attentions to Laura, retired to his country villa at Vaucluse, where he gardened and read his favorite authors, playing for awhile at solitude. Dante, when disappointed of all his hopes for Italy, deprived of friends, and home, and Florence, betook himself to the savage wildernesses of the Apennines, and thence shot the arrows of his indignant letters against the city of his birth and the princes of Italy. Dante refused the poet's wreath when it was offered him by Del Virgilio, saying, he would assume it nowhere but at Florence. Describing his own genius, Petrarch writes :—" My intellect, like my body, was more powerful by reason of its suppleness than strength. I had a comprehensive rather than a piercing quality of mind, fit indeed for every good and wholesome study, but chiefly bent toward moral philosophy and poetry." Nothing could better distinguish him from Dante than this. Dante, the deep, the definite, the trenchant, the intense— —Petrarch, the intelligent, the dexterous, the somewhat superficial in his breadth of intellect. Dante was a prophet; Petrarch, a man of culture. Dante's letters bite like vitriol, and scald like boiling lead. Petrarch's are studied compositions, fervent at times in their rhetorical invective, but smacking of the desk and lamp. In politics, as we have seen, Dante was an idealist, a *doctrinaire*, passionate for the monarchy revealed by God, earnest in his expectation of a Messiah. In politics Petrarch was no less an idealist, anxious for the unity of Italy, and eager to restore the splendours of Rome. But he did not draw his patriotism from fountains of personal fervour and religious passion like Dante. It was a matter of antiquarian interest, of literary zeal, of the educated Italian asserting the past glories of Rome against modern barbarism. Dante denounced the enemies of his country in his *Comedy*, and refused to transact with them: when entrance was offered him to Florence he trampled on what he deemed a base proposal. Petrarch, on the contrary, complied with the wishes of Visconti, Carraras, Correggi, Scalas, Colonnas, and lived like an honoured parasite at their court; while in his epistle to Rienzi he denounced these despots and destroyers of his country's freedom. Petrarch had no faculty for centralizing his life. He liked ease, leisure, money, the company of the great; but he warmed his soul with sentimental dreams of liberty. Dante used literature as a means to an end: he wrote in order to shake the hearts of men, caring for words only as they expressed thoughts, and for thoughts only as they were intrinsically valuable. Petrarch, on the contrary, was the first of modern *literateurs*. He loved the *Belles Lettres* for their beauty; his curiosity was insatiable; thought and language were to him the instruments of art. A thought that could be rhetorically or poetically turned, a phrase that might be polished, pleased him for their own sakes, not for their inherent value. Looking at the two men from without, we see Dante solemn, acrid, unconciliating, bent on the elaboration into verse of all the life of his age; we see Petrarch honoured as the great national orator, the supreme scholar in Latin composition, the refined courtier, the discoverer and preserver of MSS., the friend of men of letters and of princes, the voluminous correspondent, the eager student, the ambassador, and the poet of a romantic and fashionable love. If to set forth the most vital aspirations, the deepest fears, the intensest passions, the most solid thoughts of humanity, in language always adequate, and nearly always sublime, constitutes a great poet; then Dante is one. If to recast thoughts and sentiments that are common to humanity, so as to make them dazzlingly beautiful by force of style—if to give the final and perfect expression to feeling, be the proof of consummate genius; then Petrarch ranks below no poet of any nation or of any age. In his hands commonplace thoughts become novel, and simple emotions sublime.

From this comparison it is clear that Dante, with his grasp and force and weight of intellect, was fitted for the epic; Petrarch, with his exquisite sensibility and grace of style, for the lyric. Dante's poems of love, beautiful as they are, sink into nothing when compared with his *Comedy*. Petrarch's Triumphs of Love, Death, Time, and Eternity, in which an epical imagination and real originality of genius were required, are poor compositions when compared with his canzoni, and still more with his sonnets. Of his epic poem, *Africa*, no good can be said. When, therefore, we come to compare the *Vita Nuova* of Dante with the sonnets of Petrarch, we are measuring the weakness of the one poet with the strength of the other.

Dante's *Book of Love* is a short collection of a few sonnets and canzoni, each of which was inspired by a definite event, and formed the record of an important moment in his life. Petrarch's is voluminous, and extends over a period of more than twenty years. Dante's lady was taken from him by death when she was quite young; Petrarch's survived the birth of several children, to die at last of the plague, when she had reached the period of declining beauty and extinguished passions. What would have been the fate of Dante if his Beatrice had lived so long? The charm of the *Vita Nuova* is its almost infantine purity and freshness; it forms the idealization of a young and spiritual love. It is such love as the "young-eyed cherubim" might feel. The charm of Petrarch's collection is far different: in his innumerable sonnets we read of a smart that lasted through a lifetime; of love indulged at first with pleasure, then turning into pain; ineffectually suppressed at intervals, revived by accident; greeted with delight, abandoned with despair. In Petrarch's love for Laura is written the whole history of a sensitive and introspective nature, indulging a soul-desolating, yet delightful sentiment. "His verses," says Shelley, "are as spells, which unseal the inmost enchanted fountains of the delight which is in the grief of love." In Dante's love for Beatrice is written the simpler story of a young and passionate heart, raised from the life of the world and common things into a higher region by enthusiasm. Petrarch's sentiment is on the verge of being morbid. Dante's is as pure and healthy as a flower that opens to the dawn. If the world were compelled to choose between the *Vita Nuova* and the *Rime di Petrarca*, I for one should unhesitatingly select the latter, as the full and complete exposition of love by a genius exactly suited to that kind of work. The *Vita Nuova* I should abandon with regret, but with the satisfaction of remembering that its author had expended his real strength upon the *Divine Comedy*.

Why was it that Dante became forgotten, and that Petrarch filled Italy with his name? Dante belonged to the Middle Age, and made its monument. Petrarch had his foot upon the soil of the Renaissance. Enslaved Italy could not endure the stern singer of Hell, the inspired prophet of the political Messiah. But courtly, gentle, supple Petrarch, with his splendid phrases and polite accommodation of the dreams of freedom to the facts of servitude, suited the Italians of the Medici and Sforza period. The pure and religious tone of the *Vita Nuova* found little favour among men whose love daily became more sentimental and more sensual. Petrarch's exquisite diction, dedicated to sentiment not devoid of languor, and not without a touch of sin, seemed exactly framed for imitation by lovers, who sought to dignify the vulgarity of their amours by a pretence of philosophy, and who trifled with the elegances of language instead of bending it to serve the purposes of masculine or impassioned thought. The spirit of bye-gone centuries summed itself up and took the life of art in Dante. Petrarch initiated the coming age—an age of criticism and study, in which the personality of the individual was sacrificed to erudition, and force of style was exchanged for harmonious correctness. It is the glory of Dante that he stands like an Archangel at the closed gates of Freedom and of Faith. It is the glory of Petrarch to have unlocked the portals of the modern treasury of knowledge and culture. No nation but Italy can show two such men, so nearly contemporary, so unsurpassed in genius, so representative of the mediæval age and the Renaissance. The sculptor who should seek to represent by figurative art the genius of the modern world, would have to model a colossal statue of Italy in chains, with Dante at her feet, brooding upon the past, and Petrarch looking forward to the future, which is ours.

THE END.

www.ingramcontent.com/pod-product-compliance
Lightning Source LLC
Chambersburg PA
CBHW031938230426
43672CB00010B/1959